ROADS TO CHANGE IN MAYA GUATEMALA

ROADS TO CHANGE IN MAYA GUATEMALA

A Field School Approach to Understanding the K'iche'

John P. Hawkins

Walter Randolph Adams

UNIVERSITY OF OKLAHOMA PRESS : NORMAN

ALSO BY JOHN P. HAWKINS

Army of Hope, Army of Alienation: Culture and Contradiction in the American Army Communities of Cold War Germany (Westport, Conn., 2001; Tuscaloosa, Ala., 2d ed. 2005)

ALSO BY WALTER RALDOLPH ADAMS

(ed., with Frank A. Salamone) *Anthropology and Theology: Gods, Icons, and God-Talk* (Lanham, Md., 2000)

(ed., with Frank A. Salamone) *Explorations in Anthropology and Theology* (Lanham, Md., 1997)

Published with the assistance of Brigham Young University.

Library of Congress Cataloging-in-Publication Data

Roads to change in Maya Guatemala : a field school approach to understanding the K'iche' / [edited by] John P. Hawkins, Walter Randolph Adams.
    p.   cm.
    Includes bibliographical references and index.
    ISBN 0–8061–3708–8 (alk. paper) — ISBN 0–8061–3730–4 (pbk.: alk. paper)
    1. Quiché Indians—Guatemala—Nahualá—Social life and customs. 2. Quiché Indians—Guatemala—Santa Catarina Ixtahuacán—Social life and customs. 3. Ethnology—Guatemala—Nahualá—Research 4. Ethnology—Guatemala—Santa Catarina Ixtahuacán—Research. 5. Social change—Guatemala—Nahualá. 6. Social change—Guatemala—Santa Catarina Ixtahuacán. 7. Nahualá (Guatemala)—Social life and customs. 8. Santa Catarina Ixtahuacán (Guatemala)—Social life and customs. I. Hawkins, John Palmer, 1946– II. Adams, Walter Randolph.

F1465.2.Q5R613 2005
972.81'00497'423—dc22

                                                                2005041865

1   2   3   4   5   6   7   8   9   10

Respectfully dedicated to
Florentino Pedro Ajpacajá Tum of Santa Catarina Ixtahuacán,
and
León A. Valladares Sáenz of Guatemala City,
anthropologists and colleagues,
who died in 2002 and 2003, respectively.

TABLE OF CONTENTS

ILLUSTRATIONS

ACKNOWLEDGMENTS

In many cases, the editors of jointly edited volumes write acknowledgments individually. Here, because we have both enjoyed the assistance of each individual named—whether directly or indirectly—we believe it important to make these acknowledgments jointly. Writing acknowledgments is always a delicate task because of the likelihood of missing someone. For a book that took a decade to come into being, that likelihood approaches certainty. Forgive us the sin of omission.

We begin with a heartfelt thank-you to all the residents of Nahualá and Santa Catarina Ixtahuacán—whose names are myriad—for having welcomed us and our students into their lives and homes, housed and fed us, tolerated our endless and repetitive questions, and served as translators and culture brokers. These countless individuals helped us mold our students into professional scholars. Whatever thanks we offer are insufficient to adequately express our debt.

We also appreciate their patience, which we know we taxed, while waiting for the arrival of this volume. Each year, we were asked, "When will the book come out; when will we be able to see the results of our time spent with your students?" While this edition in English will not be completely helpful to many of them, it is a start; we are currently exploring how to translate this volume into Spanish so that it will be more accessible to those who have helped us.

Although there have been many in the communities who have been of assistance, we want to especially acknowledge five individuals. These are Manuel Tum, a leader in the reconstruction of Santa Catarina's old municipal center; Lucas Tepaz, the postman of Santa Catarina Ixtahuacán; Father Santiso, the senior Catholic priest in Nahualá from 1995 through 2002;

Dr. Miguel Rodas, the director of the Centro de Salud in Nahualá; Father David Baronti, PhD, the Catholic priest in the original municipal center of Santa Catarina Ixtahuacán; and the late Florentino Pedro Ajpacajá Túm, linguist and lexicographer, also of Santa Catarina Ixtahuacán. Each of these gave invaluable assistance in helping our students find their way in the two communities throughout the ten years of our project.

The mayors and municipal councils of Santa Catarina and of Nahualá have been instrumental in according us permission to be present in the communities and allowing us to be received well by the K'iche'. Between the years of 1995 and 2004, they include, for Nahualá, Antonio Guachiac Tambriz, Alonso Xocol Tambriz, and Miguel Tzep Rosario. For Santa Catarina Ixtahuacán, they include Manuel Tambriz Carrillo, Diego Bonifacio Tzuy Tum, and Francisco Tambriz Tambriz. (Out of respect for the residents of these two communities, we have used pseudonyms throughout the chapters that follow.)

We express deep thanks to Dr. Richard N. Adams and his wife, Betty H. Adams, parents of Walter R. Adams. Each year for the past decade they have graciously offered us the use of their home for our two-day interim conference. During all of these conferences, Richard Adams has been present to critique the student presentations, provide insight and wisdom, and sometimes even to offer access to his extensive library, thus enabling the students to improve their methods, data, and interpretation. We, too, have benefited from his thorough critiques and excellent library.

More than just intellectual sponsors, Richard and Betty Adams have also provided the students, now more than 135, with a home away from home. Indeed, each year, one or more students have spent a few days under their care while recovering from intestinal parasites or other maladies.

To Carol Lee Hawkins, John's wife, and Marilyn Baade, Walter's former wife, we also express deep gratitude.

To Clayne Pope and David Magleby, successive deans of the College of Family, Home, and Social Sciences within Brigham Young University, and Joel Janetski, chair of the Department of Anthropology, we give thanks for having let John engage in this activity. To the David M. Kennedy Center for International Studies at the same institution, and in particular to David Shuler, we give thanks for having helped us recruit and train students and student facilitators who have gone to Guatemala these past ten years. They have also provided the logistical support necessary in the year prior to the field season so that students have been better prepared to meet the challenges of work in the field. Kellee Koenig constructed the maps with subsequent modifications by Whitney Taylor. Both worked under the direction of Dr. Brandon Plewe, director of Mapping Services, Brigham Young University Geography Department.

We appreciate especially two editors at the University of Oklahoma Press: Jo Ann Reece early saw the merit of what we were doing although we had hidden it in too large a manuscript. She sent the manuscript to two anonymous reviewers who made invaluable suggestions; we have incorporated almost all of their recommendations. Assignments changed and Charles E. Rankin took on our project. Like a good personal physician, he indicated we had to lose weight or die, guided us through the liposuction, and became our best advocate when we succeeded. In addition, Anna Stone and Katrin Flechsig edited the manuscript as it approached completion, catching many problems of tense and wording.

We acknowledge the diligence of the chapter authors in this book and the many other students who have accompanied us to the field. We appreciate their maturity and intellectual companionship. We could not have brought this book into being without their enormous volunteer effort, both while in the field and long, long after.

This volume has benefited indirectly from recent funding under the National Science Foundation's Research Experience for Undergraduates program, (grant numbers SES–0139198 and SES–0354014). While all of the papers in this volume were written before we secured funding from NSF in 2002, the grant has enabled us to sustain a vigorous program of undergraduate research in the area and has affirmed the value of what we have been doing to bring student work to publication.

In spite of all this help, we must take responsibility for all of this book's shortcomings, which are many.

Walter Randolph Adams
John P. Hawkins

PREFACE

This book presents our response to two current trends in the university curriculum: project-based learning rooted in real-world situations, and the effort to involve undergraduate college students in authentic research. The two are clearly related. Project-based learning entails research and discovery. In addition to transforming the researchers themselves with new insights, project-based learning may reveal authentically new knowledge to the communities of physical and social science. Intellectual inquiry at the frontier of knowledge is, necessarily, a special instance of project-based constructivist learning. The two trends in current education are thus eminently compatible; indeed, they are simultaneously accomplishable and mutually supportive. In this book we show that project-based research by undergraduates can contribute to the knowledge base.

Both project-based learning and undergraduate involvement in research are revitalizations of long-standing movements. John Dewey, for example, championed reality-based learning by doing. One hundred and fifty years ago, an undergraduate degree was the most advanced degree available in many of the disciplines. As the knowledge base of different disciplines became increasingly large and theoretically sophisticated, however, undergraduates receded into a status of absorbers of available knowledge rather than creators of new knowledge.

The same is true in anthropology. Theory has become complex and daunting; some theorists who are required reading are frequently undecipherable, even to fellow PhDs. Methods, too, have multiplied. Book length is one crude measure: H. Russell Bernard's widely used methods textbook has expanded from a 457-page first edition (1988) to a 659-page third edition (2002) set in smaller type on larger pages. It has approximately twice the number of words as the original. Number of volumes is another measure of the complexity of anthropological methods. Werner and Schoepfle's (1987) text on basic methods embraces two large volumes. Sage Publications, which specializes in anthropological and social research methods texts, offers a full 48 titles on qualitative methods, 143 titles on quantitative social science methods, 47 titles on applied social research methods, and five different multi-volume sets. For the determined methodologist who wants a complete but afford-able summary of it all, Altamira Press, a division of Sage, offers the 1,640-page, seven volume *Ethnographer's Toolkit* (Schensul and LeCompte 1999).

In spite of such apparent complexity of methods, one can more easily imagine involving undergraduates in research in anthropology than in some other disciplines. Many unique social and cultural systems exist that need to be documented and can thus stimulate the development of theory. Anthro-pology is not alone in this, however. The biological sciences are just as overwhelmed by the vast quantity of what is not known, and for the same reason: a lack of labor power to carry out the necessary observations and write up the results. Our friends in biology tell us that, placed in the right envi-ronment, a biology undergraduate might find the discovery of new species to be a daily and even dull event. Documenting the ecological intricacies of a species in the web of life can be done anywhere and still needs to be done everywhere. Only the culturally totemic species (the bald eagle, the wolf, the bear, for example) and the disease vector species (mosquitoes come to mind) have been well studied. Less culturally exciting worms, insects, and other forms of life languish in relatively unstudied obscurity.

When working with such species, a general sense of the discipline acquired by ordinary undergraduate education, combined with a determined effort to find and absorb the relatively few books and articles related to a particular aspect of a species would bring an undergraduate to the table of research armed with the proper set of manners and utensils and able to read the menu and order something fresh to chew on. That being so, mentoring and motivation, time on task, and disciplined recording in field notebooks become more important to research success than the level of one's degree.

In emphasizing the capabilities of undergraduates, by no means do we denigrate the more professional doctoral-level studies. Advanced degrees help most recipients provide polished and more thorough understandings of the wider-ranging implications of their discoveries. But there is much still to be discovered and insight to be had. Undergraduates can be a part of the enterprise if they are coached well; instilled with enthusiasm; and taught to be careful, persistent, and diligent in recording and writing about their observations.

Moreover, undergraduates will learn more from the formal study of their core discipline and other subjects if they are engaged meaningfully in the enterprise of serious research for which they are going to be held accountable through scholarly presentation and publication. Once engaged in this process, students realize the importance of effective writing skills, the value of good statistical logic, the context provided by Western intellectual history, the necessity of comprehending theory, the value of covering the literature, and the importance of using appropriate methods. If the research expectation comes early enough in undergraduate education, other courses take on vastly greater meaning, and there is time for the undergraduate to produce repeated rewrites as a result of peer and faculty critiques of their work.

By contrast, when a capstone project or supposedly serious research effort is crammed into one's senior year, students lack the time to mature in the task. Faculty feel less inclined to invest in the student who is soon to graduate and move on. The ideal timing would be to teach students general qualitative and quantitative methods during their freshman year; have them prepare for a specific project in their sophomore year; engage them in independent and mentored research their junior year; and write and rewrite, present at conferences, and submit for publication in their senior year.

Early involvement in the complex enterprise of research would better motivate students in their undergraduate years and enable them to discover problems, provide solutions, and monitor results in the worlds of business, professions, and government. Students will be more likely to feel capable of and interested in seeking advanced degrees because they will have savored the energy inherent in the practice of original research. Moreover, having learned from experience how to engage a task, students who have independently passed through the research process as undergraduates are likely to materially shorten the time it takes to prepare for and complete doctoral programs.

Such is the promise. To prove it, though, someone needs to compare the results of undergraduate education that early integrates research participation and course work, with traditional undergraduate education that relies on classes and lab exercises. This, then, is a project that a motivated undergraduate in education could begin to work on that could mature into a fine doctoral dissertation and might well lead to a path-breaking career.

Thus far we have considered how incorporating college undergraduates into the research process early in their careers might improve undergraduate education. Successfully pursued, the process would of course change the participating university faculty. Faculty who mentor undergraduates in research will find themselves co-authoring papers with their students, editing books (such as this) that present the research, and producing broad syntheses of the work of undergraduate students done over a number of years. Through this collaboration, students, faculty, and the larger research community benefit.

This book details the evolving process by which we mentored and shepherded undergraduates and documents the research they produced. It is, however, but one of many ways that one could have gone about fostering undergraduate research. Please let us know of your own experiences in involving undergraduates in research, in whatever discipline, whether on paths parallel or divergent with ours. We are truly interested because we have enjoyed the undergraduate associations and reveled in the quality of research that has been the result. We invite you to join us in a collaboration because we suspect that there may be an edited interdisciplinary volume that ought to be written about involving undergraduates in research. We would like to hear about your approach to fostering undergraduate research in your discipline. How did you go about motivating, eliciting, and shepherding undergraduate student engagement in mentored research and publication? What institutional activities or resources most helped, hindered, or were needed? If you would like to participate in an edited volume on this subject, send us a brief description of your experience. From this we will select an array of exemplary approaches and invite those selected to submit full-fledged chapters. If your collective response overwhelms us, we will pick a few diverse exemplars for an interdisciplinary volume to lead a series, and farm out the rest, by discipline, to willing volume editors.

The photographs that might have accompanied this book did not reproduce well in black and white. We invite you to see these and other visual representations at our website, *http://maya.byu.edu.*

John P. Hawkins
john_hawkins@byu.edu

Walter Randolph Adams
walteradams@guate.net.gt

July 2004, Panajachel, Guatemala

ROADS TO CHANGE IN MAYA GUATEMALA

FOSTERING FIELD SCHOOL ETHNOGRAPHY

John P. Hawkins and Walter Randolph Adams

For a discipline that considers intensive fieldwork its distinguishing and most valuable characteristic, we anthropologists have a curious reluctance to teach the necessary methods and organize students in mentored, on-site fieldwork practice. McGoodwin (1978:175), for example, remarks:

> Field-work experience is practically a *sine qua non* in the training of professional socio-cultural anthropologists. Ironically, however, few American educational institutions offering graduate degrees in this subject provide training for field work. For generations of aspiring novices, the crucial rite of professional initiation and passage usually begins abruptly . . . [and] is often admitted to have been a trial-and-error, stumbling experience. . . . The process is analogous to expecting a student pilot to solo without ever having been in an airplane.

Reporting thirty-five years ago, Alan R. Beals recounts his effort to get help with methods. He departed for fieldwork in India, stopping in England en route. Hoping he might get some insights from E. E. Evans-Pritchard, a masterful fieldworker, Beals sought audience and asked for his best recommendations. "Never accept free housing and always carry a supply of marmalade," Evans-Pritchard suggested (Beals 1970:38, 1980:102). Sage advice, given that Evans-Pritchard could not offer a course or tutorial in the time available to a drop-in student. The brevity of the professor's response, however, is perhaps indicative of a certain reluctance to apply formal teaching methods to something as inventive and artful as participant observation and interviewing. Therein lies the conundrum: how does one formalize the transmission of the informal practice of formally practiced informality? Many schools simply do not try.

Let us give personal examples. John Hawkins attended a field methods class as an undergraduate at Brigham Young University around 1968 that used Epstein's (1967) *Craft of Social Anthropology* as a text. The class, however, had no practical field exercises. As a graduate student at the University of Chicago, Hawkins received no formal field methods training; no course was offered and certainly no field school or direct on-site mentoring. Before going to the field, beginning graduate students listened to the fieldwork "war stories" of those who had just returned from the field. Absent that, we sought what we could in the library, but no one intimated that we needed training in field methods.

In a similar vein, Walter Adams received no undergraduate field methods training while attending Beloit College. His only exposure to methods to that point came from tagging along with his father in the field. Subsequently, at the University of Pennsylvania, Adams's core curriculum for a master's degree in anthropology included a field methods course, but it came long after he had returned from conducting his first ethnographic study (W. R. Adams 1988b). His Michigan State doctoral program required no field methods training either.

Although we have not conducted a survey, we suspect there are more on-campus field methods courses now, for both undergraduates and graduates, than in previous decades. We hope so, because good fieldwork is crucial to the discipline and because interdisciplinary connections have vastly increased the range of methods appropriate to anthropology.[1] Undergraduate students with field experience enter graduate programs, regardless of discipline, at a considerable advantage: they have a grounded and cross-cultural sense of social reality, methodological practicality, and theory. Nonetheless, we continue to neglect the direct, disciplined, mentored teaching and demonstration of fieldwork techniques in dedicated, full-emersion field school contexts.

Such neglect is surprising, given that a number of ethnographic field schools have made impressive contributions to the discipline. One is tempted to begin with Boas's Jesup North Pacific Expedition in 1897 (Boas 1974) and Cambridge's Torres Straits Expedition of 1898 (Rivers 1901), both fundamental to the emergence of modern fieldwork methods. These, however, do not qualify as field schools because both expeditions employed practicing professionals and did not attempt to teach novice students how to research. The Rhodes-Livingston Institute, established in 1938, mentored many British doctoral and postdoctoral fieldworkers, often of the "Manchester School," but was not a field school and certainly not a place to develop undergraduates (Gluckman 1945).

Several field schools have been prominent in recent times. One thinks immediately of Sol Tax's work among the Illinois Fox. The Fox project included only graduate students (Tax 1988:8) and entailed relatively little mentored teaching (Foley 1999), although it gave those students valuable experience early in their careers. The most successful field school and field opportunity, to our knowledge, centered around the Harvard Chiapas Project of Evon Vogt. His field school began taking undergraduates in 1960 and did so at least until 1980. Many of these undergraduates went on to important careers in anthropology and other social sciences, and at least three of them published their undergraduate work (Vogt 1994:196, 342). On the basis of the impressive number of undergraduate students who later matured into anthropology PhDs, we judge Vogt's Chiapas Project the most successful undergraduate mentoring experience in the discipline.[2] Vogt's record is not clear, however, on how much was formally taught to undergraduates and how much was learned from mentoring and modeling in the field. Richard N. Adams (1970) took graduate students to Guatemala to work with him on a project from 1963 to 1967, but he did not consider it a field school though it included in-field mentoring (R. N. Adams, personal communication). June Nash took undergraduates to Chiapas between 1986 and approximately 1991 with funding from the National Science Foundation's (NSF) Research Experience for Undergraduates program. Aspects of that experience enrich her analysis (Nash 2001) of globalization among the Chiapas Mayas. Oswald Werner ran Northwestern University's successful field school among the Navajos beginning in about 1973 and running for many years. The field school included undergraduate students recruited from a variety of universities (Werner and Schoepfle 1987:16). Today, Northwestern continues to sustain ethnographic field school opportunities that study both Chicago urban issues and environmental resource management topics. Finally, we note the exemplary activities of Spradley and McCurdy (1988) and Kottak (1982), who have taught field methods to undergraduates in an academic-year class and published exemplary essays regarding American cultural life that are based on carefully mentored course projects. A true field school experience, however, would be separate from the rest of a semester's courses and should be more of an immersion and a fully focused effort.

As we write this in summer 2004, a mere handful of ethnographic field schools can be readily found on the Internet and most are but six weeks or less in length. They range geographically from the circumpolar area to Baja California to Peru. While we suspect there are a number of unadvertised ethnographic field schools serving particular campuses, clearly, we do not suffer from an oversupply. Thus, McGoodwin's remarks quoted above are still largely apropos.

So why the neglect of field schools for undergraduates? The answer is necessarily complex. In part, this neglect derives from expectations—in large part false—regarding undergraduate students' maturity and commitment to research. On the whole, the stereotype is that undergraduates have inadequate training in the discipline and are less committed to research. It may be argued that they are not ready.[3] Undergraduates, by comparison with graduate students, are, by and large, still trying to "find themselves."

The lack of field schools also derives from the nature of the faculty commitment to and investment in field training and the reward structure and resources in place for such activity. Because undergraduates' research outcome is much less sure, a given investment of faculty time is more risky.[4] Faculty in a field school setting may be able to accomplish a fair amount of direct fieldwork, but they must also be available twenty-four hours a day to monitor and assist students when needed. That can be taxing. And, of course, the younger the students are, the more likely they are to need assistance.

Finally, the economic and career rationality of running a field school hinges considerably on the nature of the reward structure within one's university. If a university values and rewards good teaching and on-the-job mentoring (an investment of time that takes away from one's own research), then operating a field school is favored. Often, however, such orientations prevail at colleges and universities where there is a lack of cash resources to cover the initial costs of such a program, so the positive climate is economically dampened. On the other hand, if the university primarily values and rewards research publications, then operating an undergraduate field school, while nominally bringing a faculty member closer to the research field, may appear to be a losing proposition. Time invested in administering and solving problems could have gone to the professor's own publications. Thus the field school can be seen as a risk to publications, pay, advancement in rank, and retention—a heavy set of risks no matter how much one values close involvement with the intellectual development of undergraduates. To alleviate such professional drawbacks, one must make astute initial student selections, reduce problems to a minimum by institutionalizing good administrative practices, find ways to nurture the students into producing high-quality papers, and bring the papers to publication individually or collectively.

A few anthropologists who have led field schools have tried to remedy the lack of information and offer suggestions about operating a field school. We will not attempt to summarize their findings, but we wish to make the references accessible. Grant et al. (1999) ran a field school that coached some sixty graduate students in and around the home campus of Athens, Georgia. They provide detailed material on what worked and did not work in their field school.[5] Coombs, Hess, and Killorin (1977) detail the procedures of the Urban Anthropology Field School sponsored by the University of New Mexico and give excellent advice on issues of content, structure, and timing. Vogt (1994) evocatively describes the participation of undergraduates in a research-oriented, faculty-mentored field situation in Chiapas, Mexico. Ward (1999) details the management of culture shock in the University of New Orleans's field school in the Italian Tyrol. Finally, Wallace has published two fine essays (Wallace 1999; Gmelch and Gmelch 1999) on the management and educational results of field schools. All of these articles lay out details that would help any field school director improve the operation of a field education program. In the remainder of this chapter, we will share how we conducted our field school each summer from 1995 to present in Santa Catarina Ixtahuacán and Nahualá. In particular, we explain how we selected and prepared students before going into the field, how we coached them in the field, and how we fostered more effective ethnographic description after returning from the field.

ORIGIN OF A FIELD SCHOOL

The idea for the field school that led to this book percolated in a coffee shop in Mexico City between sessions of the 1993 International Congress of Anthropological and Ethnological Sciences. John Hawkins had organized a symposium that focused on various approaches to the study of ethnicity,[6] to which Walter Adams was an invited panelist. We had not met before, having only read each other's work. Our approaches differed. Hawkins emphasized structural, cultural, and symbolic approaches to social life, while Adams employed ecological, material, and numeric perspectives. Yet, as we discovered in the conference and discussed further in the coffee shop, we were investigating many of the same issues and asking many of the same questions. We also realized that the pure analytical frameworks that we each had emphasized in our earlier works impeded analysis. Thus, Adams had begun developing questions regarding the meanings of ethnicity and the acceptance or nonacceptance of Western culture in indigenous communities, which suggested that a symbolic facet should be added to his material perspectives. Likewise, quite independently, Hawkins now explored the meanings of symbolism by examining the impact of material conditions on ethnic self-attribution and did so with a strong ecological orientation. Moreover, we both realized that a traditional anthropological study—focusing attention on a single community—would not permit an understanding of the dynamic aspects of culture change. First, studying a single community allowed no frame of reference against which to compare observations and assertions regarding change. Second, vastly accelerated globalization had by now shattered the convenient assumption that communities could be understood if approached as relative isolates.

We sought, therefore, to identify two communities in Guatemala, preferably with a common origin, that had been subjected to differing social and ecological pressures. We hoped to carry out studies of change that would parallel the work carried out at Oraibi and Old Oraibi (Sekaquaptewa 1972) or in the Methodist and Catholic Ojibway communities on Keweenaw Bay (W. R. Adams 1988a, 1997, 2000). The two communities needed to be close enough to share many of the same ecological constraints but far enough apart so that one could clearly identify the transformational differences between them and the factors involved in their different manifestations of change. Realizing that few field sites would be appropriate, we mulled over the towns we had both visited during many years of research in Guatemala. Almost immediately we came up with the same thought: to conduct the study in Nahualá and Santa Catarina Ixtahuacán.

Several factors influenced the choice of field location. First, we were inclined to select an area that offered both of us interesting opportunities in relation to our distinct theoretical backgrounds. Given Adams's research on differential rates of change in communities that had fissioned, and his research on alcohol and its abuse, Santa Catarina and Nahualá were attractive settings because the two communities had been conjoined and later split (McCreery 1994:151–57). Moreover, even to the casual observer, they showed obvious differences in alcohol use and abuse. Given Hawkins's prior research in Ladino and Spanish-speaking Indian communities (Hawkins 1984), he desired to study an indigenous community that was conservatively Indian, in which the use of Mayan language was dominant. Nahualá and Santa Catarina Ixtahuacán shared an origin in a documented, century-old fission.[7] The communities also offered the prospect of a clear exploration of processes of change, given their differing access to transportation and markets.

For both of us, a key factor in returning to Guatemala was the desire to include undergraduate and graduate students in a supervised field study experience. We decided to recruit students from Brigham Young University, where Hawkins taught, and Brown University, where Adams did research. We would place half of each year's group in residences in Nahualá and half in Ixtahuacán. Because of the more prominent use of alcohol and public displays of drunkenness in Nahualá, Adams resided in and assumed primary supervisory responsibility there, while Hawkins lived in and supervised students working in Santa Catarina Ixtahuacán.

Before we go on we should note that for us, running this field school has been an evolutionary learning process. We got a few things right from the beginning, but we learned much when our best-laid plans did not produce the desired results. We will walk you through this evolution and share the problems we experienced and the lessons we learned for each of the three phases of a field school: recruitment and preparation, in-field study, and post-field write-up and professionalization.

PRE-FIELD CONSIDERATIONS

A successful field school begins with the thoughtful selection of well-qualified students, followed by explicit instruction on the kinds of conditions they will encounter in the field and our expectations for their response to those situations. Once recruited, students should be given as much training as possible before departure to develop their knowledge about the region, hone their research topic, and acquire basic methodology.

Recruitment

Recruitment has been a relatively easy, though time-consuming, matter. In the first two years, we tried to recruit from both Brigham Young University and Brown University. Brown University, however, would not accept transfer credits, which seemed to squelch any interest among Brown students. For the first seven years, all our students came from Brigham Young University, including two from BYU's Hawaii campus. Starting in summer 2002, we received NSF Undergraduate Research Experience funding which enabled us to recruit additional students from each of three universities that became affiliated with the project: University of Illinois at Chicago, Texas State University San Marcos, and University of Texas Panamerican.

Hawkins has supervised the recruitment effort throughout the program thus far. Each year, we have picked the most charismatic and reliable student from a prior year's group to be the current year's student "field facilitator." The facilitator's duties include keeping track of the recruitment process during the two semesters before the summer field effort. At Brigham Young, all out-of-country courses, projects, and research must be coordinated through the university's international center. When the international center had its regular open houses for recruitment, for example, the field facilitator or previous participants staffed the desk and displays, while Hawkins came as much as he could. Announcements were made in classes, posted to bulletin boards, and e-mailed to departments.

We required a fairly extensive range of documents from our applicants. Hawkins, the current facilitator, and a previous facilitator would interview the candidates and include Adams in the final decision.

We required conversational ability in Spanish and preferred students with anthropology backgrounds.[8] Beyond this, we looked for maturity, resilience, mental toughness, and ability to get along. We asked how candidates had handled problems in previous foreign encounters. We gave them hypothetical problems and asked for solutions. We showed them pictures of wretched outhouses and board-hard beds and advised them that they would be sleeping for three months in a sleeping bag. We talked about reactions to dogs, fleabites, rain and mud, and getting sick. We noted that much work had to be done after the summer was over, because writing up multiple drafts of papers and becoming involved in professional presentations took time that would not necessarily earn them course credit. We held back nothing about the difficulties and were perfectly happy if people dropped out during recruitment because the prospective endeavor was more demanding than they wanted. We emphasized, however, that independent fieldwork, write-up, professional conference presentations, and interactive writing in response to hard-hitting critiques of drafts of their work would take them a long way toward their professional goals in any discipline. We let them know that they would be changed forever—for the good—because of the experience.[9]

During recruitment we explicitly discussed behavioral expectations that would be in place for the duration of the field school stay in Guatemala. At a symposium on the conduct of field schools in 1995, we had listened to exasperated field directors lament the amount of time they spent resolving problems related to alcohol abuse or love trysts between students and local residents gone wrong. To avoid such problems, we put in place six explicit groups of behavioral expectations.

1. Guatemala, we told our candidates, could be a dangerous place, and we needed them always to have unimpaired judgment. Thus, all forms of alcohol consumption or illicit drug use were prohibited during their stay in Guatemala, and any infractions would result in immediate dismissal.

2. The young men and women of the villages we studied had to make their lives there in a system that enshrined honor and thrived on gossip. Students signed a contract agreeing to conduct themselves so that there would be no behavior that could be construed as courtship or flirting in the idioms of any of the three cultures involved: indigenous, Ladino, or American.

3. Participants agreed not to smoke or wear dark glasses while in the research communities, because both activities were strongly associated with Ladino ethnic interpersonal dominance over Indians, and we wanted our students to minimize their symbolic social distance from indigenous residents.

4. Students agreed not to leave the communities without letting a compatriot student know their travel routes and return expectations. For all trips beyond resupply efforts in nearby Quezaltenango, students agreed to go in threes, so that in the event of an accident or illness, one could stay with the injured and one could find help and inform the field directors.

5. Participation in political demonstrations (indeed, even going near them) or casting judgment or aspersion on the politics and practices of the local and national culture were forbidden.[10]

6. Both because of anthropological ethics and because religion and religious change were highly sensitive issues in the communities, we explicitly asked for and got student consent that they would not proselytize. This issue seemed particularly important because not all of the students were anthropology majors schooled in concepts of research-oriented cultural relativity. Moreover, many of the Brigham Young University students had formerly been volunteer missionaries in the style of the Church of Jesus Christ of Latter-day Saints (the Mormon Church). Even though BYU's general policy required that students refrain from advocating their own faith while participating in any study abroad program, we made the agreement not to proselytize an absolute condition. We reiterated frequently that we went to

Guatemala to learn about other people's cultures, not to preach,
teach, or persuade them about any aspect of ours.

We made clear that infringement of any of the rules would result in an
immediate exit ticket from the program, and we reiterated the rules from
time to time throughout the preparation and field stay periods. We have
not had a serious infraction or a single student expelled in the ten years of
our program; we think clear and unequivocal behavioral expectations made
the difference. We completed recruitment during September through October so the chosen students could take the appropriate preparation courses
during January to April. All in all, time invested in recruiting good students
greatly affects the well-being of the field school and results in more professional essays.

Preparing for Research

For the first seven years, we urged students to choose to study some
aspect of Maya society that related to their intended future careers. We made
no attempt to define a coordinated topic area for each summer group. Thus,
education majors studied in the local schools or examined informal education, social work students investigated aspects of familial care or concepts
of disability, and premed students explored a facet of local health care. Film
students made documentaries, and anthropology students investigated
whatever aspect of village life interested them most. We encouraged students
to read in the literature on their topics before going to the field, but the effort
was not fully successful until we implemented a preparation course and
incorporated that goal into class assignments. Undergraduates, for the most
part, need structured demands.

Beginning in 1998, and with the assistance of BYU's International Center,
students had to take a preparation course that oriented all students, regardless
of major, to the rigors and procedures of fieldwork. This course gave them
the basic concepts of anthropology, oriented them to Guatemala, helped them
design a field project, and made sure they had their shots, passports, gear, and
tickets. In addition, we also required students to take the anthropology department's field methods course and its Guatemala-focused Mesoamerica course
before going to the field. Both in the International Center's preparation course
and in the anthropology field methods course, each student prepared a research
proposal for the field experience. In these initial years, we learned there is no
substitute for preparation.

IN-FIELD CONSIDERATIONS

Once in the field, a variety of new tasks require attention. These include arranging housing, monitoring health, insuring logistics, developing the teaching content of the field school, and supervising reserch.

Housing arrangements

The first on-site task is to make board and room arrangements for each student. To secure the housing, we have had a faculty member or the student field facilitator go to the communities about a week before students arrived. This approach generally secured suitable housing for 70 to 90 percent of the students. The rest we readily arranged during the day or two after arrival. Because Nahualá's only "hotel" has but three dingy rooms, each with a five-foot-eight-inch-high concrete ceiling, no windows, and no bath, we secured permission to sleep on the floor of the Latter-day Saints Church building, the only one in town with multiple toilet stalls and adequate space. Arriving on a Monday, we have generally had all students in their homes by Tuesday or Wednesday evening. During the rest of our stay, we avoid use of church facilities so that the students will not be confused with missionaries or identified as religious partisans.

All program students (the total number reaching over 135 after ten summers) have lived with local Indian families. In the early years, we deliberately chose Catholic families, some from among the most respected *principales* (elders), for most of the students; only a few host families were Evangelical. Since 2000, religion has seemed not to be an issue in family choice and the distribution has matched the population's roughly fifty-fifty split. As indicated, whatever the family faith, students were prohibited from proselytizing their own faith.

We were determined to have the students live with families to enhance the cultural experience. During the first summer field school in 1995, we arrived with eighteen students in tow. Being uncertain of the residential possibilities, we housed most of the students in pairs with families. This turned out to be a mistake, because students spent too much time in retreat, talking with each other rather than with their families. In subsequent years, each student has lived alone with a family. As a result, these students generally have had much richer and more culturally penetrating experiences. Married students accompanied by their spouse generally live as a conjugal pair with a family.

We ascertained the ordinary board and room rate for local students and decided to make our presence and its inherent disruption attractive by paying above the going rate. This enabled us to secure housing quickly. Our board and room payment helps maintain student health because it gives us leverage to ask for plates and utensils to be washed and dried well, and for water to be boiled sufficiently to reduce health risks. Generally students have their own room, but sleeping in a room with "adopted" siblings of the same sex, or, in poorer homes, separation from the family by a plastic curtain, also occurs.

In Ixtahuacán, a family that had prior experience hosting Catholic Church exchange groups volunteered to broker our entry into the community. This family adopted us and provided housing quickly and reliably, and we acquiesced to the convenience of the arrangement. After about three years, however, we became aware of resentment in the community because the families that housed us were closely related kin and among the wealthier in the community. The flow of income to such a limited circle generated envy, and we started to seek independent housing. Over a three-year period we have moved to significantly less dependence on the originating families, and we seem to have extracted ourselves from this initial linkage with some grace and goodwill. Nevertheless, for a variety of reasons, primarily associated with student comfort and health, we still have a tendency to favor families at the upper end of the village wealth scale. For example, the originating sponsor family purchased a double bed and box spring. Married students in our research groups much prefer residence in that household, with a private room, to other options of wire-mesh cots.

For the last three years (2000–03), we have tended to select homes that had a cell phone in order to maintain communication and rapidly assess the safety and health of our students. In 2002, however, we purchased cell phones for some of our students, and by 2004 all students had project-issued cell phones. As a result, we can now disregard this attribute of wealth in selecting residences, and students feel more securely connected to each other in these politically troubled times.

Perhaps there will always be a tendency to favor the wealthier half of these poor communities, because we still prefer to send students to homes where previous students have had little or no problem with health and sanitation, and we also like to send students to current and former political leaders in the communities as a form of contact and goodwill maintenance. We recognize our biases, but we strongly believe that keeping our students healthy is one of our primary obligations both to the student and to the overall success of the program. In ten summers we have had just four cases of serious illness, though most of the students have had to deal with one or more episodes of gastrointestinal parasites.

We encouraged students to be as helpful to their families as possible. They often went out for a day of field labor, hoeing corn, for example. They could not, however, acquiesce to difficult or illegal requests, such as helping family members migrate to the United States. They were not to lend money, and we encouraged them to cite project rules and us, the professors, as the reason. Students frequently left clothing, sleeping bags, and other goods with their families when they returned home to the United States.

Informed Consent Procedures

Simultaneous with making housing arrangements, we renewed our informed consent arrangements orally each year. The BYU Institutional Review Board approved verbal informed consent because many of the community members are illiterate and justifiably leery of signing documents they cannot read. Each year we communicate with the Catholic priest in each town, asking permission to be there. We explain the non-proselyting contract and indicate that the priest can at any time ask us to leave the community if he feels we have become unwelcome guests. We give the same message to some of the ministers of the many Evangelical Protestant congregations, and, of course, to the mayor and the municipal corporation as well as the leader of the local police detachment. We invite them to talk to project leaders or students if they sense a problem. We tell them that any of them can request that we leave the community, and that we will do so within twenty-four hours if they feel that we have become a problem. We believe such statements ward off any need for community leaders to use coercive methods to get rid of us if someone felt we were making him or her uncomfortable. It seems to have worked; we approach our tenth summer without difficulty.

Class Activities

During the first three years, we did not require students to take preparation courses before joining the field school, although we offered recommendations. Thus we found ourselves teaching basic methods and ethics in a series of classes held separately in each of the two communities. Because transportation was so infrequent in and out of Santa Catarina Ixtahuacán in the afternoons, holding a joint class together in one community was not an option, because half the students would have been stranded regularly. Yet the pattern of monsoon rains made afternoons the attractive time to be inside and hold class.

The gatherings, held twice weekly in each community, accomplished a number of purposes. First, formal classes helped students learn basic anthropological field methods, discuss ethical issues, and acquire a basic understanding of Guatemalan culture. Second, after class we met with the students individually to discuss their projects, concerns, or cultural difficulties.[11] In this way, if students found themselves in any sort of distress—including illness, problems concerning their projects, or other issues—the matter could be dealt with promptly. We encouraged students to let us know if they needed more immediate or more sustained attention. In preparation for these individual conferences, students wrote an essay describing what they accomplished during the week, how the information and their activities helped them understand their research topic better, what research goals they had for the following week, and how and with whom they would accomplish those goals. These questions enabled us to help students use their limited time wisely.

Holding separate classes in Nahualá and Santa Catarina, however, resulted in divisions in the student group and in the intellectual perceptions of the directors. We—both students and faculty—were too connected to and isolated within our separate communities. Students wanted more contact with one another. Indeed, students complained that the friendships they had developed with other members of the group had been negatively affected as a result of their isolation in the two communities. The students of one town tended not see those of the other town or discuss the research they were doing, except perhaps when they arranged joint travel on weekends. We also realized that although we had been keeping abreast of each of these projects on a week-to-week basis, we had no way of knowing whether the students were obtaining the kind of information that would result in a good field project paper.

To address these problems, all students now attend class one full day per week in just one of the communities. The requirement of an anthropology field methods class prior to arrival enabled us to shift the focus of the classes in Guatemala toward a review of specific methods tailored to individual projects. Faculty time could be devoted toward counseling students and encouraging them to report on their projects to one another. In spite of their prior course work, students often forgot important aspects of methods they had presumably learned during the school year. Moreover, with students now from several universities, we need to ensure that all have comparable knowledge and skill. Thus, we review anthropological field methods on-site each summer. During an hour-long class on methods, students make summary presentations from a field methods text (Bernard 1995) and we guide discussion on the application of various methods to their particular projects. We devote an hour to ethics and an hour to the topic (religion, health, or whatever), again inviting students to present textual summaries and lead discussion on applicability. We end with an hour of faculty presentation and class discussion on the country and culture and the relation of these to the students' projects.

Prior to 1998, BYU Anthropology required no independent field experience of its sociocultural majors. Yet the success of our field school in Guatamala and of another in Namibia suggested a need. In 1998 we formalized a curriculum change requiring of all sociocultural students an independent field experience, and we provided a course credit mechanism for doing so. Now students could register for "independent research" while in the field, and we correspondingly made the area study class and the field methods class prerequisites. The main requirement for the independent field experience course was the daily maintenance of a field notes journal demonstrating the application of a range of previously learned methods. We created an additional course that centered on reading two ethnographies from Guatemala. We asked students to write a half-page summary of each book's chapters. Then, once a week, they were required to review these summaries and write a paragraph or more relating a current experience of that week to three relevant chapters in each of the ethnographies. The goal, of course, was to have students relate their reading to their experience. Thereby, the students increasingly were made aware of the relations between their field experience and the major positions taken in the ethnographic literature on Guatemala. Both measures helped: the prerequisite courses in field methods and Mesoamerican culture got students going more quickly when they arrived in the field. The in-field research credits and lengthening the field season to twelve weeks gave them critically important additional time in the field and credit toward their graduation requirements.[12] With these improvements, after 1998, more of the students started producing thesis-quality studies.

Not surprisingly, all of the students complete minors in anthropology. The reason is simple: a minor requires sixteen hours of course work. Our field program students take nine hours of courses to prepare themselves for the field and another nine hours of anthropology courses while in the field. Indeed, several students added anthropology as a double major because it would only take six additional courses to complete.

Interim Conference

From the beginning, we instituted an interim conference. Approximately two-thirds of the way through the field season we hold a "retreat"—a weekend in touristy Panajachel on the shores of stunningly beautiful Lake Atitlán—during which the students present their work to us, each other, and, often, other visiting scholars. Each student delivers a fifteen-minute synopsis of his or her data and interpretation to date. We, the professors, provide a critique of the presentations and offer suggestions.[13] Equally important, students query each other about what has been presented and offer suggestions of their own. This post-mid-term presentation enables the students to determine what they have documented sufficiently and what aspects of their project need further work. Thus, in addition to giving the students a much-needed break and a chance to renew friendships, the conference enables them to become aware of any critical gaps in their data on which to focus their remaining time. Subsequent groups have encouraged us to keep the mini-conference as an integral part of our program.

Field School Duration and Course Content

From 1995 through 1997, we held the field school for seven weeks, equivalent to the university's May-June spring term. We discovered that the field session was too short. With a couple of weeks consumed in getting one's bearings and a week devoted to closing down at the end, the data collection and field implementation portion was truncated; though, as the papers in this volume show, the results were still good. The students themselves recommended we lengthen the field school to twelve weeks. We made these changes in 1998, simultaneous with the institution of required preparation courses.

Internships and Community Service

For the first three years, we tried to associate each student with a community member, group, or activity setting that related to the student's life goals and individual project orientation. To help students participate in the community, gain rapport, and succeed in research, we encouraged them to associate several hours a day with some institutional setting or to apprentice themselves with some person so that they could give service in a kind of internship and learn about the institution in the process.[14]

Did the internships work? Mostly. Some of the students tried to study broad topics, such as gender or cosmology, that lacked a specific focus on a person or place. Such topics usually proved too big for a summer and typically overwhelmed those students determined to try them. As directors, we gave advice, made recommendations, and urged compliance, but we always left it to students to make the final determination of their topic and take the consequences. As the student projects increased in scope, the internship setting proved too limiting. This was one factor that led us to discontinue the concept, although we continued to suggest that students begin their research in an internship-type setting.

Our laissez-faire approach to project selection shifted considerably, however, in 2002, when we secured National Science Foundation funding under the Research Experience for Undergraduates program. The NSF funded ten to twelve students each year with a stipend, board and room, and transportation. Additional students joined us who were not funded by NSF. These latter received support from BYU that covered travel and board and room, but not a stipend. With many projects completed on randomly chosen topics during the seven prior years, we sensed that we had to impose some topical focus upon each summer's efforts and aim for a coordinated set of studies related by a theme if we were to maximize the probability of each student producing something publishable. The incorporation of students from three other universities also led us to formalize the on-site field methods review because such a course was not offered by some of the other under-graduate institutions. In addition, NSF's recommendation that Research Experience for Undergraduates sites include ethics instruction led us to include weekly discussion of ethics issues in the field instruction. Adams handles the ethics component because of his five year experience on the Brown University Institutional Review Board.[15]

In addition to giving service in an internship within the context of their research, we encouraged students to donate five to ten hours a week in some labor contribution to the community not related to their study topic. Students tried a number of things. Some taught English. Some formed after-school homework study groups that attracted children from around the neighbor-hood who needed help or wanted friendships. Some translated various documents requesting funding for medical supplies, children's aid, or municipal projects. Some helped municipal leaders make requests to international aid foundations for additional developmental funding for the communities. Although some students ignored the task entirely, most enjoyed the break from the often alienating experience of pure research. Some kind of directly visible service in the community helped students feel less exploitative or self-centered; many wanted to give something back as immediately and as concretely as possible.

Translators and Language Issues

We provided each student with access to a language translator who also served as a guide and broker into the community. Securing good translators was essential, and we have not yet solved the task of training and coaching people to assist us in these ways. This summer (2004), we will experiment with a small school for translators that will meet once a week. Obviously, there has not been time to develop substantial language facility in the students, in spite of some introductory language teaching in the pre-field preparation course offered by the International Office. Having students come with conversational Spanish[16] and teaching them basic K'iche' greetings and a smattering of specialist word families related to their projects seemed the best we could do.

If we had infinite resources, a multi-semester K'iche' course would have been wonderful and would have satisfied Brigham Young University's foreign language requirement. But funding was not available and students probably would have invested their time in more politically dominant languages, such as Spanish. Clearly, lack of facility in K'iche' language imposes limitations on our depth of penetration into K'iche' culture. We have not figured out a way to get undergraduates better ready for research by requiring that they learn a third and somewhat obscure language, especially one that they were not likely to use again. Or so we thought until 2003.

Between January and April of 2004, we experimented with a one-semester K'iche' class, mainly for students at Brigham Young going to Guatemala. To our surprise, all ten of the BYU students going to Guatemala took the course, together with five additional students preparing for the following year's field school. We had not required the course for acceptance. The students simply wanted to be able to converse in the local language, even if only a little, during their residence with families in the community. All of the BYU students preparing for the 2005 field season also took (and some re-took) the course, again without our having made it a requirement. We had underestimated the motivation of undergraduates to prepare solidly for a research experience and we wish we had offered such a course years earlier. Doubt regarding student willingness to prepare was our own worst enemy.

Meeting Difficulties

The above gives the evolutionary details of the structure of our endeavor. What actually happened in the operation of the process? There were problems, of course.

Helping students maintain good health has always been an issue. Over the years, Adams has taken on the responsibility of keeping informed of student health and has converted his vehicle into an ambulance on several occasions. Because of Adams's awareness, local residence, and access to a vehicle, we have had surprisingly few serious medical crises during the first ten summers. Nevertheless, we have to repeatedly remind the students regarding conservative international health practices, to include not eating most fresh fruits and all raw vegetables, avoiding food offered by street vendors, and washing their toothbrushes in bottled water. Some do not listen, and all get sick a time or two, though not all need attention from us.

Culture shock was an issue we faced, primarily in the first two years. To our knowledge, we have had only two students that were incapacitated by (and did not overcome) the initial culture shock that all experience to varying degrees. One student holed up in his room and drank soda pop, making little contact with the villagers; the other became whiny, homesick, and dependent on other students. The latter student got quite sick and yet did not attempt to alert us or seek treatment. When we discovered the extent of her illness and took her to the hospital for a week to get over amoebas and severe dehydration, she requested to return home. We did not discourage her decision. That was the first summer of the field school (1995). I (Hawkins) confess I did not catch the symptoms of culture shock early or deal with them adequately in either case. Efforts to include the afflicted students in other group activities helped to a degree but ultimately were not effectual.

Why did we have so little of such culture shock in subsequent years? For one thing, we learned to choose tougher and more adaptive people. For another, we addressed the phenomenon of culture shock and depression in the preparation classes and encouraged students to counter culture shock by working more vigorously on their defined project, increasing their social contact with the surrounding residents, and sharing their anxieties with fellow students and faculty.

Gender expectations constituted another area of concern. In several ways the female students, just by existing as independent students, contravene the local logic of male-female relations. They do not appear to be properly protected and under the responsibility of a father or husband. In Guatemalan cultural symbology, unchaperoned women appear to be "available," and some men (especially when drunk) have tried to flirt or invite a relationship. For the most part, female students are direct about their lack of interest, and that has defused most circumstances.

Student responses to the occasional inebriated villager posed another concern. In indigenous society, alcohol erodes normal culture inhibitions. For the most part, men express this alcohol-induced freedom by engaging in conversation with our students in surprisingly good English. Sometimes it results in a playful proposal for marriage, also in English. If an inebriated person becomes too insistent, students simply walk away. On occasion, another alert student has rescued the recipient of unwanted attentions. In a society where public contact between males and females is extremely limited, a female student can simply slip her hand into the crook of a male student's elbow to communicate that she is definitely not available. A rumor will brew for a few days that the two students are *novios*, a committed couple. Such rumors can be a useful cultural misperception.

In one instance, however, the obvious escaped us: we had a young male translator work for a female student of similar age. The translator's parents interpreted the frequent proximity of the student with their son as willingness to be married. The student felt she and the translator were just friends, but she had a tendency to plant a kiss on both cheeks of the translator in casual Ladino and Chicano style as a form of initial greeting. Community members interpreted that greeting as advanced pre-marital behavior. Lesson learned: we now require students to select translators of their own gender and we do not assume that students understand the details of local courtship symbolism even if told.

In our worst case, we discovered after the summer was over that a student had made a trip to Mexico without informing project leaders. Although the trip took time away from her research project, we were more concerned about the student's failure to inform anyone of her itinerary. Had there been an accident or a failure to return for whatever reason, we would have not known where to look. If we had found out about such an unannounced journey during the course of the project, we would have immediately dismissed the student from the program. We now are exceedingly explicit about requiring notification regarding travel plans, and we require everyone to have traveling partners for long-distance excursions.

On the whole, over ten summers, relatively few difficulties have been caused by student immaturity. Indeed, the problems now seem inconsequential. We attribute this felicitous state to careful selection and clear standards, known and assented to by the students from the beginning.

Brigham Young University has had some advantages in regard to student selection. In the first place, a number of students in each group have been more mature. Those who had been missionaries for the Mormon Church were two years older than the norm and had learned self-motivation in the missionary process. We also readily accepted and have had several married couples go into the field. They created a stable, home-like, solid atmosphere and invariably helped the younger students acquire serious research study habits. Also, BYU students are preselected as non-alcohol users (by religion for most and by campus honor code for all, alcohol use is not part of the university culture). Moreover, a pervasive and accepted ideology of restrained courtship ideally confines sex within marriage. As a result, we have not had to worry about hurting members of the Maya community as students went about their highly independent existence in the field.

We have tried to duplicate this reliability in the students who have joined us from affiliated universities. Notwithstanding their status as part of the Mormon moral code, the above-mentioned behavioral requirements are basic to the conduct of professional research and provide increased insurance that the students will conduct their studies ethically. By careful screening for maturity and by explicit discussion of the behavioral rules and their reason for existence, we have had little problem with behavior that might endanger our students or offend our local hosts.

Exiting the Field

By the end of twelve weeks, most students have developed extremely warm relationships with their host families and with others in the communities. During the final week, we invite students to visit the various families they have associated with to say their good-byes, leave photographs, and ask a few gap-filling last questions. We encourage students to refine their outlines and begin writing a rough draft of their papers during the second-to-last week of the field season.[17] We believe that writing some of the results of the field experience while still in the field helps students further identify where and what additional information is necessary to complete their research project.

POST-FIELD CONSIDERATIONS

Each summer, as we prepare the students to leave the field in mid-August, we remind them what we told them from the beginning: getting ready for the field and conducting the field investigation, though difficult, are the easy parts of the task. When they go home, their true mettle will be tested by the task of organizing and writing up a mass of field notes and impressions, converting them into a coherent description placed in the context of the literature. We assure them that if they persevere in the lonely task, they will receive valuable criticism and eventually take their work forward through a series of rewrites and public presentations in preparation for eventual publication. If they do so, we tell them, they will have molded themselves into young professionals.

Writing Up

From the beginning, we sought to have students participate in the full round of scholarly activities within the discipline. It was not enough to prepare and then go to the field. It was equally important to write up some part of the results in a paper demonstrating the thrust of their work. Herein lay the greatest difficulty for students and faculty: how to move from the mass of daily field notes to a relatively refined paper after the field school portion of the experience was over and students returned to their universities to begin fall courses. With a slate of fall courses and perhaps a part-time job making demands on their time, students found that self-discipline and regular encouragement from faculty became key elements in the completion of a good paper. While we had warned students that this final phase of completion was the most difficult of the entire project, for many it came as a shock how much data they had to sort through, how difficult it was to write a concluding paper, and how easy it was to write far more than could be contained in a single chapter study.

In the first year, we realized we lacked a mechanism to help students draft and polish papers after returning from fieldwork. Adams distributed a detailed treatise on how to turn a term paper into a paper of publishable quality. After the second summer, Hawkins, realizing further need, organized an informal evening writing seminar for post-field BYU students during the winter semester. This post-field seminar greatly helped students develop the implications of their research.

The success of the seminar led us to formalize the requirement. For a couple of years, Hawkins taught an evening seminar in which the group assembled and went over their papers. In the meantime, Hawkins worked with the department faculty, showing the nature of the problem for all ethnography students. As a result, we changed the department curriculum to include a supervised post-field analysis and writing seminar that aimed at having all students turn field materials into professional, publishable papers. Toward this end, we also examined other university requirements that would assist us. The university's general education program required all students to take an advanced English writing course. We encouraged our students to take this course post-field and make their field project the primary paper for both the English course and their anthropology department writing seminar. Students who took both courses simultaneously thereby had six hours of credit and time allocated to the post-field write-up. In the process, four professors—Adams, Hawkins, and the instructors of the anthropology seminar and the English course—gave suggestions to improve their work.

We have tried to arrange with the English department to tailor a special section of the university's required advanced English course to the needs of post-field anthropology students. So far, that has not happened. Nevertheless, most of the advanced English instructors have course writing assignments that facilitate the development of an ethnographic paper. Thus, while the first groups of students wrote and polished in competition with other courses and job requirements, more recent students benefit from time protections, grade incentives, and advice from several faculty.

Perhaps the most difficult issue has been to upgrade the theoretical grounding and familiarity with the literature for undergraduate students from a variety of disciplines. It is unrealistic to expect any but the most motivated anthropology majors to pursue the existing literature on both Guatemala and anthropological theory to a depth equivalent to a doctoral field proposal. Nevertheless, we have encouraged greater literature control in pre-field seminars and in the post-field write-up classes. Where possible, we provide students with references and guidance on how to use bibliographic tools such as *Social Science Abstracts*, MEDLINE, and the *Social Sciences Citation Index*. We wish we had a ready solution, but the reality is that in a multi-disciplinary context, only a few have taken the time and had the motivation to thoroughly immerse themselves in the requisite literatures of discipline, topic, and geographic area.

Making Conference Presentations

The public oral presentation of research in scholarly symposia is part of the academic process. Early in 1996, we held our first public forum of research papers at BYU with parents and one representative of the International Center attending. We immediately realized that the session could be a panel at a regional academic conference, so, in April 1997 students from the previous summer read their now-polished papers at the Utah Academy of Science, Arts, and Letters annual meeting. Deadlines and the fear of public failure sped the write-up. Succeeding years followed this same pattern. First students present at a local BYU meeting in January. They then read improved versions at a regional professional meeting in April. In 2000, our students delivered an integrated panel of papers at the national meetings of the American Anthropological Association, and we have continued to do so with new groups of students in 2002 and 2003. In 2004, thirteen undergraduate students from the NSF phase of the project plus former undergraduates now studying in anthropology PhD programs and professional schools anchored three panels of papers on religious change in Guatamala at the international congress of the Latin American Studies Association. Encouraging students to prepare for and competently deliver papers at regional and national meetings has fomented quantum leaps in the theoretical grounding of their papers.

As students have moved through the process, they have benefited from professional exposure and successively more rigorous critiques, and their papers become ever more polished. The conference presentations energized the students, who acquitted themselves well and gained confidence from the experience of reading papers to active scholars and responding to their questions.

Other synergies developed: as student papers became available, we created an archive that students in the pre-field preparation course consulted to help orient their research design, and the conferences helped recruit for the following summer's field school.[18] The better students recognized the value of what we were doing and did not mind that the process entailed far more work than was represented by the summer credits given. Less motivated students self-selected not to go. We, the directors, benefited on both counts.

By trying out new ideas and dropping the least effective ones, we were learning how to promote the professionalization of students and stimulate their written output. The attendance at first local, then regional, and finally national conferences develops an esprit de corps, and each increment renews student dedication. We judge these post-field supports to writing—both class and conference experience—critical to student success. Our judgment seems sustained by the observation that about a third of the first three year-groups produced usable finished papers, while about half of the fourth through sixth year groups students did so under informal arrangements. By contrast, about three-quarters of the recent groups of students—operating under our full post-field activities—are producing usable work. Moreover, the most recent three years of student papers have more consistently and thoroughly tied their research projects into existing academic literature, whereas few of the first several year-groups did so. In short, we, as directors, were learning how to marshal and support undergraduate student research efforts more effectively.

For the directors also, the post-field phase was critical to success and yet the most difficult for us to attend to because of competing commitments. Current teaching obligations made it difficult to read and critique the many papers from previous summers, coming at a rate of thirty or more papers per year of first, second, third, and later drafts, sometimes years after the fieldwork on which they were based.

OVERALL STAFFING CONSIDERATIONS

Running such a project takes an enormous commitment of time and attention. While much of the detail work can be delegated to a good student facilitator (or a full-time administrator, had we been able to afford one), we do not recommend faculty take on the task without having considerable devotion to undergraduate education, preferably within an institution that both directly rewards and fully supports undergraduate development.

Our two-person primary division of labor has worked well. Hawkins has been resident at BYU and has managed the day-to-day details of the recruitment and post-field phases. Adams lives in Guatemala, where his close access to the villages has enabled him to reliably provide classes and counseling once a week and respond to emergencies. Adams's residence in Guatemala has been essential to another facet of the program: political risk analysis. It has been enormously helpful to have someone in the country, assessing the nature of political risk in Guatemala with access to real-time, personally experienced data. State Department reports are inadequate because they have been too inflammatory relative to the fairly calm state of daily life in the rural villages.

Finally, the existence of two directors has allowed a consultative "reality check" throughout the endeavor. Having a co-director to talk to has resulted in better and more refined implementation of good ideas and the quick death of some thoroughly bad ideas. Moreover, we have each been able to cover for the other when events have demanded our attention or presence elsewhere.

We have consistently found that our differences in perspective and mutual interest in alternative paradigms have benefited the students. They have been disabused quickly of the illusion that there is only one way to do things in anthropology. Our students, as undergraduates, have already had to confront the dilemmas that master's degree and doctoral students face: diversity of opinion between us, like diversity of opinion in a doctoral committee, forces students to evaluate the suggestions they receive and ultimately take control of making field and writing decisions for themselves.

Hiring a responsible student from the previous year as field facilitator greatly reduces the burden on faculty. All of our facilitators have been undergraduate senior anthropology majors who attended the field school the previous year. The facilitator manages appointments and correspondence during the next year's recruitment phase; meets twice a week with the student group during the pre-field preparation phase; and handles basic cultural orientation, trip preparation details, and assignment grading. In the field, the facilitator both conducts an independent research project (entering graduate school with six months' fieldwork and one or two ethnographic papers) and deals with many student problems that might not be brought to director attention. The facilitator provides additional peer assistance to junior students having difficulty in data acquisition. Post-field, the facilitator orients the next summer's facilitator and teaches or co-teaches the Guatemala-focused component of the International Center's preparation course.

The Impact of National Science Foundation Funding

In the summer of 2001, we applied for National Science Foundation funding under the Research Experience for Undergraduates program. The Foundation liked our project and negotiated with us to cut costs by eliminating funds for post-field professionalization. The compromise resulted in funding for twelve students in each of two summers (2002 and 2003) and ten students for each of 2004, 2005 and 2006. Students receive transportation, board and room, and a substantial stipend for the twelve weeks.[19] The grant was specifically oriented to enhance minority recruitment to the social sciences, so we connected BYU with three universities with large minority-Hispanic student populations: University of Illinois at Chicago, Southwest Texas State University, and University of Texas Panamerican. We modeled the grant proposal on what we had already been doing and did not anticipate big changes.

We were wrong; however, the changes stimulated by the funding have been positive. We detail some of them here.

With funding, we found we needed to recruit much earlier in the pre-field stage—in September and October rather than November and December. At each university, an affiliated Mesoamericanist anthropologist helped us find the best-qualified Spanish-speaking students (of any ethnicity) in their programs. In 2002, funding was secured in April, just a month before our departure and there was no time to adequately prepare the students from the affiliated universities. We did much better in subsequent years in preparing the affiliated university students and connecting them with the BYU students, mostly by webcasting the preparation course. Beginning in the fall of 2003, Hawkins and Adams also traveled to the affiliate universities to assist in recruitment. Students seem less fearful about going to Guatemala if they have seen us in person. A single visit to the affiliated universities greatly increases the application rate of their students.

In the field, the primary change in response to the participation of non-BYU students entailed reviewing field methods and covering research ethics. These classes were held with all the students once a week in one town. The joint class sessions enabled students to discuss their topics with each other and with the faculty. While we had always held class and advised students before, the larger size of the group and the fact of different backgrounds emerging from the differences in four participating universities forced a greater degree of formalization of the classes.

It is in the post-field activities that the NSF funding decisions have let us down. With no funds to take the students to national meetings or hold the group together, we have not had a consistent means of assisting the affiliated university students to endure the cold, hard, lonely task of writing. The affiliated students have had to conjure up research liaisons with faculty at their own universities to imitate some of the post-field writing support that we now have standardized in our program at BYU. We do not yet know the full consequences of this difference in post-field access, support, and sociality for non-BYU students.

EVALUATING THE PROJECT

In the first three years, we did not recruit students early enough for them to gain the tools to set up a research design or prospectus for their project.

As a result, while all papers reflect contact with Guatemalan cultural reality, the early ones do so without significant reference to published academic discourse. Nevertheless, we find significant thematic resonance between the student papers from all the field summers and the issues and findings of academic Mayan studies. The chapters in this volume, some ungraced by academic citation, confirm and add detail to the findings of academics.

Some of the papers, however, are at odds with the published findings. For example, several students were unable to identify a difference in Catholic versus Protestant orientation to market activities, such as Annis (1987) notes. Transformations associated with the passage of time or the difference in location perhaps account for such divergent observations.

Some of the papers have value in that they explore issues that professional anthropologists, absorbed in the topical norms of the discipline, have not examined. For example, Tarra Lynn was an anthropology major who knew she wanted to pursue a master's degree in social work, which led her to explore the cultural nature of disability. Her paper covers ground that might not have been examined by students emerging from traditional anthropology graduate programs. Papers by several premed students, designated for another volume, likewise cover unusual material.

One anonymous reviewer of an early volume of this manuscript lamented the difficulties of operating a field school and eliciting a final write-up:

> My own experience with running a field school in Mexico was that a lot of my time was spent handling student issues, from logistical things like providing suitable living arrangements to personal issues like homesickness, work ethic problems and the like. [Hawkins and Adams] make it all sound so normative and easy to resolve. My experience was just the opposite, and that solutions were only partial. . . . I found field schools to be an incredible drain and I got little of my own work done, which is especially problematic since field schools tend to be run in the summer, the one chunk of time ethnographers have to do independent research in the course of the year. I also discovered that in academia there is little recognition of the contribution one makes by running a field school. Do [Hawkins and Adams] have doubts about doing this? How has it played out in career terms since they have obviously made a big commitment to it?

These candid observations certainly push to the core of the problems of running a field school. Indeed, both of us (Hawkins and Adams) spent a considerable amount of time assisting students and solving problems. In the process, however, we made contacts with many K'iche' families and community leaders that, because of the essential goodwill of all of the students, helped us be seen as good people within the community. Both of us were known as the "professors of [name of student]," and therefore almost kin to students now incorporated into the family life of so many households. We would have had great difficulty generating the broad trust in two communities that we now benefit from had we operated as lone ethnographers. The field facilitators, who were experienced students, were also key to the early discovery of and solution of problems. We simply trusted the facilitators and the married couples to give wise advice to the younger students, and they generally did. Thus, many problems were resolved by students caring for each other.

Regarding individual work, Adams has used his contacts in the community and residence nearby to do the research underlying one published paper on alcohol abuse (W. R. Adams 1999) and another in preparation. Hawkins has a paper nearly completed on the general education value of fieldwork and another on K'iche' and Spanish code-switching. That is not much for an investment of nine years and ten summers. Indeed, like the anonymous reviewer, Hawkins has gotten little of his "own work" done to date, but he is currently living with the traditional shamans of one hamlet precisely because one exemplary, well remembered and loved student opened the doors ten summers ago. By this connection, and because two recent facilitators were particularly conscientious, Hawkins has been able to immerse himself in language and ritual studies more than in previous years.

Nevertheless, as the reviewer mentions above, research-oriented universities pay relatively little attention to the time and effort that a field school entails. We therefore share some similarity with the athletic coaches of a university: the success of our own careers is tied to our ability to coach and cajole students into performance beyond what they thought possible or reasonable. Do we experience a bit of angst in the endeavor? You bet! Winning the conference, in this case, requires motivating good undergraduate students to do research successfully, write well, stay motivated, and keep training (writing and doing literature searches) long after the obvious game (fieldwork) is over. They thereby bring the whole to publication. That is the win at the bowl game. Fostering and witnessing student development is a worthy goal in itself. But, in the context of a university that praises good teaching but more directly rewards publication, we would have torpedoed our careers had we not succeeded in publishing this book.

The students, though, have sensed our mutual interdependence and most have striven to succeed. They have done so for multiple reasons. Many have wanted to improve their prospects for admission to graduate schools, though we have not managed to bring this to print quickly enough to do them much good in that regard. Most have delighted in the field experience itself and in developing excellence in research and writing. And most have appreciated the investment the coaches have made in them and have done their best to accomplish what the coaches wanted: in this case, to add to a corpus of worthwhile knowledge about the K'iche' through publication, and in the process, to turn undergraduates into budding scholars.

In bringing this volume to publication, without doubt our careers will benefit; or at any rate, the research part of our careers will not have been undermined. If we succeed in bringing other volumes to publication—we have separate volumes under development on health practices, community fission, village economics, religious transformation in the Maya villages, and public health problems—the research facets of our careers will more than benefit. Moreover, we will have succeeded in exemplifying one successful approach to the emerging national trend that seeks to involve undergraduates in legitimate research experiences. We were willing to take these career risks both for the rewards of being involved in mentoring fine young people from a variety of universities and, as called for by Marcus and Fischer (1986:40–44), to demonstrate a new experimental mode of anthropological representation, in this case, via cumulative cultural documentation through many coordinated small projects done by undergraduates.

We mention such considerations because in university situations where publications significantly influence retention, pay, and promotion, the system conspires against investment in undergraduate research unless the research can be published. Within anthropology, student field data can not be absorbed into a professor's database in the same way that undergraduate student labor in a science lab might be. Perhaps bringing these tensions to the fore will facilitate their resolution at a time when involving undergraduates in research increasingly becomes a national mantra.[20]

To summarize, one solution to developing undergraduate research in anthropology, exemplified here, involves dedicated commitment from both faculty and students long after the formal end of a field school season. For those contemplating launching a field school, be prepared to make the follow-on investment of labor and guide the students into interlocking, mutually supporting projects so that in any given year, and long term, the whole exceeds the sum of the individual undergraduate parts. The result should permit direct student publication and not just provide the directors with fodder to produce a summation or synthesis.

Finally, we note that we face a dilemma between our role as field directors and our role as editors. As field directors, we would like to publish all of our students' papers. As editors, we recognize that only a few of the best papers will see print. To do justice to other excellent works, we have set up a website (http://maya.byu.edu) to make papers available that for reasons of space or duplication of message could not be included, though they contain valuable information. To maintain academic integrity, only the better unpublished papers are posted to the website; others necessarily remain in the project files as unpublished manuscripts. In addition, the website will provide pictures to accompany this book.

FIELD RESEARCH AS GENERAL EDUCATION

We believe that anthropological field research engages students in the purest form of general education. Students experience the culture shock of encountering a different reality. The experience is not just theoretical, mediated by books and professors; it is visceral, acquired through interacting with others, but also through the direct experience of hunger or the shocking feeling of having diarrhea with no easy access to medical attention and realizing that the family one lives with has virtually no access at all. Through such experiences, students acquire greater understanding of other conceptual realities and empirical constraints. In these papers, the students confront critically their own "-isms" and gain cultural insight about their own background in the process.

Many of the papers display a gradually increasing awareness of a student's cultural ethnocentrism. We have tried not to edit out such developing realization of their own naiveté, because it is of value to others to see fellow students struggle against the bands and blinders of our own cultural background. This, of course, is a primary value of cross-cultural immersion. The degree to which the experience changed their lives comes out clearly in some of the following chapters and in the biographical sketches provided at the beginning of each chapter. Such transformation of perspective—the ability to contemplate and evaluate the roots of cultural and societal constraint and one's place in the process—is the essence of good general education. All this is acquired through intense, interactive, reflective research experience in the field school context.

At another level, the intern experience provides students with an opportunity to apply their school-acquired knowledge to the real world and provides each community with exposure to another perspective and context for interpreting the student outsiders. In this process, students overcome the alienation that seems to be inherent in intense academic training divorced from context. The intern experience has at least two benefits. First, it provides them with the acute shock of encountering a reality not often described in the texts they read in academic institutions. In applied situations, students experience the important value of coming to understand other conceptual realities, including the experiential and empirical constraints that "real people" contend with daily. At the same time, the training they have received has value, and by virtue of that training, students are in a position to provide assistance to those in need. Students involved in an internship, then, have the opportunity to reciprocate by providing a service to those who are helping them. The internship and service components of the participant-observation research experience add a "service learning" facet to the general education they are acquiring. In our "I-centered" society and culture, such learning is general education of the most radical kind.

One complaint often leveled at the ordinary undergraduate classroom experience is that it does not provide students with the skills they will need in graduate school. For example, many (if not most) students in anthropology do not engage in fieldwork until they are conducting research leading to their doctoral dissertation. By this time, it is often too late for students to realize that perhaps they are not cut out to do research under the rigorous conditions imposed by the field experience. Having students engage in fieldwork as undergraduates gives them a sense of what to expect when they do go into the field for their doctoral dissertation research.

We believe that too much of undergraduate education is essentially rote learning and paraphrasing of existing literature and does not permit students the opportunity to attempt to integrate their own experience with the existing literature or to effectively critique others. By contrast, the fieldwork experience and the encouragement to refine, publish, and present the results of this research in professional fora require that students develop these skills. We have learned slowly, and continue to learn, how to help students develop these professional skills.

Beyond the enhancement to student general education, if we succeed in bringing additional materials to print, we will have coached students to produce a unique corpus of writings about many facets of K'iche' culture in an otherwise little-studied region. That will truly constitute success in the standard coin of the academic realm; and, in doing so, this project will have demonstrated that serious undergraduates with reasonably competent mentoring under a focused long-term project can indeed contribute to the accumulated fund of knowledge about the richness of human existence. We encourage others to improve upon our methods of collaboration with undergraduates, report those improvements, and employ them to intensively document culture, society, and human agency in other regions of the world.

NOTES

1. Coombs et al. (1977:155) likewise note, "we have found it necessary to become acquainted with a substantially broader range of methodological tools for dealing with the complexities of modern industrial society."

2. Vogt (1994) reports the substance of the experience in his autobiographical *Fieldwork among the Maya*. See especially chapters 6 and 7 for evocative descriptions of the placement and achievements of students, and chapter 11.

3. Such, for example, is the suggestion of McGoodwin (1978:149).

4. McGoodwin (1978:181), in retrospect, suggests he would prefer to take only graduate students next time, because "their greater maturity and better understanding of anthropology . . . would . . . offer more to the director, members of the host culture, and anthropology itself."

5. See also a separate comment by Levine (1999:249–50) in the same issue, addressing the fact that education need not be entirely in the classroom. We would argue that culminating educational experiences are best not conducted in the classroom.

6. *Ethnicity in Guatemala, Mexico, and Belize: Latinos, Mayas, and Theories of Ethnic Process.* 13th International Congress of Anthropological and Ethnological Sciences, Mexico City, August 1993.

7. Eric Foxtree (personal communication) has found evidence that the community of Nahualá and its conflict with Santa Catarina have much deeper historical roots, reaching back perhaps four hundred years.

8. Only about a third of our students have been anthropology or sociology majors.

9. Even in the few cases where culture shock or illness led to a difficult experience, the students were changed for the good by the cultural experience and learned more about themselves than would have been possible otherwise.

10. As a result of this restriction, the reader will not find much information about the internal political conflict that engulfed Guatemala.

11. The student facilitators also participated in these discussions, absenting themselves if topics of a personal nature arose.

12. In addition, many of the students needed the nine credit hours during the spring and summer terms to activate scholarships or receive Pell Grants or loans.

13. We also invite one or two other scholars working in the area to attend these conferences so that students receive a wider range of critiques. The conferences have been well received by the students.

14. Spradley (1979) recommends this approach to student field projects.

15. The inclusion of ethics in fieldwork discussions was further prompted by the "Darkness in El Dorado" controversy (Tierney 2000; Fluehr-Lobban 2003).

16. A few students each year have elected to go to one of several Spanish language schools in Quezaltenango for a few weeks to improve their Spanish prior to the field school.

17. The weekly documents that students prepare regarding their activities facilitate this preliminary write-up.

18. Copies of the papers and field notes are also available in a project library in Panajachel, Guatemala, in the care of Walter Adams (walteradams@guate.net.gt).

19. For 2000–03, $275 per week. For 2004–06, $300 per week.

20. As evidence, we cite both the Research Experience for Undergraduates program of the NSF, and a consortium of some 850 universities allied in the enterprise of fostering undergraduate research involvement.

CHAPTER 1

NAHUALÁ AND
SANTA CATARINA IXTAHUACÁN
IN CONTEXT

Walter Randolph Adams and John P. Hawkins

The municipalities (*municipios*) of Nahualá and Santa Catarina Ixtahuacán stretch from the lowlands to the highest ridges of the Pacific volcanic escarpment in the western highlands of Guatemala. From Nahualá, 162 kilometers of sinuous highway lead east to Guatemala City, the republic's capital; 45 kilometers wind west to Quezaltenango, the republic's second largest city; and about 35 kilometers of road sprawl east and south, dropping precipitously to Sololá, the departmental capital. The Pan-American Highway passes through the municipio of Nahualá, about one kilometer by trail and two kilometers by road to the south of Nahualá's municipal center.

Santa Catarina Ixtahuacán's municipal center is quite isolated. From Nahualá, the Pan-American Highway climbs steeply for about six kilometers to a junction where a rough-cut dirt road joins the highway at a dangerous but spectacular ridge-top curve. The Pan-American Highway continues on, rising further to Sija, the windswept 3,100-meter pass claimed by both Santa Catarina and Nahualá. From the junction, the ten-kilometer, intermittently graveled mountain road climbs briefly, flattens, and then descends steeply and sinuously to Ixtahuacán's plaza and principal church.

The steep final descent and change in vegetation give the impression that Santa Catarina is much lower than Nahualá. However, Santa Catarina's municipal center, at 2,320 meters above sea level, is just 147 meters lower than Nahualá's municipal center, at 2,467 meters above sea level (Direción General de Cartografía 1961, 1962).

Much of Nahualá's land and population is located at a higher altitude than the majority of Santa Catarina, with the exception of Santa Catarina's

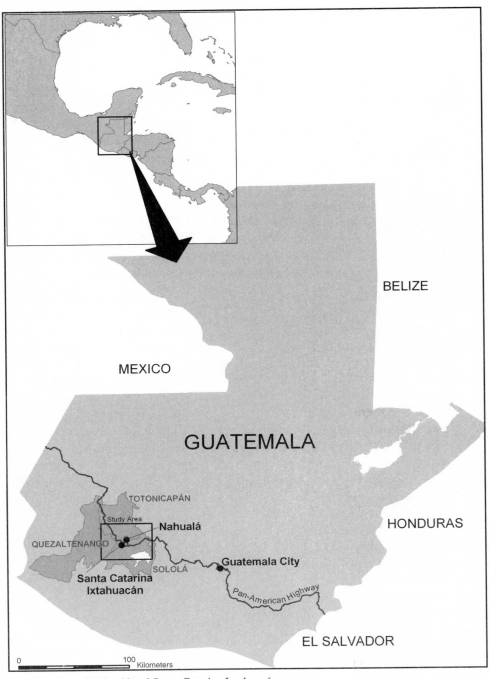

Location of Nahualá and Santa Catarina Ixtahuacán.

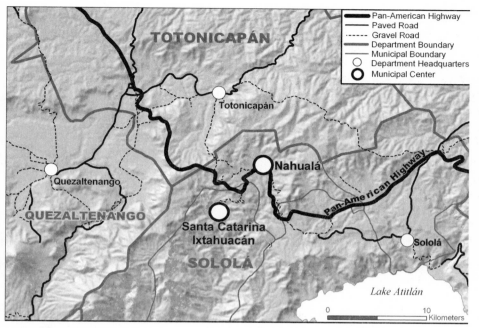

Study area.

large hamlet of Chirijox and the high, desolate, area, called Sija locally, and known as "Alaska" throughout the western region because of its cold temperatures.[1] Nahualá, on the whole, is much rockier, the vegetation sparser and more adapted to cold temperatures. Frost is a greater problem in Nahualá, and individuals have been known to die from exposure during December and January.

These conditions impose limits on what crops can be grown successfully in Nahualá. As might be expected, *milpa* horticulture—the hoe cultivation of corn and occasionally beans—predominates. There is, however, some cultivation of potatoes and wheat. Both of the latter are hardy enough to withstand the colder temperatures. Santa Catarina, on the other hand, with its greater variety of climates, produces corn, beans, potatoes, and vegetables in *tierra fría*, while coffee, bananas, and cardamom are planted lower on the Pacific slopes (Proyecto Salquil 1992:24).

Some say that thirty years ago the slopes and tops of the mountains of both Nahualá and Santa Catarina Ixtahuacán were covered with pine trees and some hardwoods. Today, only Santa Catarina has extensive visible forest land. In Nahualá, the slopes are comparatively barren, the trees having been cut down to open more land for agriculture, to warm the homes of a population that has increased by almost 50 percent between 1981 and 1994, and to provide raw materials for the wood-carvers who produce furniture, masks, and figurines (Gall 1981:712). Indeed, many erstwhile sawyers in Nahualá have complained that they have had to learn a new trade because they find it difficult to obtain wood with which to work. However, there is no evidence of effort to ameliorate deforestation there. In contrast, one sees considerable effort to protect the remaining trees of Santa Catarina.

Population Distribution

The total population of the municipio of Nahualá in 1994 was 40,737, while that of Santa Catarina Ixtahuacán was 34,198 (Dirección General de Estadística 1994). Like most municipios in Guatemala, the municipios of Nahualá and Santa Catarina each consist of a single nucleated town center, called the *cabecera municipal*, surrounded by numerous rural hamlets. The 1994 census shows that 6.7 percent of the inhabitants of the municipios of both Nahualá (2,761 persons) and Ixtahuacán (2,250 persons) live in the municipio centers. The rest of the population lives in rural hamlets located between thirty minutes' and seven hours' walk from their respective municipal centers. In 1961, Nahualá consisted of a town center with twenty-four subordinate *"caseríos"* (small hamlets) and two *aldeas* (larger hamlets) with ten and six subordinate caseríos, respectively. Ixtahuacán was less focused, its town center having just three attached caseríos, but it had seven aldeas, one with thirteen caseríos and the other six with an average of three caseríos each.[2] The similar proportion of individuals living in the urban area of both municipal centers may reflect the carrying capacity of the service sector (R. N. Adams 1988).

The 1994 census also shows that only 0.61 percent of the residents of the municipio of Nahualá identified themselves as Ladino (signifying a mix of European and Indian descent but maintaining symbolic orientation outside the indigenous municipio), while 1.53 percent of the residents of the municipio of Santa Catarina Ixtahuacán identified themselves as Ladino.[3] However, fully half of those who identified themselves as Ladino in Santa Catarina Ixtahuacán lived in a *cantón* (hamlet) located on the coast. This region of Guatemala is predominantly inhabited by Ladinos. If one removes this cantón from consideration, the percentage of Ladinos in Santa Catarina is about the same as that of Nahualá.

HISTORICAL ORIGIN OF THE COMMUNITIES

Santa Catarina Ixtahuacán was founded during the colonial period and has long had municipal status. It was a governmental and commercial center for the region, serving as a way-station on the *camino real* between Guatemala City and San Cristóbal de Las Casas, capitals of the colonial kingdom's two major provinces. By one account, the first reference to a town called Nahualá occurs in a document describing the period from March 15, 1884, to March 15, 1888 (Morales Urrutia 1961, vol. 2:579). Undoubtedly, its settlement began some time before that.

Much of what is known about the origins of Nahualá comes to us from oral traditions rather than documents. As might be expected, there are many varied accounts of the separation of Nahualá from Santa Catarina. Santa Catarina's leaders have recorded one colorful account in an economic survey created by a non-governmental organization (NGO) to solicit funds:

> According to the Comité Pro-mantenimiento de Bienes Comunales y Título Territorial, before 1862, peace, tranquility and unity reigned in the municipalities. Problems began in 1862, when Governor Manuel Tzoc began the problems between him and Miguel Salquil, Principal of the same people, due to personal intrigues and because both had an interest in the same woman. As a result, they could not agree on all that would be done, primarily with regard to the construction of the church. Manuel Tzoc wanted the construction of carved stone, while Salquil wanted brick; Tzoc also wanted a live crucifixion of Christ, sacrificing a person for this purpose. This caused conflict among both leaders and their followers.
>
> The situation became more difficult because Tzoc already had in mind the idea to separate and sent a *regidor* to a place called Pak'isis. On Friday, April 17, 1865, a great confrontation began, during which Tzoc announced that from this date he and his followers were no longer residents of Ixtahuacán and that they would form a new cantón, independent of Ixtahuacán. A battle erupted, in which approximately 3,000 people died.
>
> Proyecto Salquil (1992:21, 23)

The same document offers a second rendition of the tale which emphasizes the active combat participation of Ixtahuaquense women in the battle.

Besieged by the followers of Tzoc, no one was allowed to enter or exit the combat zone for some days.

> Anyone seen attempting to leave by some footpath or exit was immediately attacked with a cudgel. For this reason, authorities had no knowledge of what had taken place until a group of merchants arrived. When they were told what had taken place, they went to break the news to the authorities, who intervened and, for once and for all, separated the cantón . . . [that] later was called Nahualá.
>
> Proyecto Salquil (1992:23)

In this second version, Santa Catarina is saved by women and itinerant merchants, both prominent aspects of indigenous society vis-à-vis the Ladinos. Regardless of versions, there is strong circumstantial evidence that Nahualá achieved municipal status in the 1890s. The split into two municipalities set conditions for boundary disputes that continue to the present. Most often, one hears the rivalry expressed in the form of bantering and ribbing. The separation is by no means total, for a number of individuals from the two communities have married each other. But, sometimes, the rivalry gets expressed with more vehemence. In 1998 and 1999 the tension over land use in Sija boiled over and resulted in the loss of life as the two communities again engaged in hand-to-hand combat.

We recognize that this is not a thorough history of the two communities, a matter that we will treat at greater length in a subsequent volume on the fission of the town center of Santa Catarina Ixtahuacán. This is sufficient, however, to establish that the towns share a single cultural origin, and it sets the stage for the next historical event of consequence—the building of the Pan-American Highway through Nahualá.

ROADS AND CHANGE

First cut as a gravel track in the early 1950s and paved in the 1960s, the Pan-American Highway passes just south of Nahualá's municipal center because community elders prohibited passage of the road through town (Gall 1981:712). Access roads, about two and three kilometers in length, connect the east and west ends of town to the highway. The same highway passes further from Santa Catarina Ixtahuacán, to which it connects by a rough, dirt spur road, ten kilometers in length, marked by steep descents.

Although the Pan-American Highway did not pass through Nahuala's town center, its construction led to the commercial florescence and transformation of Nahualá and to the concomitant decline of Santa Catarina Ixtahuacán. The weekly market that developed in Nahualá, for example, is at least twenty times and perhaps as much as fifty times larger than its counterpart in Santa Catarina Ixtahuacán. This estimate of relative size difference applies to the physical area covered by vendors who lay out their wares on mats or set up portable stands. It applies also to the number of sellers, because Nahualá attracts a large number of itinerant vendors from other towns, whereas Santa Catarina attracts only a few. Moreover, Nahualá's market attracts vastly more buyers than Santa Catarina's market. Frequent buses bring many hundreds of out-of-towners to market in Nahualá. Only one bus plies the steep, rocky road to bring potential customers to Santa Catarina's plaza. The quality and variety of products also is much greater in Nahualá.[4]

In addition to ubiquitous one-story, tile- and (increasingly) tin-roofed houses, there are several two-story and a few three-story concrete commercial retail stores in Nahualá, in addition to a general store, gas station, and several relatively substantial pharmacies. By contrast, in Santa Catarina one finds only single-story storefronts attached to homes; it has no gas station, no general store, and only two small pharmacies, one of them in a tiny general store on the plaza and one in the entry room of a home.

NAHUALÁ AND SANTA CATARINA IXTAHUACÁN IN LOCAL CONTEXT

The Department of Sololá, the administrative home to both Nahualá and Santa Catarina Ixtahuacán, is among the poorest departments in Guatemala, in spite of the presence of major tourist centers such as Panajachel. Furthermore, Nahualá and Ixtahuacán are among the poorest of Sololá's municipios.

The Local Economics of Nahualá

Nahualenses are primarily subsistence agriculturalists who work small plots of land. According to employees of Dirección General de Servicios Agrícolas (DIGESA, Guatemala's agricultural extension service), the average family needs at least six *cuerdas* of land to provide the corn they would consume in a year.[5] The population explosion and inheritance practices requiring that offspring inherit land equally result in most families owning

Table 1 Land holdings reported by 95 youths in Nahualá.

Amount of land (*cuerdas*)	0	1 to 2	3 to 4	5 to 6	7 to 10	11+
Percent of responses	68	4.2	11.5	6.3	6.3	4.2

Source: (W. R. Adams 1999).

land parcels that are too small to provide enough food to feed a family for the entire year.

Employees of DIGESA and others consistently told Adams that most families in Nahualá had four cuerdas or less. In 1997, W. R. Adams (1999) conducted a survey of ninety-five young men between the ages of fifteen and twenty-eight, asking how much land they had access to. The average was 2.3 cuerdas. As seen in Table 1, most individuals had access to no land at all. A nurse at the health center stated that roughly 70 percent of the families in Nahualá had to purchase corn in June, an indication that many families could not depend entirely on their production to meet family needs. In this respect the youth in our sample may reflect the demographic conditions of the community.

Deforestation, lack of terraces,[6] and the constant use of the same parcel of land without letting it lie fallow have combined to reduce agricultural yields (Leonard 1987). Most Nahualenses are aware of the need to invest in agricultural inputs such as chemical fertilizers and pesticides to keep agricultural yields high, because DIGESA and Peace Corps volunteers tell them so. Because these products are expensive, many families can not purchase enough to provide yields high enough to warrant their use. Consequently, many farmers either use these products in a way that limits their value or do not use them at all. Per capita corn yields thus continue to decline, pushing families to seek additional or alternative sources of income.

The population pressure has increased the demand for land, which, in turn, results in a scarcity of unowned land regardless of agricultural quality. Even if land were available for sale, its cost has skyrocketed over the past twenty-five years, so that most families find it difficult to acquire more. The best agricultural lands sold for 35 U.S. dollars per cuerda twenty-five years ago. Today, that same plot of land sells for about 600 dollars. In 1970, a man had to work approximately 50 days to buy a cuerda of this land; he would have to work 230 days to purchase it at current wage-labor prices. In 1970, lower-quality land sold for about 6 U.S. dollars; today it sells for about 150 U.S. dollars. A man would have had to work 9 days for it in 1970; today, he has to work 50 days (W. R. Adams 1999). Moreover, today, there are many more things on which to spend the money that comes from the land. These include Western-style dress, radios, chemical fertilizer, galvanized tin roofs, pickup trucks, and even fast food in nearby towns. As a result, the accumulation of capital by wage labor to buy needed land is even more difficult than before.

We have seen very few head of cattle in Nahualá; pigs are also relatively scarce. Some herds of goats and sheep in both towns, especially in the portion of Nahualá with the highest altitude, subsist on the harsh grasses characteristic of such elevations and climate. Chickens and turkeys are also present, but in fewer numbers than one might expect. One possible reason for the low number of livestock is the absence of food. The high, rugged terrain provides tough and less-than-adequate natural vegetation for most animals. The absence of natural fodder imposes the need to provide concentrates or corn. Most families cannot purchase the concentrates due to lack of capital, and the corn is needed to feed family members rather than livestock.

In the past, Nahualá was also known for producing quantities of wheat, sold to make chicory coffee and to bake bread. With the passage of the North American Free Trade Agreement (NAFTA), however, better-quality baking wheat from the United States flooded the Guatemalan market, and wheat production in this area has declined precipitously.

Nahualenses also produce and sell home furnishings such as chairs, chests, and dressers. Some use the income to supplement their diminishing crops; others, to provide their primary income. Vendors of these products have often complained there are few customers for their products. A local Evangelical church provided vocational education in carpentry, but carpenters said they found it difficult to obtain wood. With few customers and a shortage of raw materials, many men trained as carpenters no longer practice their trade.

Historically, Nahualá was known for the textiles it produced primarily for personal wear and for sale to tourists. However, the tourist interest in traditional textiles plummeted during the civil war and has not recovered to any great extent. Moreover, few tourists go to Nahualá, preferring instead tourist towns such as Antigua, Chichicastenango, and Panajachel. Thus Nahualenses have to travel to the primary tourist towns to sell their wares, where they compete with hundreds of vendors from many other communities.

Nahualá is justly famous for the production of manos and metates, tools made of volcanic rock for grinding corn. This industry, too, is on the wane, a victim of the shift from grinding corn in the home to grinding corn in a gas-powered *molino* (mill).

To obtain cash, many males, and sometimes entire families, used to travel to the Pacific coast to work as wage laborers on coffee and cotton plantations. This was a last resort because working conditions were poor, and the plantation workers often brought home tropical diseases such as malaria and dysentery. Even this source of income, however, has been closed to many Nahualenses because falling coffee prices have diminished the need for labor in the coffee-growing areas along the south coast, and the fluctuating labor demand is now more than met by permanent coastal residents, who suffered unemployment as high as 45 percent in 1994 (B. H. Adams 1994).[7] Coffee growers also prefer local workers because they have known work records and backgrounds, important matters in a country still struggling to recover from a guerrilla war (B. H. Adams 1994). These factors, then, mean that few individuals from Nahualá find employment as wage laborers on distant plantations.

In short, none of the traditional economic patterns are viable for most inhabitants of the municipio. The lack of employment and economic opportunities has especially hurt the males, who, by cultural norm, are supposed to be economically active providers. Those men who own some land keep busy by working on their milpas or going into the mountains to cut firewood. Younger males help their fathers in the fields or play with their siblings or friends.

It is no wonder that many individuals (some as young as fifteen years of age) have left the community to seek their fortunes elsewhere. A number of families have a relative living in the United States, most of them illegally.[8] Remittances provide an additional source of income, but many families remarked in 1995 and 1996 that such windfalls were both small and infrequent.

These conditions may be the reason that Nahualenses continue to produce subsistence crops rather than cash crops: given the absence of any viable means of obtaining cash while living in Nahualá, the production of subsistence crops is the only way they can ensure that their families will have food to eat at least for some part of the year. In this regard, the situation in Nahualá is the opposite of what Cancian (1992) reports in Chiapas, Mexico. There, the capitalist economy has provided continual infusions of capital, and this has allowed the Chiapanecos to rely more fully on the cash economy rather than subsistence agriculture. In Nahualá, by contrast, there is no regular infusion of external capital, and subsistence agriculture is the only option available.

Under these conditions, then, it is not surprising that individuals find ingenious ways of obtaining needed cash. In Nahualá, one of the responses has been the production of an illegal alcoholic beverage known as *cuxa*. No one knows for certain how much cuxa is produced in Nahualá. Municipal authorities, however, know that one *cuxero* produces three thousand liters per month. They also know there are between twelve and fifteen operations in the area. From this they estimate that total production is around thirty thousand liters per month (W. R. Adams 1999). Most, if not all, of this is consumed locally.[9]

The Local Economics of Ixtahuacán

Many Santa Catarina Ixtahuacán residents must also supplement their agricultural subsistence production with other kinds of work. Although they have, on average, more agricultural land than Nahualenses (Proyecto Salquil 1992:63), they generally do not have enough to provide a comfortable subsistence that also covers the cost of market purchases.[10] Ixtahuacán embraces a wide ecological span, having land from alpine "Alaska" to the semitropical "*boca costa.*" Thus, Ixtahuaquenses can plant a variety of crops in addition to corn if they have suitable land. Those living lower on the mountain cultivate lowland crops including coffee, and they labor on the plantations (*fincas*) when they can. Even those living near the upland municipal center participate in lowland coffee wage labor, but to a lesser extent. The same ecological diversity has enabled a few intrepid farmers to try their hand with cabbage and, beginning in 1997, broccoli. The latter has not yet been seen in Nahualá, and cabbage is not as common as in Ixtahuacán, presumably because of less favorable climatic conditions.

Several minor economic activities help Ixtahuaquenses supplement their incomes, though not to great prominence. Some Ixtahuaquenses herd sheep. Women weave primarily for their own use; we have never seen a tourist buyer come to Ixtahuacán center and only occasionally do they appear on the streets of Nahualá. Ixtahuaquenses sell their work to intermediaries in Nahualá or in the nearby tourist centers. The few who lack a commercial intermediary must travel to one or another tourist center and hawk their wares directly, but they are less likely to do so than women from Nahualá. Two or three of the residents of the Ixtahuacán town center make furniture and other carpentry products. A number of residents make extra income by exploiting the communal and private forests for timber and firewood.[11] Two primitive sawmills operate in town, and a hike along any mountain trail reveals occasionally the site of legal or illegal logging and the makeshift stands for hand-sawing rough planks. With the possible exception of Chirijox aldea, Ixtahuaquenses do not produce manos and metates.

Certainly Santa Catarina Ixtahuacán presents none of the developed commercial aspects of Nahualá's town center. It has seven small sheds serving as permanent stores. A half dozen more stores are scattered about the town, operating out of people's houses. A mall of sorts faces the plaza; its six concrete cubicles function as a pharmacy/general store, a butcher shop, and other shops proffering sundries.

In all, Santa Catarina Ixtahuacán remains dominantly agricultural and displays the classic characteristics of Indianness—*encomienda* foundation,[12] corn dependence, refuge location, community focus, ethnic affirmation through Mayan language use, relatively persistent indigenous clothing traditions (older males and all females), and unequivocal self-identification as Mayan, in about as pure a form as one can expect in the bus-connected, television-fascinated world of Guatemala in the early years of the twenty-first century. The verdant forest and quiet agricultural panorama easily deceive the outsider into a romantic notion of Indian well-being; however, for town center or rural inhabitant, having too little to eat is a constant concern that dominates the majority of their daily efforts.

These aspects of economic life in Nahualá and Santa Catarina reveal that poverty is endemic in both municipios. In spite of some economic diversity that allows a few persons to enjoy relative security, for most inhabitants of both communities, life is a daily battle to provide for the next meal. It is made all the more galling by the images of wealth flooding into a few homes on television sets or readily seen on trips to nearby cities or in the public media of movies, video parlors, billboards, newspapers, and the occasional magazine.

Domestic Social Organization

The residents of both communities organize subsistence production through the household. Among the rural residents of both municipios and many residents of Santa Catarina Ixtahuacán's municipal center, fathers and sons work the fields together until a son's marriage, after which the birth of one or more children precipitates a separation of accounts. The married son then builds, usually on a plot near his father's household, often along the edges of an increasingly congested common yard shared by other siblings and kin.

Mothers and daughters share the tasks of converting *ixim* (corn grain) into *wa* (corn foods and also food of any sort). Mothers and daughters work together until impending marriage or common-law union divide them, because, usually, daughters marry out and move into the house or compound of their husband's father. Depending on wealth, young couples slowly or quickly move to the edge of the compound, progressively achieving familial and economic independence. Men of unusual prestige or considerable wealth are sometimes able to retain their daughters by attracting less wealthy sons-in-law to settle around or near the compound. The result, over time, is a town center or rural hamlet composed of compact zones of kin who reside in patrifocally kin-related sectors of town. Men work scattered plots of land they inherited, bought, or acquired through their spouse's inheritance.

Thus men raise corn in many dispersed fields and send what they have raised home to a single location. Women raise daughters in a single location and send them out to dispersed locations. Super-men manage to accumulate both corn and daughters and concentrate them both, creating social networks that empower them with respect in community government.

Community Government

Our field school still needs to study the nature of community government in both Santa Catarina Ixtahuacán and Nahualá. We have seen its surfaces but have not penetrated its heart or complexity. Daily, one sees a core of elected and employed municipal leaders (relatively young, bilingual and wearing Western dress), surrounded by delegates and counselors from the hamlets (older, Maya-speaking, and wearing indigenous dress) being consulted by delegations of a man with his sons, wife, and daughters, earnestly inquiring about matters as diverse as land boundary disputes, taxes, spouse abuse, theft, or marriage. The young leaders broker between the worlds of the Maya and the Ladino, trying wherever possible to avoid sending a case up to a higher authority, for that almost invariably means having it decided by Ladino authority, according to principles other than their own. In Ixtahuacán, as far into the past as anyone can remember, the justice of the peace has been Ladino and has never remained in office for more than three years. In Nahualá, only one recent justice of the peace was a K'iche' from nearby Totonicapán.

In Santa Catarina Ixtahuacán, a town meeting is a common enough event. The local town crier walks the streets, his helper beating a drum, informing the citizens of the municipal center that the men or parents or women, as the case may be, should gather at the municipal hall at a particular time. In as many months of residence in Nahualá, we have no record of such a meeting or call-up procedure there. If it occurs, it is by no means as prominent, reflecting something of the lessened sense of community in Nahualá. Three times during our first stay in Santa Catarina Ixtahuacán, the wild ringing of the church bells drew hundreds of men and women to the central plaza to hear of some insult or offense against the community (one involving illegal harvesting of wood), whereupon they could take collective action. Although informants report that this has occurred in Nahualá in the past, no such event has occurred in Nahualá during our repeated stays.

We have witnessed collective mob action in Nahualá, however, as hamlet residents imposed self-help justice, beating and threatening to lynch the foreign or domestic malcontents who offended them, dragging them to the town center and asking permission to deliver a coup de grace. Collective anger and anxiety overflow in Nahualá. Collective deliberation and discussion in the traditional indigenous model of participants ever so slowly advancing their incremental possibilities to see what the collective will might allow comes closer to describing Santa Catarina Ixtahuacán.

IXTAHUACÁN AND NAHUALÁ IN REGIONAL CONTEXT

We have already discussed how fission and proximity, under the umbrella of disinterested national government, have led to frequent land disputes between Ixtahuacán and Nahualá, and between these and adjacent municipios.

Because of Nahualá's access and Ixtahuacán's distance from the Pan-American Highway, Nahualá has flourished commercially relative to Ixtahuacán. As a result, Ixtahuacán has lost its place as a prominent trading center and has become subordinate to Nahualá. Ixtahuaquenses have to travel to Nahualá or Quezaltenango for most of their commercial needs.

Santa Catarina Ixtahuacán also has de facto subordinate status in the quality of government services. For example, although Ixtahuacán has a post office, the post office's employee must travel to Nahualá twice a week to pick up mail sent to Ixtahuacán and to drop off outgoing mail. The lower level of services is the result of Ixtahuacán's smaller size, more difficult access, and increasingly subordinate status.

Nahualenses can access all regional towns by hailing a bus passing on the Pan-American Highway, a mere three kilometers by road and less than a kilometer by path from the town center. Seldom does one have to wait more than ten minutes, during daylight, for transportation in either direction. Nahualá also has two bus companies of its own. These buses leave the town center to Quezaltenango and Guatemala City daily, except Sunday.

By contrast, between 1996 and 1998 Santa Catarina Ixtahuacán was connected by one bus to Quezaltenango, departing once a day in the early morning, except Thursday and Sunday, when travel was redirected to Nahualá for the market days. When we first began conducting fieldwork, there were two buses offering this service. An accident in 1996 reduced the access from two to one. Between 1995 and 1999 any car, pickup, or truck taking the road out of Ixtahuacán would be besieged with persons waiting at the plaza for a ride out, and anyone needing to enter or exit the town could anticipate a delay of one to several hours waiting for transport if they did not exit on the 4:30 A.M. bus or return with it at 1:00 P.M.

SANTA CATARINA IXTAHUACÁN AND NAHUALÁ IN NATIONAL CONTEXT

The two municipios have an unmistakable Maya character. This is seen in the predominantly rural orientation (more than 95 percent of the inhabitants live in rural areas) and by the heavy reliance on subsistence agriculture (almost 90 percent of the population are subsistence farmers). Most women and many older men continue to wear the distinctive handwoven clothing that identifies them as Nahualenses or Ixtahuaquenses. The dominant language—spoken in the homes, in the streets, and in the municipal offices—is K'iche'. In the community-level ethnographies written during the 1950s and 1960s, these qualities are reported as characteristics of "Indian" communities. It is not surprising, then, that most of the inhabitants identify themselves and are identified by others as *indígena* (indigenous), *naturales* (in this case meaning natives), or "Mayan." Ethnic homogeneity, communal orientation, and resistance to outsiders make it difficult for other ethnic groups to reside in the municipio (R. N. Adams 1995).

From the point of view of the national political system, the small size, Indian ethnicity, and lack of commercialization in the two communities, especially in Santa Catarina, have relegated them to second-class status in the municipal hierarchy. Nevertheless, a variety of national institutions currently play a role in the life of the community, providing education, medical services, and the infrastructure of government.

The residents of both Nahualá and Santa Catarina Ixtahuacán send their children to a range of schools. The town centers and all of their rural hamlets have an elementary school. In the town centers, the schools are large, with multiple classes for each grade level and separate classrooms for each grade through level six. In the larger and nearer hamlets, there may be fewer classrooms, with some doubling of grades in a room. In the more distant hamlets, course work sometimes extends through the third grade only, so that those older children who continue must walk to another hamlet or to the town center. In both town centers, a government-funded junior high school, grades seven through nine, serves the older children of each municipality. In Nahualá, a church-sponsored high school and a private commercial-skills academy offer high school training. In Ixtahuacán, a private high school with some international funding—the *Paraíso Maya*—completes the formal educational opportunities available in the community. Some students from both communities reside in other communities to complete high school, and a few attend university classes in Quezaltenango or in the capital.

The national government provides preventive and emergency first-aid health care through its health care outposts. Nahualá center hosts the region's main health facility, the *centro de salúd*. In addition, Nahualá has a *puesto de salúd* (a subordinate health outpost) in one of its larger hamlets. Santa Catarina has only a small puesto de salúd in its center. Finally, each of the hamlets is supposed to have a health promoter, a man or woman modestly trained in preventive care and in the treatment of the most common, simple ailments. This system and its relation to traditional medical practices and practitioners will be dealt with extensively in a subsequent volume.

The national government penetrates the municipality by paying for local government, the leaders of which are connected to Guatemala's byzantine national parties. Thus, the justice of the peace is appointed by the judicial branch of national government. A post office clerk, with access to radio communications, channels messages to designated recipients.

Finally, the non-governmental processes of national commerce, labor migration, television and radio access, and use of the Pan-American Highway all connect Nahualenses and Ixtahuaquenses, in varying degrees, to the national pulse.

IXTAHUACÁN AND NAHUALÁ IN INTERNATIONAL CONTEXT

During the 1970s, the availability of products from world markets surged in importance due to road construction and participation in international labor markets. The economic momentum was lost in the 1980s, however, due to declining tourism, civil war, global recession, and depressed market prices for primary agricultural products such as coffee, sugar, and other commercial exports. The period became known as the "lost decade." A 1995 cover story in the weekly news magazine *Crónica semanal* brings the economic picture into clear focus in one sentence: "If Guatemala is to regain the 1980 standard of living within ten years, the Gross Domestic Product of the country has to increase at the rate of 5 percent per year" (García Kihn 1995). This would be a phenomenal growth rate in any country for one year, and stupendous if that rate of growth could be repeated for more than one year in sequence. Guatemala has not achieved the necessary rate, and many of its people experience impoverishment relative to their status in the 1970s.

Since the 1990s, world communication through television and video has penetrated both Nahualá and Santa Catarina. Because electrical connections serve virtually every home in the municipal centers and many homes in the nearby hamlets, audio and video recording and playback devices of every sort have been purchased by community members. In 1995, only a few individuals from Nahualá had migrated to the United States, most seeking work. The first migrants from Santa Catarina municipal center left in 2000. By 2003, migration was a common occurrence from the hamlets and town center of Nahualá.

The economic decline of the 1980s under the ravages of war, and the growing market in the United States for illicit drugs, have made this source of revenue important for many countries. Guatemala is not an exception. Indeed, Guatemala is recognized as being a transshipment area for cocaine originating in Colombia. The discovery of some ten thousand heroin poppy plants, enough to produce 4.5 kilos of heroin, was the only known foray into this activity in Nahualá and Santa Catarina Ixtahuacán. There has been no indication that anyone has tried to reestablish this cultigen since the Guardia de Hacienda destroyed the crop in 1994.

The arrival of international organizations, including the United Nations, human rights groups, and development NGOs, in the aftermath of the war, as well as the award of the Nobel Peace Prize to Rigoberta Menchú in 1992, have clearly opened protected space for indigenous nationalism throughout the country. In Santa Catarina one finds two such projects. In one case, a person seeks to raise consciousness of indigenous land rights through his connection to a variety of national and international organizations. In another case, community members have succeeded in connecting with a Norwegian development group and have built a private school, the Paraíso Maya, that teaches a Maya-centric curriculum.

As of 1995, at least one Nahualense had acquired an international university education, having left Nahualá in the early 1990s. He returned to the community for a brief visit in late 1996 or early 1997. Our conversations with his family suggest that he has departed from the community and Guatemala permanently. We are not aware of any individual from Santa Catarina Ixtahuacán who had left the community prior to 1995 to pursue an international education. By 2004, several from Nahualá center and one from Santa Catarina center had studied in international universities.

An Interpretation of Current Cultural Processes

The residents of Nahualá and Santa Catarina Ixtahuacán now struggle to integrate three levels of social interaction and ideology—community, nation, and world—as they pursue their daily lives. At the local level, they combine "milpa logic" (Annis 1987), local orientation (Hawkins 1984), and an emphasis on the community rather than the individual (W. R. Adams 1993b). Within this orientation, they must adapt to the limits of corn subsistence, the realities of land shortage, their unequal access to the cash and market economies, and the constraints rooted in 450 years of ethnic subordination. Until very recently, these factors have contributed in large part to the maintenance of a subsistence economic orientation, which has served, at least in part, as a buffer against the vagaries of fluctuation in market prices of foods and basic needs.

The Mayas have traditionally viewed themselves as *milperos* (those who practice subsistence cultivation of corn by hand labor). The *Popol Vuh*, the ancient sacred book of the K'iche' Maya, says that human beings were made from corn (Tedlock 1985). The ethnographies written in the 1950s and 1960s (Reina 1966; Valladares 1957) and even more recently (Annis 1987; Rojas Lima 1988; Valladares 1993) consistently state that to be a highland Guatemalan, to be Mayan, means to be a milpero. Males take great pride in knowing that they can give their family sufficient corn from their subsistence plots and that they do not have to purchase this dietary staple. In Nahualá, almost every adult male proudly proclaims that he produces enough corn to meet his family's needs. However, typically, their sons and neighbors have told us that these statements are false. The nurse's opinion that 70 percent of the families have to purchase corn in June, and the results of our survey, suggest that the detractors may have been more truthful.

The frequency of the proud but false statements points to the continued importance of being a good milpero. Adding support to this interpretation are the comments made by two of Nahualá's highest municipal authorities. These individuals, as paid civil servants, do not have as much need to practice subsistence farming, nor do they have time to do so. Both men, however, state that they practice milpa agriculture "to get back to their roots."

Indians must also deal with the nation, which, to a large degree, means they must deal with Ladinos, imposed hierarchies of status difference, and pervasive, systematically entrenched discrimination. When the national system penetrates the community, community orientation to some degree can be maintained and is protective. When the individual travels outside the municipio, however, the value of community is less apparent.

Finally, Indians must now, more than ever before, deal with a world system that is at once penetrating their communities and giving them new opportunities to overcome the limitations of the corn economy and the micro-parcel land tenure system that exist at the local level. With the penetration of world products (beginning in 1940s) and concepts of ethnic protection (beginning in the 1990s), local Indians have begun taking tentative steps to synthesize a variety of ideologies, manifested by such movements as Cosmovisión Maya or Movimiento Maya (Cojtí Cuxil 1997; R. Wilson 1995), material development, personal education, and the blurring of traditional Ladino-Indian demarcations. These new ideologies must deal with the colonial legacies of enduring corn-based subsistence, persisting ethnic control by the Ladinos, and inadequate access to capital, goods, and services. Concurrently the people of Nahualá and Santa Catarina Ixtahuacán must contend with the emerging context of increased but incomplete world markets and the penetration of goods and services. They must also address external concepts of equality, diversity, and human rights promulgated by international agencies. Finally, they must increasingly absorb worldwide electronic communications. The result is communities in foment.

For most Mayas, the effect is life on the edge, more so now than perhaps at any time since the conquest. They face life on the edge of economic catastrophe due to a huge and rapidly rising population living on an inelastic land base with no obvious sources of alternative income. Given the poverty of hillside soils, one can only chop down so much forest higher on the volcano. No one from Santa Catarina or Nahualá expressed any interest in opening new land to the north in the Petén. In a cash-short economy, buying expensive fertilizer is risky; most do it but they lament the way they must stretch to meet the up-front cost.

The cash economy has penetrated differentially. Market mechanisms have made the basics of Western material culture available in the local market. At the same time, the whole range of Western consumer culture is visible but inaccessible behind glass, either in the stores of nearby Quezaltenango or on the screens of the increasingly numerous televisions that all can watch in local households. Yet the market has made jobs and cash available to only a few in Santa Catarina and Nahualá. Consequently, a lack of access to cash makes the purchase of these known goods and other services difficult. Yet, new commodities are being bought and the trend makes the shortage of land for subsistence all the more critical because the penetration of new market products adds to the pressure on the land; without a job, new consumption patterns must be purchased with corn that is sold rather than eaten.

Village Mayas exist not only on the edge of survival, but also on the periphery of world civilization. They evaluate what they have in relation to what they see via the penetrating new modes of communication and transportation. *Dallas*, as portrayed in TV hyperbole, becomes the world they do not have, and the difference further impoverishes the place where they are.

These transformations place Nahualá and Santa Catarina on the edge culturally because these Mayas must further adapt to the new conditions of international penetration. Yet, many Mayas are uncertain and have inadequate information regarding how to proceed and insufficient capital to do so. The result is endemic anomie—in the classic sense that Durkheim (1951) intended—with the behavioral consequences of perceived chaos. These take the form of personal and interpersonal insults. Examples of the former include the current abuse of alcohol (W. R. Adams 1999) and potentially the use of other drugs, as well as suicide. Examples of interpersonal insult include spouse abuse, homicide, the rise of youth gangs, and both the fear of and the fact of rape, theft, assault, envy, and witchcraft accusation. Evidence that these events are occurring in these communities can be found in the following chapters.

These observations bring to focus one inference: that these people are fearful. Fearful of the uncertainty of the future. Fearful of outsiders and yet aware of the importance of making contact with them because they must do so if they are to connect to the world economy. One hears from the rooftops of every town the response of fearfully strident religions, desperate to provide new pathways of action and deeper understanding of an increasingly complex reality.

In this context, Maya activism (Wilson 1995) and Maya pride, new religions, the rush to education, and the surge toward economic development and international support—together with a simultaneous repulsion of these drives and a movement toward traditional culture—all converge. Given the past of inadequate access to market goods and services, refuge-traditionalism makes sense, because there is no assurance that Indians will be awarded adequate access to markets, capital, or institutions of today or tomorrow. In this context, the only insurance Mayas have is to rely on subsistence agriculture using subsistence techniques, locally proven technology, and traditional forms of social organization. Yet the techniques and technologies are inadequate to meet the demands placed on an increasingly impoverished soil, while some traditional social organizations have collapsed and no longer provide the protection they once did. Hence, even for the few refuge-traditionalists, life is on the edge. Moreover, the next generation sees the uncertainty and largely abandons refuge-traditionalism for highly modernized forms of indigenous status, including a few who pursue the politics of international indigenous protection as neo-traditionalists.

In the remainder of this book, we will see how these factors articulate, in a complex and sometimes contradictory manner, with the experience of each student ethnographer and his or her topical focus. Jesse Morgan examines the life of a respected elder in one hamlet of Nahualá and shows how, paradoxically, the transformations of tradition and the influx of new religions make some desire a "return" to a distinctive neo-traditionalism. Kelly Araneda details how courtship and marriage expectations are moving from parental arrangement rooted in economic expectations to personal choice rooted in personal attraction expressed as love. Ryan Thompson and Heather Hanamaikai show how deeply-rooted gender expectations lead to the mistreatment of women within local and national legal systems. Rebekah Semus reveals the tensions between the binding yet protective ties of kinship and the urgent striving of women to find improved earnings in the market for weaving. In "Sit Properly," Tara Seely Hatch shows how teaching is limited by a lack of resources and by a variety of bureaucratic inefficiencies. Hanamaikai and Thompson examine gender bias in the classroom and provide statistically compelling evidence that males generate a disproportionate amount of the problems in the classroom, receive less than their fair share of negative sanctions, and are given more than their share of positive attention and praise. Checketts explores the variety of development groups in Santa

Catarina Ixtahuacán, showing that Protestants interact less with aid groups than Catholics. They limit their contact because they dislike compromising themselves by receiving money whose provenance is unknown. Their behavior is intelligible if viewed in terms of older indigenous concepts that blame an evil outside source for excess wealth acquired by members of the village. Nuttall's paper shows that women are active, capable agents who anchor many family and community development projects in Guatemala.

Together, these papers exemplify Anthony Gidden's concept of "structuration," wherein active, self-aware agents create new layers of behavioral variation based on core patterns laid down by prior performances (Cassell 1993:122–26). In the conclusion, we tease out themes within Guatemalan indigenous society that these papers share with each other and with the existing anthropological literature.

NOTES

1. Nahualá and Santa Catarina Ixtahuacán have disputed their territorial boundaries since their separation in the mid-1860s. In 2000, four-fifths of the residents of Santa Catarina municipal center resettled in Sija, in "their" territory, from their point of view. From the point of view of Nahualá, however, the resettlement was a land invasion.

2. In 1992, Proyecto Salquil (1992:21) asserted that Santa Catarina Ixtahuacán consists of "1 pueblo (town), 7 aldeas, 54 caseríos, and 4 parajes." The increase in number of caseríos attests to the population explosion witnessed in subsequent years.

3. The meaning of the term "Ladino" is complex and considerably contested both in academic literature and in popular usage (R. N. Adams and Bastos 2003). At the risk of oversimplification, we may say that the term connotes persons who claim a European heritage and make that claim by manifesting symbols that derive from outside the indigenous community.

The 1994 census is unique in that for the first time it required individuals to designate whether they regarded themselves as indígena (indigenous) or Ladino. Previous censuses had required the interviewer to impute the ethnic status of the respondent (R. N. Adams 1997).

4. We anticipate publishing descriptions of the two markets by Jeremy Rabe (n.d.) and Jared Kulbeth (n.d.), or posting them to our website at http://maya.byu.edu.

5. The concept that six cuerdas is sufficient to supply the subsistence needs of a family may be merely a rule of thumb. W. R. Adams (1993a) received the same

ratio while conducting fieldwork in Jalapa in 1993 and in the arid southeastern part of Guatemala and in El Salvador in 1992 (W. R. Adams et al. 1993). It may therefore not reflect real-life conditions. If this is the case, it is likely that the information provided by Brandon Lee (n.d.) may be more accurate for conditions facing inhabitants of Santa Catarina Ixtahuacán and Nahualá.

    6. Elsewhere in Guatemala, the Mayas learned about terracing through various development projects. Development agents had been prohibited from entering Nahualá until recently. Today, however, many Nahualenses resist constructing terraces because they feel they will lose land, and therefore production, by doing so. We only saw two terraces in the municipio.

    7. The coffee crisis deepened between 1999 and 2003 (Inter-American Development Bank 2002; Oxfam International 2002; Villa Cases 1999), and the industry still has not fully recovered.

    8. The desire to travel to the United States was so dominant a thought in the minds of Nahualenses that all of the students and Adams were approached virtually daily by individuals asking for assistance in obtaining visas, information on the cost of travel to the United States, and so forth. It was not as prevalent in Ixtahuacán.

    9. Informants in Santa Catarina Ixtahuacán told us that about twenty years ago there were cuxeros operating there. However, Nahualenses informed the Guardia de Hacienda, which entered the municipio and destroyed all of the stills. The legacy of that event continues in the ethnographic present: there is only one known cuxero reported to be operating in the municipio of Santa Catarina Ixtahuacán.

    10. Proyecto Salquil's *Diagnóstico socioeconómico* (1992:63) avers that 22.14 percent of the population owns between one and four cuerdas, 26.57 percent owns between five and nine cuerdas, and 19.19 percent owns between ten and fourteen cuerdas.

    11. Ixtahuacán residents express a strong recognition of communal lands and the community's right to prohibit the sale of land to outsiders. We noticed no such emphasis in Nahualá, except the restriction of land sales to outsiders. Nahualá does have some communal land, but its protection does not appear to be as focal an issue there as it is in Santa Catarina.

    12. Encomienda is the tax obligation of an indigenous community (*congregación*) whose residents were required to give tribute to Spanish overlords.

About the author: *After completing my BA in cultural anthropology and humanities in 1998, I spent two years in Asia before entering law school at the University of California, Berkeley, in 2000. During law school, I interned at the Office for Legal Affairs on the Drug Policy Alliance (Oakland, California); the U.S. Embassy in Kuala Lumpur, Malaysia; and the Jakarta law firm Mochtar, Karuwin, and Komar. Since completing law school (JD in 2003), I have been employed as a legal trainer in Jakarta.*

Reflections on the 1995 field experience: *Javier's village stands at a crossroads—but, likely as not, so does mine and yours. Since leaving Guatemala, I am discovering that, for people everywhere, costume, language, and religion matter a great deal. In places as ostensibly dissimilar as Indonesia and Utah, opinions regarding how women (and sometimes men) should dress are common. In Malaysia, the comparative importance of the English and Malay languages within the national curriculum is vigorously debated. Finally, perpetration of and response to the increasingly troubling crime of terrorism is often interpreted by reference to religion. Nevertheless, I believe that millions around the world share Javier's belief in the imperative of tolerance.*

The same highway that brings missionaries, anthropologists and Hollywood movies south to Nahualá invites Guatemalans to the North—to California, say, where every ethnic group (including mine) is a minority. In the near future, villages, regardless of global location, are likely to experience rapid change and a barrage of new ways that seemingly endanger the old ones.

To me, in the misty, verdant summer months, Berkeley, California sometimes looks and smells like the Maya highlands. I continue to marvel at a Maya elder's tranquility and optimism in the face of enormous uncertainty.

CHAPTER 2

STANDING AT THE CROSSROADS
Culture Change in Nahualá
as Seen through the Eyes of Javier, a Maya Elder

Jesse Morgan

Three hours west of Guatemala City, the bus stopped on the shoulder of the Pan-American Highway. Excited undergraduate students with backpacks, duffel bags, and laptop computers began to emerge. In both directions the winding highway disappeared into a rumpled patchwork of bright green maize fields. Only a few miles further, the road would reach an altitude of nine thousand feet, the highest point in its transcontinental traverse. The sharp curves, sheer drop-offs, and deep ravines that border the highway in this alpine region make travel difficult and dangerous.

As the bus pulled away, I felt somewhat abandoned. Other than two houses at the junction, I could see only green mountains, fields, and to the southeast, the tops of the volcanoes that ring Lake Atitlán, a tourist mecca. New sport utility vehicles whizzed past Indians in traditional dress hawking homemade furniture at the edge of the highway. Our pile of luggage was already under inspection by some curious goats. The scene could not have contrasted more with bustling Guatemala City, where we had been only a few hours before.

Eighteen of us were about to be distributed among indigenous families of Nahualá and Santa Catarina Ixtahuacán. Each of us would try to fathom some aspect of Maya culture. I wanted to investigate the nature of religion and religious change in the indigenous community. Through pure luck, I would try to do so by coming to understand my Indian foster father, Javier Tzoc, and his friends.

In the process, I think I came close to understanding a key component of traditional Indian culture: the process of shared communal accommodation and syncretic absorption—a sort of co-optation—of things foreign. Such accommodation and absorption, paradoxically, were the essence of Maya continuity and yet lay at the root of the most profound changes that have occurred within the Indian community. What was changing most fundamentally in Nahualá and other indigenous communities was not clothing, language, or economic mode of production, though these changes were having their impact. What had changed fundamentally was that the Maya were no longer able to absorb new religious and political ideologies because these new ideologies invited—even demanded—division and difference rather than accommodation and absorption.

ENTERING JAVIER'S WORLD

Soon after arriving in the village, we met with one of the two Catholic priests caring for Nahualá's parish. After consulting with his advisory committee of respected elders, he and they agreed that the Catholic elders would provide for those of us still needing families to live with. Probably no less anxious than the students, the priest told us how the community would expect us to behave and then presented us to the families who were to host us during our stay.

Javier, my host father, was stooped and wrinkled, with a kind face and bright eyes. He dressed in the handmade costume (*traje*) of the Nahualense man: a brown sweater made of wool, decoratively embroidered in yellow, orange, and red at the collar and cuffs; white shorts; and the brown, skirt-like *koxtaar*. In the chilly mornings and evenings Javier often wore a *tzut*—an embroidered cloth that is wrapped around the head and fastened in front. Javier described himself as a farmer (*agricultor*). While never failing to plant his milpa each spring, he had also been employed as a carpenter, stone carver, educator, civil servant, and agricultural consultant. Gracious, dignified, and serene, Javier Tzoc was one of Nahualá's elders (principales) and his name was well known throughout the municipio.

Two of us were to room with Javier's family. Telling us that he lived "a short distance from town," he shouldered a piece of our luggage and told us to follow him. After climbing for forty-five minutes we stopped to catch our breath. We found ourselves enveloped in clouds, not much lower than the summit, the forested ridge that we had seen from the village. This particular pleat of mountainside, bordered on each side by deep ravines, is Palank'ix— the cantón or "neighborhood" where Javier had lived all his life and now presided as principal. The Tzoc family home reflected a small degree of prosperity relative to some of their neighbors in the same cantón. It was a four-walled family compound that united a small adobe "kitchen" (where Javier, his wife, and three children slept); a slightly larger structure made of cinder block (where John, one of the sons, and I slept); a small adobe *tuuj*, or sweat house, where we took steam baths; and a makeshift lean-to dedicated to Javier's carpentry projects.

Much of my time in Nahualá was spent in Palank'ix with the Tzoc family. Javier—who said he was too old to go out much—also spent a good deal of time at home, eating, doing carpentry work, or chatting with friends. His wife Juana, who spoke no Spanish, was rarely idle. She spent much time sitting on the dirt floor of the sooty, dark kitchen grinding corn for tortillas with mano and metate. At other times she would be busy weaving, washing the clothes, or preparing the tuuj for the family's baths. She and her shy, almost secretive, eighteen-year-old daughter rarely sat on chairs, preferring to leave them free for the males. In the damp evenings, after a dinner of tortillas (and little else), family and guests would remain in the kitchen talking and listening to Javier's stories. We would all gather as close as possible to a sand-covered table on which Juana maintained an open cooking fire, rather optimistically positioned below a makeshift stovepipe. Juana made popcorn in a frying pan and smiled appreciatively whenever anyone remembered to translate portions of the conversation into K'iche'.

Florentín was seventeen and showed more interest in my tennis shoes and my tape recorder than in my research. Above his cot he had pictures of Tex-Mex singers and department store fashion models cut out of the newspaper. Like his sister, Florentín was his mother's child from a previous marriage. Friction between Javier and his stepson was not uncommon. Although he was reserved around me, Florentín's Spanish was good and we soon became friends. He had a few tapes with pop music recorded from the radio and was more than happy to swap them for some of the music I had brought. After school, Florentín could be found visiting his buddies in other cantones, fetching firewood, or going to weekday church services.

Little Javier—or Mateo as he was usually called—was a darling boy. Although ten years old, he looked no older than eight. He was sometimes too shy to try out his budding Spanish but loved to listen in on the conversation. Born to both Javier and Juana, Mateo was clearly his father's favorite.

Javier, the Elder

Javier was officially an elder (principal) of Nahualá. This title stemmed from years of unpaid service in the municipio's civil-religious hierarchy before the collapse of the "old ways." The system incorporated a rotation of responsibilities (*cargos*) and upward mobility; sometimes against their own will, those who had the most to offer the community eventually reached the upper ranks.[1] From 1952 to 1957 Javier served in the municipal hierarchy as *primer consejal*, the position second from the top. When a Nahualense man retired from such a position, he automatically became a principal. The principales were also leaders and servants, but at a cantón rather than municipal level. Residents of Palank'ix, for example, looked to Javier for guidance in resolving disputes and spearheading neighborhood improvements. Within the greater community, Javier served as a representative of the cantón's needs and viewpoints. Thus, his familiarity with the history of Nahualá, a lifetime of public service, and a diverse occupational history had given Javier an excellent grasp of political, economic, and social systems within the town.

Javier had a broad understanding of Nahualá's religious landscape. "I was born on a day that is good for ideas," Javier once told me, referring to the quality of days in the 260-day calendar the Mayas once used for divination purposes. He often used the Spanish word for "ideas" to refer to thoughts and mental faculties. He referred to those he admired and respected as "having many ideas."[2] Another time he said, "I've never been to a day of school in my life, and yet I have not stopped learning." Javier taught himself to read and write at a time when he realized that no one else in the municipal government could. He possessed a philosophical turn of mind in a society that had little use for philosophers. When I asked him why he was so interested in learning about religion, he turned the tables on me: "I'm like you. I like to investigate things—find out how they work." Some of the same raw curiosity that drew me to the Maya highlands must have drawn him to invite a pair of unknown North Americans into his cantón and household.

By virtue of being born in 1930, Javier had a particularly good vantage point from which to consider the cataclysmic cultural change that Nahualá had undergone in the last part of the twentieth century. One of the reasons that Javier concerned himself with Nahualá's past may have been that he was also concerned about its future. The changes that had already occurred over his lifetime may prove to be only the tip of the iceberg—cable TV and Internet cafés were already commonplace in some of the Indian villages surrounding Lake Atitlán and in Quezaltenango. In this respect I saw Javier standing at a historical crossroads.

He seemed to sense this, too. "My son [Florentín] does not understand. He does not know anything about the way things used to be. And he does not care. He has his own ideas." On the other hand, Javier seemed to have a fairly good grasp of his son's world. Although Javier remembered Nahualá's past in a special way, he lived exclusively in its present. I think it was this, as much as his storytelling, that drew me to him: he was no less interested in learning about my laptop computer than in teaching me about traditional divination practices. The way that Javier enthusiastically engaged and examined the new influences pervading Nahualá continually surprised me.

The World of Javier's Roots

Javier's great-great-grandfather, Diego Tambriz, probably came to live in what is now Palank'ix in the 1860s. Nahualá had yet to be founded and was little more than a preferred grazing area for the livestock of nearby Santa Catarina Ixtahuacán. Led by Manuel Tzoc, certain of those from Santa Catarina—including Javier's ancestors—determined that instead of remaining a part of Ixtahuacán, they would begin to reside independently and permanently at the present site of Nahualá. Various political, personal, and religious factors may have played a part in the now-mythologized schism between Miguel Salquil and the secessionist Manuel Tzoc, overcoming the powerful community-oriented valence that has traditionally held together the diverse minds within a Maya municipio.

Using a metaphor that struck me as particularly relevant as we talked on a steep mountainside covered with cornfields, Javier described himself as "one of the roots" (*una de las raíces*) of his cantón. One of the first settlers in what must have been an outpost of an outpost, Javier's ancestor, Diego Tambriz, eventually became the mayor (*alcalde*) of Nahualá. Javier described Diego as a good man and a wealthy one: "The people say that he had three *caballerías* and about six hundred sheep."[3] Javier was born on land that belonged to Diego Tambriz and now belongs to Javier's brother, Lázaro.

When Javier was young, life was primarily a matter of planting enough milpa to feed one's family until the next planting season. Nahualá's social structure, economy, and belief system were centered around the production of maize, and the corn plant itself was important symbolically.

In 1930 Nahualá would have been its own world, almost entirely isolated from the national structure of Guatemala, not to mention the rest of the globe. The Spanish language was relatively unknown, and access to newspapers, electricity, and automobiles lay many decades in the future. "If an Indian left the village, he was on his way to jail, to boot camp, or to the hospital," I was told by an Indian man describing the tiny world in which his parents had grown.

To understand Nahualá as Javier knew it, one must understand the civil-religious hierarchy, also known as the *cofradía* system, which here and in most other Maya communities once served to integrate the community's power structure, economy, and religious practice. Based on "saint brotherhoods" that once existed within European Catholicism, the ostensible function of the Maya cofradías was to honor individual Catholic saints. Associates followed an elaborate protocol in creating, dressing, displaying, and worshiping wooden representations of Santa Catarina and other saints. A large percentage of a family's resources often went into the preparation of these extravaganzas, and cofradía members would sometimes bankrupt themselves buying the necessary materials. In practice, however, the saints were only one element of the complex civil-religious hierarchy, which included near-obligatory, unpaid community service functions. Indeed, the system of annually rotating responsibilities (cargos) created a structure that made almost everyone in the municipio a volunteer civil servant.

Under the old ways, community life was integrated to the degree that there was little separation between its political, social, and religious aspects. While he was primer consejal, Javier was a leader in each of these three spheres. I asked him to comment on his period of service and he said, "Hard. Very, very hard." He explained that it was an enormous sacrifice since it was an unsalaried position that required him to take time away from farming and other life-sustaining activities. "I do not choose this position," he said, "I was chosen. They choose those that have [at least enough economic security] to allow them to bear this period of service."

Nahualenses only recently had begun to expand their role in the overarching political, social, and cultural systems of Guatemala. Most of these systems had functioned previously to exclude Guatemala's indigenous peoples. Despite constituting a majority of the population (slightly over fifty percent), Guatemala's Indians, until the 1990s, had almost no representation in the national government, Catholic clergy, or any professional fields. Any attempts to include the Mayas in the national culture amounted to naive demands that they expeditiously throw off their backwardness, assimilate into the mainstream, and stop embarrassing Guatemala by being Mayan, or— contradiction though it surely was—that they remain unchanged, quaint, colorful natural history exhibits sustaining Guatemala's international tourism project. In the early 1980s, in an effort to not only root out *guerrilla* insurgents but also destroy what was seen as an important guerrilla power base—the highland Maya municipios—the Guatemalan army razed village after village, using helicopters, napalm, occupation troops, kidnappings, and torture.

In the 1990s, officially and otherwise, indigenous Guatemalans continued to be second-class citizens in the nation, and the Mayas distrusted the Ladinos and the Guatemalan national structure. Mayas assumed that if they were to survive, it would be due to their own vigilance and tenacity and in spite of whatever actions were taken in regard to them by the national government. However, even conservative municipios like Nahualá are now being greatly influenced by party politics, presidential elections, and the national system of justice and law enforcement. Yet there is no reason to assume that a transition from reliance on local institutions to national ones would take place smoothly, for what is foreign usually engenders distrust.

The World of Javier's Children: Rootless in Nahualá

Ecologically, economically, and socially, the Nahualá where Javier grew up and the Nahualá where his son, Javier junior, was growing up were two different places. Carlsen's (1997:166–67) statement about Atiteco culture applies equally well to Nahualá: "This century has seen significant and fundamental evolution in virtually all areas of Atiteco social and cultural existence that eclipses even those changes which followed the Conquest." The evolution referred to has ecological, economic, and social causes. A mushrooming population combined with the system of dividing land among one's children and increasing expenditures in external markets caused the highland Maya to become poorer and poorer every year. Nahualense families struggled mightily to obtain the corn necessary to make the daily tortillas and the sticks of firewood necessary to cook them. In 1995 there were clear signs of widespread malnutrition.[4] The dwellings of those the community perceived as being well off turned out to be very humble affairs.

Poverty resulted when those who lived from the land no longer had enough of it. Nahualá's trees had been stripped by the young firewood gatherers. Wood gathering—as I discovered—now required one to hike at least an hour beyond the pueblo and then climb forty or fifty feet into trees that, stripped of their lower branches, looked more like palms than pines. Goats and sheep were left tethered in the footpaths to take advantage of the tufts of grass that grew there. Literally every square foot that could be sown with milpa was sown. And yet, brutally, the expanding population's demand for natural resources continued to exceed the supply. The Nahualenses commonly employed lawsuits as well as machetes in attempts at preserving their farmland from similarly impoverished squatters of neighboring municipios.[5]

Sensing that the old ways were untenable, Nahualense youth like Florentín looked elsewhere, outside, to new ways. Yet, while Nahualense youth desired tennis shoes, CD players, and other elements of the fast-paced Western consumer lifestyle they saw in movies, they had very little opportunity to acquire them. Although Quezaltenango—a city of two hundred fifty thousand—was only an hour away by bus, it was a hostile place for a Maya kid whose name, limited use of Spanish, and unfamiliarity with everything from hamburgers to ATM machines made him or her an easy target for Ladino rejection and ridicule. Annis (1987:74) describes the plight of the "landless Maya son" who might "reject the prospects of a lifetime as an agricultural day laborer. . . . In every village, young men stand watchfully around the town square. They talk of migrating to Guatemala City, or perhaps of slipping into the United States. . . . Spiritually restless and drifting from his parents' values, he is at loose ends." "Restless and drifting" seemed to perfectly describe Florentín, who in 1995, had already put in a stint at a Guatemala City shoe factory. Indeed, Florentín exemplified the generational outcome of a certain siege on Indianness.

THE ROAD TO CHANGE

In Nahualá, the siege on Indianness began long ago. Perhaps Javier would have agreed that it began in earnest when the Pan-American Highway arrived at the town's doorstep in the mid-1950s. Around 1954, construction was underway on the stretch that runs from Guatemala City west to Quezaltenango. By the year 1955, when Javier was twenty-five, this forgotten corner of the western highlands would suddenly become a stop on the Pan-American Highway. When the road was eventually paved in 1967 or 1968, the effect was magnified (Gall 1981:712).

The road has had a profound influence on Indianness in Nahualá. Although anthropologists and others argue against such "essentialist" definitions (Warren 1998), if we were to ask Javier what it meant to be Indian he would probably refer to the fact that he and his townspeople dress differently from the Ladinos, speak K'iche', and plant maize. If the question had been presented to him twenty years ago, he might have also commented on some of the rituals associated with *costumbre* or "traditional Maya religion." Dress, language, sufficiency of corn, and religion—these elements of Indianness are currently under siege in Nahualá.

Construction of the highway must have been a spectacular project, with heavy machinery, foreign engineers, and barefoot Indian laborers inching their way through the rugged mountains, leaving an asphalt trail behind them. Javier recalls:

> People were angry. Where the highway is now, there was nothing there originally. Not even a path. There was only milpa. I do not remember what month it was [when the highway came] but everyone had already planted their milpa and it was getting pretty high. And so a lot of people lost their milpa. They had to yank it out and forget about it. Throw it away. And tear down their houses too, if they were in the way.

While the arrival of the highway immediately harmed some, it helped others. For many Nahualense men, including Javier, the highway provided steady employment over a period of several years. Javier was quick to point out that he did not work with a pick or a shovel. Instead he oversaw the construction of dwellings and other structures that formed a part of the infrastructure necessary to support the army of road builders. "We saw to it that the engineers and other workers were well taken care of," he said.

The Road to Clothing Change

Alonso Tambriz, a parish caretaker, recalled the day that he visited the highway site looking for work. The foreman saw his koxtaar skirt, embroidered shirt, and shorts, and told him, "Maybe I'll hire you—but not until you get rid of what you're wearing." Before the arrival of the highway, Javier, Alonso, and most other Nahualense men had never put on a pair of pants. But since there was no work available for a man wearing a koxtaar, the Nahualense men began changing their wardrobe literally overnight as Alonso describes:

> I had to wear pants in the daytime when I went to work on the highway to show respect for my job, but in the evening I'd put my traje back on to show respect for my culture. Many Nahualenses worked on the highway. And that's when they began to change the way they dressed. Some of them put on pants and never took them off. And then when their children were born, they would dress them

in pants as well. In 1955 people still wore their traje, but after that
there was a tremendous change.

Nahualenses seemed to be in a bind: while insisting that a very important
part of being Indian was wearing Indian traje, they also admitted that more
and more Indians were taking off their traje and adopting Western dress. As
fewer and fewer boys went to grade school wearing a koxtaar and an
increasing number of older men were seen wearing pants, it was clear that
the Nahualense male might soon cease wearing traje altogether.

There was no reason to think that the same thing would not subsequently
happen with the woman's traje, as it has elsewhere in Guatemala. Already
one encountered very liberal interpretations of the Nahualense *huipil*, the
handmade blouse displaying elaborate brocade designs. Many girls wore
mass-produced, store-bought, machine-embroidered versions, and some
even T-shirts, as part of their Indian outfit. Many boys in Nahualá have
probably never donned a koxtaar and would admit that it was more or less
a foreign article to them. The women, however, were under a great deal
more pressure to continue wearing traditional dress—especially the *corte*,
the dark, ankle-length skirt. For the very small—but growing—percentage
of Nahualense young women who found themselves living or studying in
Quezaltenango or other cities, it was not always easy to be dressed like an
Indian. They constantly experienced prejudice, ridicule, and peer pressure
because of their outfits. Statements like the following, made by a local man
named Leopoldo—although sincere—may be wishful thinking:

> The woman continues to play a very important part in Maya culture.
> It's harder to take away her traje. She feels more secure with her
> culture. Sometimes she'll take it off [temporarily]. Sometimes, when
> she goes to work in the capital. But she'll never take it off [perma-
> nently]. She's more comfortable with her culture [than the man].

Leopoldo relates his own experience with traje:

> I left traje when I was in sixth grade. I went to take a test so that I
> could go to high school in [Quezaltenango] and all the boys laughed
> at me. They said I wore a skirt. They lifted it up to see if I had
> something underneath. And—being human—it hurts you inside. It
> would be great to wear traje, but I know that inside I'm indígena. So
> that's how they got the Indian men to quit wearing traje—they did

not say, "Take it off, take it off." But through jokes and prejudice, step by step [it happened].

Accounts such as this help explain the ethnic valence that one felt so constantly in Guatemala. Guatemala's two principal ethnicities were locked in something of a family relationship—albeit a dysfunctional one. The roots of the family tree were conquest and rape. The Ladino offspring seemed to side with the Spanish father, the indigenous offspring with the indigenous mother. But the two siblings had more in common than it might first appear: without the indigenous Guatemalans, there would not have been any Ladinos. Without the Spanish and Ladinos, there would be no "Indians" either: when Pedro de Alvarado invaded Guatemala in 1520, he found no municipios, no cofradías, no psychedelic costumes, and no one who called themselves either "Indian" or "Maya." It is generally held that the sixteenth-century Spanish institutions of the encomienda and *reducción* were the principal force in the establishment of the closed corporate communities that are today accepted as quintessentially Mayan (Wolf 1957). Hawkins suggests that the "crucible of the conquest" made "inverse images" of the Mayas and the Ladinos, whose cultures corresponded to each other as would a molded object to its mold. The Mayas often wished to see their cultural roots reaching deeper into the past. Warren (1998:78) suggests that the inversions between the two cultures may be the result of strategy on the part of the Mayas: their wholesale rejection of the way Ladinos speak, dress, and earn their living was part of the Mayas' rejection of Guatemala's interpretation of the Indians as illegitimate, weaker, and inferior.

The oppositional, dynamic nature of ethnic identity was visually expressed in patterns of dress. To be Ladino was to not dress like an Indian, and to be Indian—for Maya women at least—involved wearing non-Ladino clothing. In postmodern Guatemala, however, these oppositions soon collapsed. Recently it has not been only the tourists who were intrigued by the dazzling colors and intricate patterns of the Indian textiles. Highland-chic designs—skirts, shirts, and backpacks that use indigenous-looking fabric in the creation of Western-styled clothing and accessories—have found favor even among the Ladinos.

The Road to Language Change

Javier said his "ideas began to grow" and he subsequently "went off to look for his life." Doing so required that he speak Spanish. While employed as a forestry official and an agricultural extension agent, he used Spanish to communicate with his Ladino superiors. Javier explained to me how he had taught himself to read numbers: "I had a yardstick. And I knew how to count. So I'd just go down the yardstick counting off the marks, and that's the way I learned to recognize the numbers." Javier seemed to be aware that living in Guatemala without being able to speak the national language was a significant disadvantage. Although he said "Guatemalans," I believe Javier referred specifically to Nahualenses when he said, "The Guatemalans are very sad. They're uneducated. My wife does not hear. She does not see. She does not go out. She's closed. The Guatemalans are poor and sad." More than once I heard Javier lament the fact that his wife was "deaf and dumb," something that had probably been brought into unusually high relief since the arrival of the foreign houseguests.

However, perhaps similar to the way that Alonso would put his traje back on at the end of the work day, Javier maintained a special attachment to the K'iche' language. When I first met Javier, it was not at all clear that we would be able to communicate with one another. During my first couple of days with the Tzoc family, the issue of language received a great deal of attention. Perhaps if he had not been so intelligible in insisting that he did not speak Spanish, I might have given up and employed a translator. Javier was adamant in his insistence that "here in Nahualá we speak K'iche'. Only K'iche'. Not English. Not Spanish. Only K'iche'. K'iche' only." Javier would say, "Our word is not your word. Her word is not your word," referring to his wife. Of course all of this was said in Spanish, but I understood the point Javier was making: in Nahualá, speaking K'iche' is more than a matter of communication—it is a matter of identity.

Of course if it were strictly true that "in Nahualá we speak K'iche'," there would be little point is saying so. In fact, in Nahualá, Spanish was used frequently. Javier alleged that his stepson Florentín's K'iche' suffered because of his Spanish. Partly because the Nahualense youths spoke Spanish at school and with their friends after school, they had less and less contact with the K'iche' language and with elements of the local culture that were expressed only in K'iche'. Sometimes when I would ask Florentín a question such as one that dealt with the cofradía system or the derivation of a K'iche' word, his father would protest, "He does not know anything about that. He does not speak K'iche' and he does not speak Spanish. So I say, he does not speak anything at all!"

Alonso, the parish caretaker, emphasized, "If you spoke K'iche' and spoke with the youth, you would realize that they do not speak pure K'iche'.

They always include Spanish words. It is a shame. Our customs are *good* customs: for example, the respect that parents have for their children and children have for their parents." Both Javier and Alonso associated a decreased capacity to speak K'iche' with a departure from other aspects of the culture of Nahualá's past. Javier told me that he wants his son Mateo to learn Spanish but does not want him to forget K'iche'.

Ironically, it was much easier to study Spanish in Nahualá than to study K'iche'. Although bilingual education played a role in some classrooms, indigenous languages served primarily as an on-ramp to Guatemala's predominantly Spanish education system. This was true because in Guatemala, Spanish literature has been available for centuries, whereas written K'iche' has existed only for a matter of decades. Once indigenous students were fluent in Spanish, there was very little incentive to continue reading or writing K'iche'. Consequently, Nahualenses of all ages read and wrote Spanish much better than K'iche'. The stigmatization of the Mayan languages also played a role. As Leopoldo explained,

> Mayan languages have been taught. But we [the indigenous people] did not learn. The foreigners learned [the indigenous languages] easily, but the Mayas themselves did not learn. The Indians did not want to learn an "under-language" because to them the Mayan languages are "dialects." When [educators] talk to us about our marimba, about our writers, we do not assimilate. The Mayas learn Ladino culture, but they cannot learn their own culture [because] they say it does not exist.

The Road to Social Connection and Cultural Change

Social contact with Ladinos as a result of highway construction began to transform more than Nahualense clothes and language. According to Javier,

> After two or three years of working on the highway, the people would stop to rest for a while. They'd ask to be relieved of their positions and go off investigating other opportunities. They traveled far and wide—to Guatemala City, to Chimaltenango, Mazatenango, and Esquintla. [While they were working on the highway] their ideas began to grow. They began to wear pants. They got interested in leaving—in going off to look for their lives. Before the highway,

people did not leave. But because of the highway, they woke up. Who knows why it works that way—but being around all the machines, with the engineers, the foreigners, everybody speaking Spanish—their ideas began to grow. Before, [the Nahualenses] wore blinders and they had their ears stopped up. Because of the work [on the highway], their eyes and ears were opened so they could have a new life. There were men from all over the world working on that highway: Ladinos, Americans, Germans, white people, black people. . . . They began to exchange ideas.

LOOKING FOR THEIR LIVES: RELIGIOUS CHANGE IN NAHUALÁ

Road construction brought Nahualenses into increased contact with a greater diversity of non-Nahualenses of all social types and introduced them to new ideas, new premises, and new symbols with which they could re-think the issues they found in the world around them. Among those new ideas, symbols, and changes, religion stood prominent.

The Old Ways

Before, we only had one religion—Catholicism. And the Maya priests—so, two religions, really. We always went to the Maya priests for help with our problems, our illnesses. The [Maya] priests would ask for a favor from God and the *mundos* [local mountain spirits].[6] That was the old way.

Javier Tzoc

Of course, significant changes have naturally occurred over the centuries. Continuities also certainly exist. The sun, earth, volcano, mountain, cave, maize, blood, *guaro* (liquor), and *copal* (resin from the copal tree) are among the symbols that have been salient in the Maya cosmovision since long before the conquest. Key religious concepts include the human soul, the intimate bond between humans and the natural environment, the existence of powerful mountain spirits, social-religious responsibilities (cargos) that the townspeople must shoulder, the importance of offering sacrifices, and gratitude to higher powers (Carlsen 1997:56; Warren 1978:56; Watanabe 1992:75, 87, 106; R. Wilson 1995:52–61, 91, 164). Under the old ways, the shaman-priest, *ajq'iij* (*zajorín* in Spanish), was the interface between the mundos and the people. Worshiped and propitiated as those who created rain and guarded the milpa, mundos were also feared as capricious demanders of sacrifice.

Javier's hesitancy to differentiate between Catholicism and the practices of the Maya priests (shaman-priests)[7] suggests the degree to which Catholicism and the old ways eventually became fused. The Mayas were able to put the Catholic saints into the same conceptual category as the mundos, and eventually the Maya pantheon and the folk-Catholic pantheon merged. The sheer physical and psychological violence of the Spanish invasion probably guaranteed that the Catholicism of the invaders would significantly influence the worldview of the (future) Nahualenses. But, at the same time, the Spaniards' subsequent reduced presence in the highlands and some four centuries of neglect on the part of first the Spanish and then the Ladinos allowed the Nahualenses to retain many of their former beliefs and practices (Lovell 2000:118–19).

Not long after I arrived in Nahualá, I had the good fortune to witness a group of Maya priests performing costumbre. All but one of them wore traje. Seventeen men stood in a semicircle around a metal tub from which flames and billows of black smoke were rising. A group of women huddled on the ground nearby. Near the men, a large heart had been drawn on the ground with white flower petals. Two ears of maize had been placed at the center of the heart. The Maya priests—many of them elderly—spent more than an hour feeding candles, incense, and copal to the flames while they prayed individually and as a group. Three Maya priests accompanied the ceremony on a large wooden marimba, playing the same minor-keyed melodies over and over. At times guaro would be sprinkled on the flower petal heart and elsewhere. Toward the end of the ceremony, the priests each produced a small cloth bundle and passed it ceremoniously though the smoke before touching it to their foreheads. A younger man, whose leather hiking boots stood out among the bare feet and sandals of the older priests, was the apparent leader. Throughout the ceremony he gave them their cues and thanked them each individually when they departed.

The ceremony took place in the plaza, a few meters from the entrance of the Catholic church; in other words, at the physical, social, and spiritual heart of Nahualá. And so I was surprised to find that, besides a few of the custodians (mayordomos) who were on duty inside the Catholic church, there were almost no spectators at the event. One mayordomo said that there were few Nahualenses in attendance because "it was a work day and everyone was at work." One of his colleagues, however, suggested that the reason for the low turnout was that "these things were done by surprise," without advance notice. They called it a "Maya ceremony" and told me that the priests were "thanking God for the sun, moon, river, and mountains, and remembering the ancestors, especially those who were pure Mayan."

When I recounted what I had seen to Javier, I found that he knew the details of the ceremony as well as if he had been there. He helped me complete my sketch of the ceremony and identified the flower petal heart as "the heart of the maize," or alternately "the heart of the Maya." According to Javier and other informants, the work of the Maya priests seemed to fall into two principal categories: giving thanks by performing costumbre and using supernatural power to benefit those seeking their aid.

The verb "to burn" (*quemar* in Spanish) is sometimes synonymous with the word costumbre. To perform costumbre is to make a fire and feed it with things such as candles, incense, guaro, bread, chocolate, and—most important by far—copal (*poom* in K'iche'). While the fire is burning, the Maya priest chants lengthy prayers that repeat the names of authority figures, including the mundos, deceased principales, judges, the pope, and the ancestors. While costumbre is sometimes performed on behalf of the entire village or in commemoration of a special day of the Maya calendar, the Maya priest usually performs costumbre on behalf of individuals who visit him seeking assistance. He accepts money or payment in kind for such services.[8] Although there are many reasons for searching out the help of a Maya priest, curing illness is one of the most common. The Maya priest also has at his disposal powerful magic stones and methods of divining the future.

As powerful entities with the ability to help or harm the Nahualenses, the mundos[9] have traditionally played an important role in the work of the Maya priest. Dealings with the mundos seemed to take place on a quid pro quo basis, and it was the responsibility of the Maya priest to determine the *regalo* or *multa* (present or fine) required in exchange for a mundo to grant the desired favor. The mundo stipulated the costumbre that had to be performed or other sacrifice to be made. Florentín said it was common knowledge that in order to complete the construction of a large bridge, located near Nahualá at the point where the Pan-American Highway crosses the Nahualá River, it had been necessary to "ask the mundo what he wanted." Florentín told me that the mundo's request was for people—five of them. Florentín assured me that the sacrifice had been made—that there was no other way that the bridge could have been built.[10] Health and fertility were two of the principal favors traditionally sought. The Nahualenses who still seek out the services of the Maya priest also ask for blessings on relationships, business ventures, academic endeavors, and other modern concerns.

Nahualenses have found it important to make a distinction between different types of practitioners of "traditional religion." Javier, for example, described a friend of his—a principal from another cantón—who would perform costumbre but could not be considered a zajorín, because he did not use special stones.

Alonso at the parish told me a good deal about the work of the Maya priest. The K'iche' word for zajorín, ajq'iij, means "day worker," or "craftsman of the days." Alonso told me that the "true ajq'iij" is "called of God." If he should refuse the responsibility (cargo) he will die. He does not put a price on his services but accepts what he is given. Someone who calls himself an ajq'iij and begins to ask the people for large sums of money is not authentic.

My informants so often insisted on the significant difference between the ajq'iij and a figure called the *ajiitz* (worker/master of misfortune) that I must assume that there were many similarities. Alonso explained that the ajiitz had the capability and inclination to use his powers to do evil.[11] An ajiitz, for example, might perform costumbre in behalf of someone who he knew could not be cured, just to get the money. An ajiitz can cast curses and even bring about death. For Javier, the character of the individual practitioner was the paramount difference between ajq'iij and ajiitz: was he doing good and benefiting others? Or was he solely benefiting himself?

Surprised by Javier's familiarity with the costumbre performed in the plaza, I was even more taken aback to discover that the officiator in the hiking boots was Javier's younger brother, Lázaro. Javier described his brother as "the leader of the Maya priests" and said, "Sometimes he goes to the very heart of the mountain[12] to burn copal." He was clearly impressed with some of the accomplishments of his brother as head of a religious movement that was presently an underdog in Nahualá. "He is not alone. He has a good number of supporters," Javier assured me, without ever making it clear if he was among them. "People come from all over Guatemala to visit him. Foreigners come from other countries, too." The family sometimes chuckled at the exploits of their colorful uncle but seemed to regard him as a powerful figure. "He makes money with what he does—he makes money daily. It's as if it were his salary," Javier said, impressed but not resentful. Yet it was always less than clear exactly what Lázaro did.

Lázaro Tzoc, Maya Priest

Eventually, I interviewed Lázaro at his own large, sturdy compound. He was polite but curt, as any public figure would be in the presence of a researcher with unknown motives. Lázaro's careful, diplomatic answers suggested that it was important to him that his work be viewed in a positive light. The first question of the interview was one that he asked me: "What do you think about the work I do? Because if you say it is good, then I will tell you more. But if you think that what I do is bad, then I will not say another word." I must have provided a satisfactory answer, because the interview continued. Lázaro recounted to me various occupations that he had held in the past: highway worker, lumberjack/sawyer, candle maker, and purveyor of corn and wheat. He said that he had received his calling to become a Maya priest when his three-year-old son was cured of a life-threatening disease by a zajorín. Lázaro said that his job was "to help people." He said that those who came to visit him found his services "efficient and upbeat" (*eficiente y muy alegre*).

On one occasion Lázaro took me into the small room enclosed in the family's compound where he did his work. He chuckled when I referred to it tentatively as a "church." I had no idea what I would find inside, and Javier and Lázaro seemed to enjoy playing up the element of mystery. It was pitch black when the three of us ducked into the church and closed the door. When the light came on I found myself face to face with two large male dolls with thick black hair and mustaches, dressed in three-piece suits. A roughly carved skeleton character with large eyes peered out from behind the dolls. Lázaro smiled inscrutably and introduced the men in the suits as "San Simón." The skeleton character was "Juan Noj." Sitting quite self-possessed behind something of an altar, Juan and the "saints" were surrounded by antique wooden icons, candles, and other Catholic paraphernalia.

San Simón was an example of the way the Maya co-opted Catholicism and integrated it into their own worldview. Known throughout the western highlands, San Simón—or Maximón as he is often called—may have felt particularly at home in Nahualá due to its proximity to Santiago Atitlán, the municipio where he had the strongest following. A huge hit with tourists but an embarrassment to the Catholic Church (and many Atitecos), the scandals surrounding Maximón, the hard-drinking gentleman-saint who always wears a suit and smokes a cigar, were the subject of articles, books, and lawsuits. Javier's half-mirthful, half-fearful description of San Simón was consistent with the dual personality of the "saint": powerful and able to bestow great favors, he nevertheless tended to charge for them dearly. In the *costumbrista* scheme, San Simón was a mundo. However, in the folk-Catholic scheme, he was "Saint Simon Judas," disciple and traitor.

Lázaro preferred to be vague about what took place in his church, but Javier later confided to me that to assist those who came to visit him, Lázaro established communication with the mundos and perhaps with other spiritual entities. Javier had a hard time describing the nature of "that which arrives" (*lo que llega*) and preferred to use the K'iche' word *juyub*,[13] meaning something like the spirit of a mountain or hill.

> Whether [the juyub] is a person, an animal, perhaps the spirit of— [he paused and did not finish]—I do not know. It's dark in there and you cannot be sure what's going on. But there is a loud whirring or rumbling. [Javier imitated a ferocious whirring sound.] But when it arrives it introduces itself. Sometimes it says, "I am Simón," or "I am Don Pedro" or "Tecún Umán" or "Santiago Atitlán."

Javier took "that which arrives" seriously, despite the humor he employed in its description. He described a brash jokester with a fiendish laugh—someone or something of a foreign nature but with a familiar personality. "That which arrives" liked to whistle and to drink, and was reportedly able to consume sixty gallons of guaro at a time. Florentín said that he had witnessed this fearsome drinking habit and that several gallons of alcohol that were set out for Simón before the lights were turned off had been drained by the time they came back on again. I was also told that Simón had been known to take advantage of the darkness to "grab the women."[14]

While we were in his church, Lázaro showed me a number of large crystals and pieces of smooth, weathered glass. He said that his baby son had been cured using stones like these. He conceived of these "ancient" stones as one of his principal sources of power. The stones used by a Maya priest, he told me, must be found by accident and by luck, often while one is walking in a remote area. One of his stones had been found while he and other priests were visiting the ancient Maya city of Tikal.

The zajorín must determine beforehand whether or not an ill person is capable of being cured. To divine this (and other things), the zajorín uses seeds called *tz'iite'*. Lázaro pointed out that, unlike the crystals, there was nothing sacred about the tz'iite'—they are merely tools. He proved this by taking perhaps thirty oblong black seeds and dumping them unceremoniously on the table. After "shuffling" them, he began to divide them into groups of four. He attempted to explain to me how the randomly occurring groups were counted off (using the days of the Maya calendar) in such a way as to produce a "yes" or "no" answer to questions such as, "will this person survive her present illness?"

One day shortly after Javier and I had returned from a visit to Lázaro's house, he admitted: "I participate with them. I have my own stones. I have my credentials as a Maya priest." He unwrapped a cloth bundle and showed me the stones, seeds, and other small objects it contained. It was clear that Javier had not only been exposed to the old ways of worship since he was young, but that he accepted them. Unfortunately, he was often reluctant to talk about this part of his religious experience. He described costumbrista practices in the passive, telling me about rituals that "are sometimes carried out," while omitting details relating to who, when, and where.

"Puro Simón"

Almost every afternoon, thick clouds would settle on Palank'ix, and even though it was summer, the dampness and elevation often made for chilly evenings in the Tzoc family's uninsulated and, except for the kitchen, unheated buildings. Once a week, respite from the cold dampness came in the form of time in the tuuj—the indigenous sauna. One night after emerging from the tuuj and putting on his koxtaar, Javier was having a hard time getting warm again. Seeing him shivering, my companion, John, offered him his two-piece warm-up suit and stocking cap. Javier was hesitant at first, but soon began to smile at the prospect of warming up his bare legs. Although the suit was a couple of sizes too large, Javier actually looked pretty good, and everyone found the situation amusing. Adjusting the stocking cap in the mirror, Javier smiled slyly and said under his breath, "Exactly like Simón. I'm only missing the cigar!" ("*Puro Simón. Sólo falta ahora el cigarrillo.*") Indeed, in addition to being a "Catholic" saint and a Maya mundo, San Simón was also a nineteenth-century Ladino landowner, as indicated by his black suit, leather shoes, wide-brimmed hat, and fine silk scarves.[15] Finding himself looking more like a Ladino than an Indian in John's clothing, Javier turned his thoughts to the treacherous Simón. The epitome of duality, the Ladino was patron and provider and, at the same time, thief, executioner, and cheat. Wealth, power, and technology come from the Ladino, but also inequality, caprice, and betrayal. That is part of the duality Javier sensed. Thus, nineteenth-century drawings and lithographs of San Simón show him seated at a place where two roads intersect.

The Demise of the Old Ways

Jesus reigns forever,
In the earth and all creation.
His heart will be our king,
For Mary's is the nation.
Song sung by Javier

Lázaro's interest in hiding the details of his work as a Maya priest is not difficult to understand; a relationship often exists between what is sacred and what is secret. But at the same time, there was at least one additional explanation for the low turnout at the ceremony in the plaza besides those mentioned thus far: "It's an embarrassment for the people," Javier said. Although he was describing some of the more underground practices of the zajorín, his statement applied to all aspects of costumbrismo and what is now thought of as pre-Columbian religion. "People make fun of things like this. Can you imagine—going to the cemetery in the middle of the night to talk with a bad spirit? As far as the people are concerned, this is wrong," he explained, without taking sides.

The question "What do you thing about the work I do?" was not really Lazaro's. It represented a powerful cultural dialectic that long had torn Nahualá apart. In the 1940s the Guatemalan Catholic Church began a self-reformation called Catholic Action. "Study groups" organized among the lay Catholics would eventually take on important social and political dimensions. In the 1960s, at the same time that various Protestant sects were translating the Bible into indigenous languages and beginning to have a good deal of success among the Mayas, "foreign priests who came to highland Guatemala encountered a [Catholic] Church that performed sporadic rituals for the community but was not integrated into daily religious life" (R. Wilson 1995:172). During this time, whenever a priest visited Nahualá, babies would be baptized and Mass would be given, but, overall, the Nahualenses had almost no knowledge of the Bible or Catholic theology. The cofradía system, which did indeed play an important role in daily religious life, had little to do with orthodox Catholicism. Following the Bible-centric example of the Evangelicals, the Catholic Action program oversaw the training of local, indigenous educators, called *catequistas*, who then passed on their newfound understanding of the Bible and commitment to orthodox Catholicism to the rest of the community. The catequistas "reinforced trends of declining authority [already present] in the civil-religious hierarchy" and played a key role in "weaken[ing] and ultimately destroy[ing] unorthodox religious beliefs and rituals of the Indian brotherhoods" (Warren 1978:88), that is, the confradías.

The collapse of the cofradía system held clear benefits for the Catholic Church. For one, the saints were partially reappropriated, and the central saints were no longer allowed to participate in the drinking, dancing, and revelry associated with the yearly festivals organized by the cofradías. But Nahualenses from Javier's generation were left to confront a difficult question: had the old ways represented one religious system or two? Had the progressive, modernizing forces of the catequistas modified a religious system or destroyed one and brought another? The catequistas' new approach to the saints and the Bible was capable of accommodation among a people who—after all—considered themselves Catholic. But what was to be done about elements of costumbre such as Juan Noj and San Simón? Were they just skeletons in the Maya closet or would they continue to have value as a part of costumbre—as part of what makes the Mayas different from the Ladinos? Javier remembered with a certain degree of fondness the days when Nahualá still had cofradías and town festivals: "It's not the same now. It was merrier then when we used to have cofradía. The church had the responsibility of maintaining the cofradías. And there were always processions. Every twenty-fifth of November they'd take the saints out for the processions. Now it's all been forgotten."

Although the Tzoc family assured me that Lázaro was doing a booming business in his church, it was only with extreme reluctance that the average Nahualense would admit that these practices still continued. One explanation is that, even among themselves, the Mayas are less likely to discuss the ajq'iij than other aspects of the old ways because he represents private, individual, even secret religious options, rather than communal, public ones (Warren 1978:75–83). Furthermore, the ambiguous nature of the ajq'iij/ajiitz opposition probably makes for a particularly difficult topic of discussion to take up with an outsider. But, without doubt, the official opposition of Catholics and Protestants, as well as the stigmatization of shamanism as "witchcraft" and "superstition" in Western society, have forced costumbre deeply underground. Many, if not most, of those in the community would have agreed that the cofradía and zajorín were "backward" aspects of the Nahualense past that have, for the most part, been "overcome." Nahualá's Protestants, for their part, would not hesitate to call Lázaro a "witch" (brujo)— as the Ladinos have always done.

For over ten years at least one voice—which is becoming increasingly louder—has countered the anti-costumbre position taken by Catholic Action and the Evangelicals. These pro-costumbre forces often hail from the ranks of the educated, intellectual Maya elite and could probably be best described as "neo-costumbristas." Their vision was trickling from urban areas into rural ones, where it sometimes made contact with the remnants of old school costumbrismo.[16] In advancing traditional, rural practices and beliefs, Javier's brother Lázaro employed up-to-date, politically savvy techniques. In 1996, I witnessed an elaborate costumbrista celebration of the Maya New Year, held in Santa Catarina Ixtahuacán, which brought together illiterate ajq'iij, Maya and Ladino intelligentsia from Guatemala City, local residents, anthropologists, undergraduate students, and a film crew. Activities like this, taking place at a much greater level of organization than was typical of earlier costumbrista practices, have led observers to suggest that a "Pan-Maya Renaissance" is currently underway in Guatemala (Warren 1998).

New Ways

When I was born, I was as blind as a chicken inside an egg. But later I found my way out of the egg. I wanted to understand the world—I wanted to know what path to take, I wanted to know about religion. My first religion was Catholicism. I was baptized a few days after I was born. That's how it was in those days. I was born Catholic. But by the time I was about twelve, I was looking around at other religions.

Javier Tzoc

The *evangélicos* emphasized biblical precepts, abstained from alcohol, and encouraged rapturous, visceral manifestations of the Holy Spirit. Economic factors were the most often cited reasons for their success. Annis (1987) suggests that within the Indian communities the "Protestant work ethic" led Indian entrepreneurs and merchants (rather than farmers) to favor Protestantism, arguing, like Weber (1996), that Protestantism inspires interest in nontraditional, market-oriented modes of occupation. Anthropological literature in general suggests that throughout indigenous Guatemala, evangélicos are more likely to accept change in the direction of national Guatemalan culture (such as Ladino dress and Spanish language), while those who are most resistant to these changes are likely to be Catholic. At

least in terms of language, the surprisingly high percentage of Spanish words
heard in Nahualá's evangélico services tended to support this view. Moreover, Nahualenses perceived a serious problem of alcohol abuse in the
municipio and the Evangelicals' teetotaling stance was seen as one of their
selling points.

As a youth, Javier first attended Protestant services while traveling to
Quezaltenango with his father. The first Protestants in Nahualá arrived
shortly after the highway. Javier remembers the less-than-warm welcome
they received:

> The first [Protestant missionaries] began arriving around 1956 or
> 1957. The people got pretty angry. They told [the missionaries],
> "Your teachings are worthless. They're from the devil, not from
> God." People would hit [the missionaries] and fight with them. The
> first real Protestant here was Patriza—the man who gave me my
> New Testament. He arrived in 1957. Patriza was a doctor, and there
> was no doctor here at that time. When people got sick . . . little by
> little, they would begin to visit Patriza. Once there was a man
> named Juan Tzep who fell gravely ill. Patriza arranged for him to
> be sent to a clinic in Xela. Juan recovered and now he's a minister—
> there are maybe 150 members in his congregation. And so that's
> how the Protestants began to grow.

Javier seemed reluctant to share his substantial knowledge of Nahualá's
evangelico forces. One day he mentioned, "I participate with them. I was
baptized." This surprised me more than his "credentials" as a Maya priest.
I had assumed that Javier was Catholic: I had seen him go to Mass and I
knew that he held a position in the parish. It was not exactly clear when
Javier began personally committing himself to the evangélico cause or when
or why (or if) he became disenchanted. He related the following experience
as the context of his 1990 conversion:

> At that time [around 1957] I used to drink a lot. That's why I
> renounced my position in the municipio—I thought I was giving
> a bad example—I was not fit to be a leader. It was not the right
> thing to do. I was not fit to be considering the needs of the people.
> I went to my house and spent some time thinking about what I
> was doing. Once I was alone up on a mountain surrounded by
> *plantillo* [vegetation]. I really began to think about my lifestyle.

Then, little by little, I started to give up drinking. People were happy about the change in me. Before, I used to spend my time out of the house—in the streets, in the *cantinas*. Sometimes I'd get mad at my wife—scare her. It was a good change for me.

Because of the far-reaching political implications of religious affiliation in Nahualá, it seemed likely that only by resigning from his position in the Catholic political-religious hierarchy would Javier have the freedom necessary to investigate Nahualá's new religious options.

Javier had good things to say about Misión Centroamericana, the denomination into which he was baptized. One of the largest of Nahuala's myriad evangélico bodies, the church maintained a medical clinic and ran a number of other projects that benefited the community. Javier said that he used to attend church every Sunday; his former pastor confirmed his activity. Javier concluded his discussion of the Misión Centroamericana by saying that he was unable to participate with the congregation because of the position he held in the Catholic parish. While this may seem an understatement given how vociferously Evangelicals oppose Catholicism, it provided a window into Javier's understanding of religion.

JAVIER'S AMBIVALENCE AS CULTURAL SYNTHESIS

Dissatisfied with a mere history of the changes in dress, language, and religion that had taken place in Nahualá during Javier's lifetime, I repeatedly asked him questions that I hoped would make him put the old ways and the new ways in the same balance—pants on one side, koxtaar on the other; Spanish on one side, K'iche' on the other, etcetera. I was particularly frustrated by what seemed to be his ambivalence regarding Nahuala's burgeoning array of religious options. How could he simultaneously identify with the Maya priests, the orthodox Catholics, and the evangélicos—groups that are more or less at each other's throats in Nahualá? Although Javier did not hesitate to point out the shortcomings of Nahualá's various religions, he did so uniformly. I began to worry that perhaps his reluctance to show his religious sympathies stemmed from the fact that he had no way of knowing where *my* political and religious sympathies might lie. Perhaps his statement, "I'm like you. I like to investigate all religions," was simply a good piece of diplomacy, calculated as the safest approach to a topic that in Nahualá does not exist in the abstract, that is, without serious political implications.

In order to set my mind at rest, during one interview I attempted to make the issue of cultural change as abstract as I possibly could, hoping to make it easier for him to take sides. I created small cards and labeled them with key words representing various options faced by the Nahualense in areas such as dress, language, occupation, religion, and alcohol. Then I asked Javier to place the cards in groups or categories according to their relative acceptability/advisability. Following phrases that I had often heard him use in his gentle critiques of various good and bad "ideas," the categories had been labeled, "wholly acceptable," (*no tiene problema*), "acceptable/advisable" (*tiene pocos problemas*), "problematic" (*tiene muchos problemas*), and "unadvisable/unacceptable" (*siempre tiene problemas*). Apprehensive that he might not appreciate being cornered in this way, I was happily surprised to find that he approached the activity with a great deal of enthusiasm. "This is the very best interview we have had. We should do this every time," he said.

Although not all of the questions that the cards were supposed to ask were good ones—as Javier pointed out—the overall results of the activity were useful. I had predicted that in his placement of the cards, Javier's ambivalence would show up in a heavy reliance on the "problematic" category. Often, however, he tended to group competing options ("wear pants" versus "wear traje") together in the same "acceptable" category. I felt that this suggested ambivalence just as strongly. However, these results were far from scientific and I have not relied on them heavily. In fact, the entire activity was conceived of primarily because I wished to see how Javier would react to the last set of cards. They had been labeled "Catholic," "Evangélico," "Charismatic," and "Costumbrista." Javier was intrigued by the proposition, and I filled several pages in my notebook recording his response. After a long discussion of the problems associated with being religious in Nahualá, Javier returned to the neatly organized columns of cards and realized that the religious options had yet to be sorted. In fact, the gist of what he had been saying was that they *could not* be sorted. "We ought to just throw these out," he joked, slightly frustrated. Although I said that this would be perfectly acceptable, he made one effort to shuffle them into one category or another—if only for the sake of completeness—before giving up.

One of the life decisions that for Javier may have been the most important and the most difficult—because it was least Indian—was that of choosing between mutually exclusive, bitterly opposed religious factions whose origins were neither entirely Nahualense nor entirely foreign. This facet of modernity was made all the more difficult because Javier had resided his entire life in a local community and in an ethnic sector that valued the outward appearance of consensus and harmonization.

The Mayas Believed in Everything

Not long after I came to live with Javier, we were returning from an interview with his brother Lázaro when he stopped and sat down next to the footpath. It was clear that my persistent questions about religion had begun to affect him, and it seemed to me that he would have liked to provide me with answers, if only to shut me up. I think he was sobered by his inability to come up with answers that even satisfied himself. He said thoughtfully,

> Who knows where we stand right now? In the old days all the families had saints, and those that did not, had a cross. Now it's very different. The Mayas believed in the saints and in the mundos. The Mayas believed in everything. The Mayas believed in everything. The Mayas believed in everything. I really would like to know what God is like. Before, the people believed in everything. Why is it not all right to believe in everything now?

Although the statement appears cryptic, what Javier was trying to say went a long way toward explaining his religious ambivalence. I do not doubt that Javier would have liked to know the nature of God—but I think it would only be a means to an end. What he would really have liked to know was what to make of Nahualá's bewildering circus of religious claims and claimants. In fact, Javier's understanding that his ancestors "believed in everything" was fundamentally incompatible with the Evangelical proposition that they were right and the others wrong. Javier seemed painfully aware that, in Nahualá today, to express belief in something implied doubting something else, thereby creating division. Accepting the authority of Nahualá's beleaguered Catholic priests, for example, meant challenging the legitimacy of the various Protestant pastors who were usurping their flock. To believe in the Maya priests and their invocations of the mundos was to reject the entire thrust of Catholic Action's mission among the Guatemalan Indians over the past half century. As Javier pointed out, in the days before the arrival of the highway—before people's "eyes and ears were opened"—belief had never been such a scarce or divisive commodity. It was *disbelief* that was traditionally harder to come by.

Javier dated the religious divisions within Nahualá to about 1957—
perhaps shortly after the arrival of the highway:

> The problems began for the Catholics [with the arrival of the
> Protestants in 1957]. [Because the Protestants were using the Bible]
> the catequistas began using the Bible too—trying to prevent the
> people from straying into other paths. And that's where the problems
> began for the Maya priest [and his followers] as well. Apparently
> the Bible says that you should not burn incense and copal and do
> costumbre. Apparently this kind of worship is not mentioned by the
> Bible. The evangélicos accuse everyone of not following the word
> of God as it is found in the Bible. They say that they alone have a
> crown—that when they die, they'll go straight to the right hand of
> God. [Javier chuckled]. Who knows if it's true?

For Javier, the role of religion was social. He saw things in terms of groups
of people, of communities rather than of ideologies or institutions. He never
referred to "the Catholic Church" or "Catholicism," but to "los católicos"
(the Catholics), meaning—in effect—those in Nahualá. Likewise, when he
referred to "los carismáticos," he did not have in mind factionalism within
the Roman Catholic Church, but the puzzling rift between those Nahualenses
who were content to attend Mass in the temple built by Manuel Tzoc and
those who insisted on holding their own meetings at other locations. During
our card sorting, Javier pointed out that the card labeled "Does not have a
religion" was redundant because everyone who did not have a religion
would be Catholic. I believe it was an indication that the relationship of
Nahualá's religious groups to one another was of more import to Javier than
the details of their doctrine. In his view, even those who never attended Mass
were Catholic, because they did not oppose the Catholic Church as the
evangélicos do.

Javier's criticisms of Nahuala's religious options were usually social
ones. For example, he pointed out that because the evangélicos held *culto*
(services) throughout the week at so many different locations, as opposed
to Mass held twice weekly at the Catholic church, they were splitting up
families rather than bringing them together. He assured me that unplanned
pregnancies were one result of young men and women "running around the
countryside," ostensibly on their way to or from culto. He may also have felt
that the evangélicos' tendency to dress up for culto threatened egalitarianism
in Nahualá.

When people go to culto these days, the girls [are] all dressed up—
shoes, makeup—it's like they are going to a fair or a festival—it's
just as bad. And that's not the way it is supposed to be. Jesus did not
go around changing his clothes. Jesus was poor, he was not rich—
he only had a couple of suits of clothes anyway.

For Javier, the competition and mistrust between the various Evangelical
sects and between the Evangelicals and the Catholics were antithetical to
what religion ought to be. In Nahualá, however, open confrontation between
religious factions was the rule rather than the exception. Lázaro's observance
of costumbre—on the front steps of the Catholic church—and the proliferation of fiery evangélico sermons that echoed off the mountains every
afternoon and evening were examples. "Nowadays," Javier said, "There are
three or four paths you can take. But people do not know which one is the
best. None of them seems very certain. None of them. Everyone is fighting
among themselves, claiming that this one or that one is the best. They make
fun of each other. Perhaps none of them will actually save you. None of
them."[17]

Paradoxically, the very flexibility and tolerance inherent in the Maya
synthetic approach to religion had been exploited by outside religious forces,
thus undermining the capacity of the Indians to retain those characteristics.
Evangélicos accused Catholics of drunkenness and sloth; Catholics accused
evangélicos of being greedy, overzealous and divisive; everyone accused
costumbristas of being backwards and superstitious.

Although it struck me as perhaps only a matter of diplomacy at the time,
I should have taken Javier at his word when he told me that he liked to
investigate all religions and that he was familiar with the religious practices
of a number of denominations.[18] Somewhat skeptical, I inquired, "Are there
many other people who are familiar with various religions like you are?" He
replied, "No, there are not. This is something I do because I am a cantón
leader. You see, it's difficult to show up and participate with a group of
people you do not know—the same as it was difficult for you to come here
to Nahualá." There was no indication that Javier would abandon his practice
of pan-denominational religious participation any time soon. Indeed, such
accommodation—a refusal to be openly divisive within the community—
may well have been a primary manifestation of his essential Indianness. The
pastor of Misión Centroamericano suggested that the reason Javier had not
been attending recently may have been due to his participation with the
Jehovah's Witnesses across the street. Javier also mentioned that Mormon

missionaries from Quezaltenango had been visiting him regularly. At the time, I failed to press him regarding his fascinating self-study course in comparative religion—still convinced that I would sooner or later find out his "real" affiliation.

"Not mixing up religion with community leadership" is "the way of the principales," Javier told me. Ironically, the community leadership he was referring to was his position in the Catholic parish. Accustomed to holding a civil-religious duty (cargo) for most of his life, Javier was hard pressed to determine what institution might inherit the claim to his service following the breakup of the cargo system. The decision would be a difficult one for anyone, because none of the existing institutions within Nahualá—social, cultural, religious or otherwise—remotely resembled this former one. I believe that Javier had chosen to serve in the Catholic parish because he associated the Catholic Church itself with a certain degree of neutrality in regard to local religious division. As Catholicism was the status quo before the arrival of "religion" in the 1950s, he sensed that by remaining Catholic—whether or not one went to Mass—instead of becoming Protestant, one was less guilty of contributing to societal discord. Given that Javier viewed his position within the parish primarily as a matter of service to his community, rather than as service to the Catholic Church or to God, his saying that he could no longer attend *evangélico* services because of his community service should not have seemed so puzzling.

When You Forget the Paths That Lead to God

Dotted with volcanoes, rocked by earthquakes, and torn by war, Guatemala is a society fractured along innumerable fault lines, including ethnic division, gender discrimination, the widening gulf between the rich and the poor, religious difference, and the politics of a recent civil war. But we need to look no further than the municipal plaza to see how the fissures have begun to pull Nahualá apart. Javier said with regret,

> The Catholic Church is just kind of dying. Take the Charismatics, for example—they are not together with the rest of the church. The only reason that any of them come to Mass at all is because the Father pleads with them and tries to force them to come: "Why in the world will you not come to Mass? Here we have this big, beautiful church, why do you not come?"

For Javier, the irony seemed overpowering. It visibly saddened him. He sensed that life in Nahualá was falling apart at the seams. He described the Catholic priest—an outsider—pleading with the Nahualenses to take better care of the town's icons: its saints. "These are yours to take care of, not mine. Do you not care about them? They are remembrances of the past." Elders of Ixtahuacán and Nahualá, both men and women, recounted to me the battles fought over the right to retain Santa Catarina—her image and her patronage.[19] She alone assured the people's legitimacy as a municipio, as Catholics, and as Mayas. Some of the battles had been fought with paper, before ecclesiastical and legal authorities. Others had been fought in the forest with machetes. In one Nahualense account, which took on mythological proportions, Catarina herself interceded in favor of Nahualá by thrusting her wooden arm into the fray.

Because it is difficult for outsiders to conceive of the degree of integration and overlap that once existed between the legal, civic, social, and religious aspects of life in Nahualá, it is also difficult to understand the way the system's disintegration affected Javier. While religion plays a relatively small role in modern American society, symbols such as Manuel Tzoc's granite church and the statue of Santa Catarina were once central to Nahualá. For most of Javier's life, identity in Nahualá was a non-issue: Nahualenses lived in Nahualá, planted maize, wore traje, spoke K'iche', and followed costumbre under the eye of the saints. Only in the last forty years have outside forces moved so quickly as to make community and ethnic identity require thought. As the population grew, farmers left the municipio to find work in the city or in the United States, Ladino culture entered the municipio, and costumbre was forgotten. It was anything but clear what it meant to be Nahualenses. Thus Javier lamented,

> Sometimes I believe. Sometimes I do not believe. I have not succeeded in finding the right path. There isn't one. There is nowhere to go. And there are a lot of people who feel like I do. It's better to just stay home. Believe in God and leave it at that. No one knows what happened to religion here. Now there's nothing you can do about it. When you forget where the paths go that lead to God, there is no God.[20]

Such a statement—Durkheimian in import—is not so much about the loss of God as much as it is about the violent changes that have occurred in a local way of life.

The Divisiveness of War

The notion of violent change is not just a metaphor. Violence, war, and kidnappings have been a physical reality in Guatemala's recent history in a process that—like religious ideology—has injected divisiveness into the community by trying through force and intimidation to achieve pure ideological affiliation. In the "counter-insurgency" of the early 1980s, the Guatemalan military capitalized on the religious and societal anomie that existed within the Maya highland municipios. Although the role of the Mayas in this conflict continues to be debated, David Stoll (1993) provides evidence that Indians were "caught between two armies"—the Guatemalan army and the guerrillas—and forced to take sides. Carlsen (1997) refers to the system of "civil patrols" organized by the army as part of an attempt to "engineer instability." While the civil patrols were ostensibly organized to protect Maya villages from guerrilla infiltration, "in fact, through civil patrols [the Indians] were drafted into being agents of the Army within their own community" (Carlsen 1997:145). Javier was a leader in Palank'ix's civil patrol, which was not disbanded until 1990. He was required to spend chilly nights in the small adobe guard station (now a roofless ruin defaced by fire and graffiti) that commanded a view of the last set of switchbacks on the trail ascending the mountain to Palank'ix.

During the violent presidency of the evangélico strongman Efraín Ríos Montt (June 1982–August 1983) the Mayas were encouraged to rationalize the army's atrocities in religious terms. Although the ugly intricacies of the war hardly justified such simplification, the Mayas came to associate the guerrilla with the Catholic Church and the army with the Protestants. The Mayas' belief that distancing themselves from Catholicism would provide the best protection from the army led to mass conversions to Protestantism. The army clearly benefited from the atmosphere of paranoia and terror. Preexisting social rifts within the communities took on lethal dimensions as members of the same community denounced each other, each whispering to the death squads that the other was a guerilla (Stoll 1993). During that time, certain catequistas and priests indeed were playing a progressive role by empowering Indian municipios through the creation of religious as well as economic and cultural organizations.

Because the army never occupied Nahualá (as it did many other towns, such as Santiago Atitlán), there were relatively few disappearances, tortures, and deaths within Nahualá in comparison with other municipios. The ex-mayor told me that during the worst of it, he was regularly required to go out to the highway to "pick up bodies." The army made a practice of dumping its victims where they would serve as a reminder to others of the danger of any kind of organized resistance. The Nahualenses were reluctant to talk about "*la violencia*"—the undeclared civil war of the 1980s.[21] For about a decade, the Indians lived in silent terror of the army, the guerrilla, and their own neighbors. One of the most horrible aspects of the conflict was that it had been almost impossible not to take sides. Yet to do so was extremely dangerous and divisive to the community. The fact that most Nahualenses refused to be drawn into and divided by the war was, in fact, fully Indian, and parallels Javier's conscious refusal to be polarized by religious divisiveness.

CONCLUSION: INDIGENOUS CULTURE AS SYNTHESIS

Although Nahualá physically survived "la violencia," the war for its heart and soul is far from over. Ethnographers of the highland towns describe the Mayas' current predicament as "baffling," "a world turned upside down," "chaotic." Carlsen's (1997:166) conclusion regarding the future of Santiago Atitlán probably applies equally well to Nahualá: "It is difficult to escape the conclusion that factors which previously undermined the functioning of the Old Ways remain in place and threaten to undermine present efforts at social stability."

Recommendations for the future are received from various quarters: plant new crops, teach new languages, print more Bibles, pass new legislation. But, in Javier's view, perhaps Nahualá's salvation lay in the past rather than the future. For all of their newfound religious zeal, the Nahualenses were walking away from God. The roads that led to God—the "old ideas" that "always worked"—were known, but they were being forgotten. While some dreamed of, others strove for, and some doubted the possibility of a cohesive, respectful Nahualá, Javier simply remembered it, and tried to live it personally by synthesizing, by accommodating, and by joining new movements while retaining his neutral underpinnings via Catholic community service.

Despite the enormous waves of cultural change crashing upon Nahualá, in Javier's discussion of them there was often a sense of patience, strategy, option, and control. Such control may well have been an illusion, but, as he calmly considered the needs of his people, it was an illusion that continued to affect him. Javier had not been converted to the linear Western gospels of "progress," "development," "modernization," and "globalization," with their inherent tendency to factionalize and differentiate. Javier's refusal to convert and his insistence on acquisitive accommodation and synthesis in the service of maintaining community were the true essence of his continued Indianness.

Yet who will guide the Nahualenses as they walk into a new millennium? Standing at the crossroads of the agrarian village life of the past and the industrial consumer culture of the future, who will choose the path that will be taken? Will Nahualenses look to their elders, such as Javier, for guidance, as they have in the past? Perhaps. After all, Nahualá is the place where both the Guatemalan army and the guerrillas were run out of town with pitchforks, where government liquor was banned, and where suspected murderers and thieves were, and still are, lynched on the spot.

Or will Nahualenses diverge at the crossroads, taking the "three or four" and more paths of ideological division? Time will tell, but synthesizers such as Javier seemed to be a waning minority. In churches, development projects, and the offices of the municipo, one commonly saw younger Nahualenses in charge. Nahualá's mayor in 1995 was no more than forty years old. Material well-being, so desperately needed and wanted, is a siren's voice. Thus, one of many cards that Javier placed in the "no problem" pile was "life after the Pan-American Highway." By contrast, "life before the Pan-American Highway" went into the "problematic" category. I do not know why this surprised me. After all, this was the highway that Javier himself helped to build. "Things were much easier after the highway," he said. "Do you know how difficult it was to get crops to market before we had that road?" Indeed, roads did make life easier in some ways, but they also made the path to God, social cohesion, and ethnic identity exceedingly difficult.

Notes

1. See Watanabe (1992:107–226) for a description of the cargo system.

2. Warren (1978:49) found the word "idea" used in similar ways in San Andrés: of the ancestors, the Trixanos say that their "ideas and words were good ones"; the Spaniards "are remembered as active people full of good ideas" (Warren 1978:41).

3. In most renditions, a caballería is a land measure comprising one thousand cuerdas.

4. See Lauri Bertrand (1999).

5. The Guatemalan newspaper *Hoy* on July 31, 1999, reported thirty people had suffered machete wounds in a recent battle between Nahualá and Santa Catarina.

6. It is difficult to generalize about the "mountain spirits" because they are conceived of differently from municipio to municipio. The Q'eqchi' Mayas recognize the *tzuultaq'a* (R. Wilson 1995:53), and the Mam, the *witz* (Watanabe 1992:75), for example.

7. "Maya priest" (*sacerdote maya*) was a new term with various political implications. It was part of a positive reevaluation of previously stigmatized aspects of the religion of the Maya municipios. It seemed that when referring to potentially controversial activities, the informants were more likely to refer to the shaman-priest as a *zajorín* or *ajq'iij* (the K'iche' term) instead of calling him a "Maya priest."

8. In 1996 a Maya priest in Santa Catarina Ixtahuacán was more than happy to perform costumbre in my behalf. He asked me to provide some of the items that would be offered: a number of candles and a bottle of soda pop. Before beginning the ceremony he needed to know my full name and where I was from.

9. My informants referred to the mundo alternately as "*el dueño del mundo*" which means "the owner of the world." It seemed that each mundo corresponded to an actual mountain known to the Nahualenses. This being the case, it seemed that mundo could also be construed as "owner of the mountain." Florentín spoke of the mundos as being inside the mountains. In his stories, the most fearsome owners were those that dwelt inside volcanoes.

10. In my opinion, Florentín accepted this anecdote very literally. He told me that his mother had indicated to him the specific location along the span of the bridge where the five people were interred.

11. It was not made clear to me whether or not any Nahualense would ever refer to himself as an ajiitz or whether the term is always derogatory. Warren (1998:175) states, "Those who felt they had been wronged could go to . . . the ajiitz (the shaman who specialized in bringing harm to others)."

12. Among the Q'eqchi' Mayas of northern Guatemala, "the heart of the mountain" can refer alternately to a cave—chosen as the ideal place to offer sacrifices to the mountain spirits—or to the mountain spirit itself (R. Wilson 1995:57).

13. Javier thought that *juyub* might be the equivalent of *nahual* (probably the root of *Nahualá*), which refers to the animal spirit that was traditionally thought to inhabit each person's body by day and could exit in dreams at night.

14. See the exploits of the zajorines in Tarn (1997).

15. R. Wilson (1995:53, 57–58) discusses the duality of the tzuultaq'a, the mountain deities of the Q'eqchi' Mayas. He also describes their association with landowning Ladinos and foreigners.

16. Malcolm Botto-Wilson, personal communication.

17. Ignacio Bizarro Ujpán, a Tzutujil Maya elder, shared many of Javier's attitudes: "What I don't like about the religious groups is that they don't behave well [toward one another]; the Catholics hate the evangelicals, and the evangelicals despise the Catholics because they respect and revere the saints" (Sexton 2001:21).

18. Although I did not entirely understand his Spanish, Javier referred to a plan by which every year and a half or so he would switch churches and was thus able, little by little, to become familiar with all of them.

19. See Watanabe (1992) for another detailed example of saint as municipal protector.

20. When Javier said, "Sometimes I believe, sometimes I do not," I do not think he was suggesting atheism. During our card-sorting activity, when I attempted to include a card labeled "Does not believe in God," he assured me, "There are no Nahualenses who don't believe in God."

21. At one evangélico service I attended, the pastor would occasionally switch off the microphone (apparently so he could be heard by the congregation but not over the loudspeakers placed outside the church). During the times when he was thus "off-mike," he was discussing "the military" and "jail," Spanish words that I picked out of the mostly K'iche' sermon.

About the author: *At Brigham Young University I majored in Marriage, Family, and Human Development and minored in Anthropology. My adventures in Guatemala inspired me to seek out other foreign research opportunities, and I soon found myself in South Africa where I investigated the impact of apartheid on fatherhood. I then continued my travels with an eighteen-month volunteer experience in Minas Gerais, Brazil. During a subsequent visit to Brazil, I met and married my husband, a native of São Paulo. Past professional endeavors include parent/family education, English as a Second Language instruction, youth mentoring, and website "localization" and translation.*

Reflections on the 1996 field experience: *As my first foreign experience, the time I spent in Guatemala opened my eyes to the complexities of living cultures and their constant effort to deal with change. The inevitable process of comparing and contrasting the evolving culture of the Ixtahuaquenses with my own Caucasian, North American culture allowed me to reexamine personal feelings and opinions, including the daily pattern of family interaction, the division of labor among family members, and appropriate dating behavior and parental involvement. I believe this helped me develop a more secure sense of self and gave me a greater degree of freedom to continue investigating the world and all its diversities.*

CHAPTER 3

"THE COMMITMENT"
Transformations of Courtship and Marriage in Santa Catarina Ixtahuacán

Kelly C. Araneda

Marriage, the linkage of men and women to households and reproduction, is a fundamental institution of all cultures, no matter how it is defined in detail. Moreover, marriage entails some form of courtship—some way to bring men and women raised in different households together. I began this study of courtship in Santa Catarina Ixtahuacán expecting to encounter an unchanging, enchanted Indian village life where time would have little meaning. It did not take long to dispel that illusion, because change is no stranger to any culture. Carrithers (1992:21) confirms that "the worlds anthropologists find are always . . . [in] a permanent halfway station between one condition and another, between a past and a future and between one society and another." Similarly, the people of Ixtahuacán were not isolated from the impacts of a changing world. Every aspect of their lives, including courtship and marriage, is and always has been subject to both internal and external forces that have led to change. This paper will focus on courtship and marriage customs and local people's perceptions of them. It will also explore some of the factors causing change in courtship and marriage practices.

THE CHANGING NATURE OF COURTSHIP

I sat across from María, a middle-aged woman, with my pen poised above note pad, eager to hear the words as they fell from her lips. Unaware of my good fortune at having scheduled an interview with one of the community's most active women, I hoped that María had something specific to tell me. "María, tell me how you met your husband. What was it like?" "Oh," she said with a heavy sigh, "things are not the way they used to be. Today the young people are allowed to meet in the street. They kiss and hug. Some boys even come into the girl's house. It didn't used to be that way. A girl's parents would hit her if they knew she had a boyfriend." This was a common preface to many interviews with women between the ages of thirty and forty. And with older women, the changes proved even more drastic.

The Traditional Era

Up to about fifty years ago, parents found a suitable bride for their son and proposed to her after the son reached the age of nineteen or twenty. Typically, his mother would approach the chosen girl in secrecy, away from listening ears. If a girl's parents discovered that someone intended to propose to their daughter, they would forbid her to leave the house or make sure that she always had an escort. Thus, the boy's mother had to choose just the right moment, perhaps while the candidate was washing at the river, carrying water, or selling at the market. The mother would propose the marriage to the girl in hurried whispers and remind her that the offer included someone who would provide her with food, clothing, a house, and a secure future. The young woman would accept or decline the offer based on her judgment of the young man and the quality of the offer. In a society of little mobility, where people have known each other since childhood and have shared a common lifestyle and similar folk-Catholic beliefs, making such a critical character judgment about a potential spouse would not have been difficult. Most people knew each other very well and were willing to divulge information about their neighbors, making it easy to learn the needed information about a person from friends and relatives in the community.

A young woman had no reason to refuse the offer if she had no evidence of faulty moral character. I experienced this continuing reality one evening while talking with my host family. "When are you going to marry?" was a familiar question to which I usually answered, "Who knows? Whenever I find the right man." But tonight this response did not satisfy them, and they continued to press the issue. "What do you think of 'X' [a fellow field school student living a few houses away]? Do you like him?" Of course I admitted to liking him as a *good friend*. "Well, is he a good worker?" Yes, he seemed to work hard. "Does he have a good character?" I could not say no. "Do you think he's handsome?" I was stuck. A negative reply would be unkind to my friend, a positive one would only confirm suspicion. I tried a casual "Well,

I guess so." My family chuckled and prodded, "Then why don't you just marry him?" This exchange manifests the criteria for accepting or declining a marriage proposal. If the prospective groom fulfills the basics of being a hard worker with good morals, and if she finds him at least somewhat attractive, there is no reason to refuse the offer.

The Transitional Era

About thirty to forty years ago, some young men dared to initiate their own relationships with young women. A thirty-year-old female informant related one way in which young men sought the affections of young women. Young women would gather at the river on Sundays to do laundry, where admiring young men often filled the nearby trails. When a young lady caught a boy's interest, he might toss a rock in her direction to get her attention. Checking to see there were no parents or tattling siblings nearby, she might dash away from her work for a quick conversation with her admirer. Over time, they might grow to know each other through secret encounters and meetings. If feelings changed to mutual affection, the boy would snatch away the girl's *pañuelo* (a woven cloth that women use for such varied activities as swatting flies or wrapping and carrying loads). A girl's parents normally objected if she lost her pañuelo, because they knew it meant she had a suitor. Parents also became aware of romantic encounters by word of mouth, particularly from children who, running through the streets during the evening, spied on sequestered couples and threatened to inform their parents. Flustered parents looked for their children and escorted them home. If a girl's parents objected to her self-made relationship (as they almost always did), they might require her to perform more than her normal share of difficult housework to prevent her from leaving the house and pursuing the relationship. Some parents locked their daughters up and even harmed them physically to discourage a relationship from developing.

The Recent Era

Although courtship was much more accepted in 1996, secrecy remained an integral part of the process. Electric street lights made it harder to court in the streets away from curious eyes, but inventive couples still found ways and places to rendezvous. They met on the few remaining dark street corners and took advantage of girls' newfound acceptance in the world of sports. The basketball court was often crowded with boys and girls of all ages in friendly competition. Equally filled were the spectator benches which conveniently served as a casual place for couples to flirt or court under the pretense of watching a game.

A changing economy provided another means for young people to consort. As families shifted from milpa economy to a market economy, children were needed less for their labor, leaving more time for them to participate in school. It was increasingly common for young people of both sexes to finish *primaria* (primary school) and continue on to *básico* (junior high school). School offered many opportunities to evaluate candidates for marriage.

Some young people in 1996 participated in official courting. However, it was very rare that a boy would directly ask a girl to go out with him. Instead, a third party—usually a friend or relative—delivered a letter or asked the girl for him. The girl had the option of accepting or declining the invitation. Some young men went directly to a girl's parents and asked permission to enter the house and speak with their daughter to avoid the secrecy and hiding associated with dating. This was risky, however, because the boy had to deal with the inevitably angry father.

When I asked the two K'iche' girls with whom I lived about their dating experiences, both claimed ignorance and denied any kind of romantic involvement. It was customary, however, for girls always to deny having a boyfriend. Sixteen-year-old Rosa surmised that all the boys already had girlfriends because she saw them through her window as they walked down the town's main street.

Those who had trouble securing a *novio* or *novia* (boyfriend or girlfriend) could seek special help from San Simón. San Simón differed significantly from other saints. He had a capricious and unpredictable nature that produced both good and bad outcomes. Although "good" Catholics and Evangelists believed it a sin to venerate or even consult San Simón, those "without religion" petitioned him for blessings and favors, bringing him gifts such as candles, food, alcohol, cigars, clothing, incense, or money. In return, patrons expected San Simón to help them with such endeavors as finding a boyfriend or girlfriend, finding work, or conceiving a male child.[1]

Courtship remained secretive and a girl still faced the possibility of physical punishment if her parents discovered that she had a novio. If the couple was successful and all went according to plan, the last people to find out about the intended marriage were the girl's parents. After secretly solidifying the decision to marry her suitor, the girl would flee her home in the middle of the night and hide at her future husband's home, where she would remain until the wedding ceremony began.[2]

The *Karelaq'aaj* or *el Robo* (the Elopement)

This part of the process, when a girl escaped from her home in the middle of the night, was called the *karelaq'aaj*, or *el robo* (the robbery), and had to be carried out in secrecy. The karelaq'aaj appears to have remained fairly constant over the generations. In the past, the boy's parents normally arranged a time and place for the couple to rendezvous. Today, the couple arranges things themselves. Both in the past and today, it has been possible for a girl to run away alone, but, more often, her novio will wait for her around the corner as she escapes and accompany her to his household. In the past, the couple's first meeting of any significant duration might take place after the karelaq'aaj, whereas in 1996, couples were well acquainted before executing the formal asking.

In her hasty flight, the girl brings nothing except the clothes on her back. Upon arriving at the groom's home, the bride can expect to receive a new wardrobe that her mother-in-law prepared during the previous months. This normally consists of four huipiles, four cortes, two *fajas* (belts), two pañuelos, two sweaters, and two aprons. Producing this marital offering requires a large investment of time, money, and effort. The average huipil takes about one month to complete and costs between two hundred and three hundred quetzales. The bride's act of forsaking all possessions and clothing may symbolize her willingness to shed her past and start a new life with her husband's family (Mair 1971:107). After a couple has safely engineered the karelaq'aaj, the danger has not completely passed. Angry parents may still search for their daughter and try to take her home. Thus, a girl might hide at a relative's home or at the novio's parent's home. A common hiding place in the past was in the large wooden box behind the house where the family kept its store of dried corn.[3]

The *K'amal B'e* (Go-Between)

The next morning, the boy's parents typically informed the bride's parents of what had occurred during the night and asked permission for the marriage to take place. Emotions would run high at this point. The bride's parents, who likely felt they had been unjustly robbed, were in a volatile state, and often had no interest in talking to those people who they felt had just wronged them. To soften emotions, the boy's parents called on a mediator or go-between for the two families, the *k'amal b'e*, who would do the actual petitioning and make several visits to the bride's parents. With the boy's parents in tow, the k'amal b'e would arrive at the girl's home to ask her parents for permission and to *pedir disculpas* (ask forgiveness) for having stolen their daughter. In the past, this process required the k'amal b'e to visit each day for up to forty days. Today the k'amal b'e visits twice a day for about ten days. How long it takes depends on how angry the parents are and how long it takes them to consent peacefully. The visits also serve as planning sessions to prepare for the wedding.

Now retired from the profession at age sixty-eight, José was one of the community's few remaining k'amal b'es. José was a gentle, soft-spoken man. His wrinkled face; thin, muscular legs; and yellowed fingernails spoke of many years toiling in the elements. He candidly admitted that his profession presented several risks. Every time he petitioned a girl's parents, he had to confront their anger and the possibility of physical harm. In extreme cases, the parents threw water on the ground in front of the door and required the k'amal b'e and the groom's party to kneel in the mud and receive a beating. These and other risks contributed to the scarcity of k'amal b'es in Ixtahuacán today. Young men do not consider the small salary received from the groom's parents adequate compensation for the risks, travel time, and effort required to learn the difficult *palabras antiguas* (old words or ceremonial speech).[4]

The palabras antiguas are used the morning after the karelaq'aaj—when the k'amal b'e petitions for forgiveness—as well as during and after the house wedding. Many of these words come from an older form of K'iche', with which very few people are still familiar. None of my female informants could tell me the meaning of the palabras antiguas or even the topics therein. According to Ixtahuaquenses, the palabras antiguas have never been written down. Instead, the k'amal b'e memorizes them and passes them on to the next generation of apprentices. José recited the palabras antiguas for me. He closed his eyes and leaned slightly forward as the words poured without pause in a soothing and rhythmic cadence.[5]

The Marriage Ceremonies

Once the k'amal b'e had fulfilled his role as mediator and both sets of parents had agreed to the marriage, the wedding festivities began. Couples participated in three different ceremonies: the house wedding, the civil wedding, and the church wedding.

The House Wedding

The first celebration was the house wedding, where the bride reunited with her family for the first time since the karelaq'aaj. This celebration was always completely financed by the groom's family.

One typically cloudy morning I was shaken from my sleep to receive a last-minute invitation to a 7:00 A.M. house wedding. I found myself hiking through the morning air to an aldea with my sixty-six-year-old neighbor, Juana. We caught up with her husband, Manuel, who greeted me with his somewhat toothless grin and asked, "Are you going to accompany us to the wedding?"

When we arrived at the household, everyone seemed busy doing his or her part to prepare for the wedding. I gratefully heeded Juana's signal to follow her into an evangélico church, away from staring eyes. We sat on a low wooden bench with several other older men and women. Women served us a meal of plain tamales and beans. After we ate, the men gathered in the doorway to hold a meeting of sorts. My roommates' sister, Florentina, explained that the k'amal b'e could not come; instead, Manuel would perform the wedding because he knew the palabras antiguas.

As preparations continued, one authority spread pine needles all around the church floor and in front of a table that held a picture of Christ, flowers, and candles. Three crates of bottled sodas, two baskets of bread, and two thermoses of hot chocolate were placed on the floor in the middle of the room. As the wedding guests began to fill the church, Florentina pointed out the bride and groom to me. She wore the traditional traje; her head was covered by a large green and purple pañuelo. He wore a black jacket and blue jeans.

With no formal warning or beginning, Manuel began speaking to the couple seated on wooden crates in front of him. The young man nodded intermittently and listened with eyes downcast. The three seemed to be holding their own conversation without regard to the other guests in the room, who talked among themselves.

After Manuel finished speaking, the couple knelt in front of the table near the front of the room, and all in attendance came in closer to kneel on the pine needles. A man dressed in Ladino clothing stood at the pulpit to read Bible passages. In contrast to Manuel's quiet voice and manner, this man's loud voice echoed through the tiny church as the congregation repeated passages and muttered prayers. After the Bible reading, spoken mostly in K'iche' with intermittent Spanish, everyone stood and the party prepared to leave, as men loaded crates of food onto their strong backs. I saw the groom slip a hundred quetzales to a young boy who took the bill and quickly ran out the door in search of supplies for the next stage of the wedding.

Led by Manuel, the party moved to the bride's home. The bride followed with her head bowed and her mouth covered by her pañuelo. Next came the groom, followed by men in colorful head wraps. Then came my neighbor, Juana, and the men carrying the food. I brought up the rear with other women and children. We walked in silence through the tall cornfields and slowly filed into a small front room at the bride's house. The bride's family sat on the left side of the room while the groom's family sat on the right. Manuel took his seat at the front of the room near a table decorated with flowers and candles.

In front, two wooden chairs remained expectantly empty where the bride and groom would sit. For the time being they sat on their respective sides of the room with their families. Before beginning his discourse which now seemed to be for the benefit of all, Manuel stood and prayed before a picture of Christ, while others also stood, crossed themselves, and prayed. Manuel paused to allow the bride's father, Alberto, to speak. Alberto, the event's honorary *chuchqajaw*,[6] projected a powerful aura with his wrinkled brow, tightly shut eyes, and booming voice. Eventually, Alberto paused and the couple moved in front of the wooden chairs where they crossed themselves and knelt. Alberto then conducted a question-and-answer session with the groom. Informants said this dialogue was an investigation about how the couple met and the length of their acquaintance.

Following these formal inquiries, the bride's relatives, in random order, took turns offering advice to the couple about how to fulfill their responsibilities. The speakers always greeted everyone in the room before and after addressing the couple. Other studies of marriage in Guatemalan villages have documented such advice-giving sessions. Saravia (1983:127–29) details this process and provides a Spanish translation of advice given to the couple, which includes:

- Be sure to pray at night for your husband and children.
- Say good night before going to bed.
- Do not answer disrespectfully to your husband (or your mother-in-law) because it shames your parents.
- Be sure to keep your husband's clothes mended.

- When you get up and you see your in-laws, fold your arms [respectfully] and greet them. Then give your *petate* (a small woven mat) to your mother-in-law to sit on. Answer her with all respect.
- Sweep the floor well and keep house well so that you will not be chastised.
- Work well and wash the clothes.
- Help your husband earn money and food, because that's just how it is for your whole life.
- Do not stop in the street to speak with a man.

Similarly, the relatives then offered the following advice to the groom:

- Remember that you are married, and you should not bother young women in the streets because it would bring shame to your parents.
- Give money to your wife every day for expenses, for food, for soap, for cooking, and for clothes.
- Get up early and greet the adults of the house.
- If you have animals, care for them.
- Eat breakfast early and leave quickly for work.
- Care for your tools: *el azadón* (hoe) and your machete. If you cut firewood, care for your ax and sharpen it.
- When you return home from work, focus on your path and think about God so that nothing happens to you.
- Return quickly so that you do not displease your wife or your parents.
- Do not forget your *suyacal* (rain protection) in case it rains.
- Be careful about picking up and putting down what you carry on your back (probably referring to large loads of firewood).
- Do not drink cold water on the path.
- If you go to the mountain, take care because rock falls can harm you.

The Ixtahuacán ceremony was free from any strong display of emotion. I did not detect any hint of nervous energy or anxiety from anyone until the bride's mother spoke to the young couple and tears revealed her feelings. Although I did not understand the words, the message of love and concern was clear, and the couple looked at each other for the first time since they first knelt.

After two hours and fifteen minutes, the couple received permission to sit on chairs amid their relatives for a brief respite from kneeling. But before long, the couple again knelt to kiss each relative's hand, beginning with the bride's father. If the relative consented to let the couple kiss his or her hand, it signified acceptance of the marriage. Meanwhile, the *mayordomo* (a friend or relative chosen by both families to assist with the wedding) began the ceremony known as *chupb'al q'aaq'* (to extinguish the fire). He walked around the circle of guests with a pitcher of water and a pañuelo over his arm. Those who wished to participate washed their mouths and hands when the mayordomo passed in front of them. Ordinarily, the mayordomo would then bring a small pitcher of cuxa and those who washed would take a small sip. This was, however, an evangélico wedding and they skipped the alcohol offering. The mayordomo then distributed bread, coffee, and sodas to the guests, serving the bride's family first.

The ceremony represented peace and union between the two families. From that time forward the two families forsook any resentments or ill feelings and addressed each other with respect. Thereafter, when any members of the two families met each other on the street, they used formal pronouns, similar to the distinction between *usted* and *tú* in Spanish. For example, instead of saying, *la utz awach* ("Good morning," literally "is good thy countenance/face?"), they will say *la utz wach la, naan* ("good morning, respected you, mother).[7]

As we enjoyed the refreshments, the bride's relatives thanked the groom's family for providing the food and drink by saying, *maltyox naan, maltyox taat* (thank you, mother, thank you, father). After clearing the dishes, one of the groom's female relatives produced two beautiful bouquets of fresh white flowers and gave them to the couple before they again crossed themselves and knelt in front of the table. Alberto spoke again and draped a brightly colored pañuelo over the bride's hair. The ceremony drew to a close, and what resembled a receiving line formed near the door, where Alberto, as chuchqajaw, paused to shake hands with departing relatives.

The ceremony then moved back to the church. Inside, the couple placed their bouquets on the table near the pulpit and reseated themselves on the crate at the front of the room as Manuel gave an animated concluding discourse. He spoke as if he knew that this was his last chance to give his counsel to the young couple and wanted to make sure they remembered every word. Meanwhile, the mayordomos served another meal, consisting of *caldo de res* (beef stew), tamales, and soda. Children played games in the back of the room and again it seemed that no one paid attention. Manuel spoke mostly in K'iche', but I heard him say "*el matrimonio es santificado*" (marriage is holy). Manuel finished speaking and enjoyed a bowl of soup while the guests socialized. Slowly the festivities ended and the guests left. The couple would now go to the groom's grandparents' home for lunch and bring an end to the day's events.

Several informants had described a process in which the bride takes a moment before leaving to say good-bye to her parents. One informant related her sad *despedida* (good-bye) in detail: she explained to her parents that she felt no sorrow or regret for her decision because she had found her life with a new and respectable family and invited her parents to come visit her new home. Her parents responded by saying that they had not wanted her to marry, but she would not listen and now it was too late; there was nothing they could do.

The Civil Wedding

According to the town mayor, the civil wedding may take place as soon as the day after the house wedding or be put off for several months. After a civil wedding, the couple is not permitted to separate without a legal divorce, as they could with the house wedding.

In the past, the law required couples to go to the mayor's office and sign a certificate declaring themselves single and unrelated to each other. The mayor would add his signature and post it outside the municipal hall for everyone to see. Members of the community had two weeks to challenge the certificate, after which wedding plans proceeded as normal. Today, posting the certificate at the municipal hall is not necessary. Couples living in Ixtahuacán meet with the mayor to arrange a date for the ceremony before acquiring a marriage license from the secretary with the mayor's authorization. Couples from distant hamlets and villages can get their marriage license and have the wedding performed in one day to avoid two trips into the town center. The bride and groom must be at least eighteen years old to marry without parental permission.

Like the house wedding, the civil wedding I attended was a lengthy family affair. The couple sat, bride on the left and groom on the right, before the mayor's desk, which was covered with a Guatemalan flag and adorned with a vase of flowers symbolizing happiness.

The civil wedding consisted of six parts. Believing that many couples were still forced to marry, the mayor began by asking the couple if they had come of their own free will. Once convinced that the couple had entered the relationship willingly, he inquired about the length and origin of their courtship, as Alberto had during the house wedding.

The second part consisted of a reading from the *código civil*, the civil code, which included passages that clearly delineate a man's and woman's individual roles and duties. The code emphasizes that marriage is based on *compromiso* (commitment) and that couples must fulfill their responsibilities to have and sustain a family. A woman is obligated to contribute to the household in any way she can, including financially, but her primary responsibility is to raise their children and care for the home. According to civil law, a woman has no right to work outside the home. If a man works diligently and does all that he can to provide for his family, he has the right to forbid his wife to work or study outside of the home. If, for some reason, the husband is incapacitated and can not provide for his family, the wife must take over his responsibilities. The same is true for the husband, should anything happen to his wife.

The third part of the wedding was a reading of the *código penal*, the penal code, explaining the fines and punishments associated with infidelity. The Guatemalan government established both the código civil and the código penal and in theory enforces them uniformly throughout the country.

During the fourth part of the wedding, the mayor stressed the importance of parents' roles in the community and the importance of the family as the base of society. He reminded the couple that they needed to cooperate and compromise. The mayor then permitted parents to speak and share their counsel with their children.

Las juramentaciones (vows) made up the fifth part of the civil wedding. Everyone stood while the couple faced each other, holding right hands, as the mayor again affirmed that the couple had entered the marriage willingly rather than by force. After the vows were taken, the families applauded and sat down.

During the sixth and final section of the wedding, the mayor read the official certificate, which had to be signed by the couple, the parents, several witnesses, and himself. After the wedding, the groom's family hosted a lunch for all the relatives in the town's social hall.

The Church Wedding

The third wedding ceremony, the church wedding, could take place immediately following the civil wedding or at any time in the following years.[8] Catholics viewed this third and final wedding as the most important one because it united the couple before God. Divorce after a church wedding was not considered permissible, yet most informants knew at least one divorced person. In Santa Catarina, the Catholic priest would not perform a church wedding until couples completed a class taught by the local catechist who further instructed them on how to fulfill their responsibilities in the home.

A week before the church wedding, the priest visits the couple and gives them a special blessing. Other preparations include choosing *padrinos* (godparents). The young couple offers gifts of bread and chocolate to a married man outside of the family and asks him to serve as padrino. If he accepts, the padrino will ask his wife to accompany him as *madrina* (god-mother), whose role during the wedding includes helping the bride put on her veil, the only special article of clothing worn for the occasion.

The bride and groom, carrying white candles, meet at the bride's home with their relatives and walk to the church to celebrate Mass. After taking Holy Communion, the priest asks the couple if they love each other and reminds them of their duties as man and wife. He then takes a long necklace of gold beads and loops it around the couple's necks. The necklace symbolizes their unification before God and that they are not to separate.

The padrino then steps forward and presents the groom with a handful of sacred coins. The groom gives the coins to his bride, and she in turn gives them back to the priest. This transaction symbolizes that the couple now has the responsibility to build their own house, have their own family, and make their own money, and that the husband, receiving from God, provides to his wife.

After the church wedding, the madrina will help the bride remove her veil and put on a *cinta*, or a *xaq'ap*, a long, belt-like headpiece with brightly colored tassels on each end. The bride's hair is divided down the middle and the xaq'ap is wrapped around each half and tied in front so the tassels dangle over her ears and forehead. She will wear this headpiece until evening as a symbol of her newlywed state. One informant indicated that young women these days prefer not to use the xaq'ap because it is difficult to make and cumbersome and uncomfortable to wear.

The church wedding is followed by another feast, hosted by the groom's family. The traditional foods include *tamalitos*, caldo de res, and coffee. The padrinos are invited. The k'amal b'e will thank all the people in attendance and close the ceremonies with a final counsel that the couple behave themselves and not argue. After the feast, it is customary for the bride not to say good-bye to her family or look back at them as she leaves, because it may cause the young couple to fight. One informant explained her own experience of passing around the circle of her relatives to bid them all good-bye. She told them, "It's the last time that I'll say good bye. It's the last time we'll see each other this way. Next time it will be different."

Case Studies of the Marriage Process

To exemplify this marriage process, I will relate several case studies from key informants that capture each era of change in courtship and marriage in Ixtahuacán.

Manuela, Age Sixty-six—A Traditional Period Story

Manuela married her husband, Andrés, now age seventy-eight, when she was eighteen. Following the traditional pattern, the couple did not seek each other out. Rather, Andrés's mother approached Manuela alone and made the proposal, which Manuela initially declined. But Andrés's mother persisted for a year. Whenever the two women met in the street, Andrés's mother would renew the offer until Manuela eventually consented. Her parents opposed the idea, but Manuela never knew why. Although she knew her parents would be very angry, Manuela was not afraid to run away to Andrés's house on the night of the karelaq'aaj, when she met him for the first time. However, she did fear that her parents would come searching for her, so she and Andrés hid at a friend's house for two days while his parents began the petitioning process through the mediation of a k'amal b'e. They petitioned twice a day for two weeks until finally her parents accepted the proposal.

They celebrated the traditional house wedding, similar to the pattern described above. Manuela remembers how she and Andrés knelt and listened respectfully for many hours while her relatives gave advice. Her house wedding included the ceremony called *chupb'al q'aaq'*, where they shared a common glass of cuxa. A few weeks ensued between the house wedding and the civil wedding, during which the groom's parents visited Manuela's parents four more times over the course of four weeks. The first time, they brought a little purse of money and left it on her parents' kitchen table. The following three times they brought gifts of food. Nowhere else did I find this type of post-wedding gift giving mentioned in my interviews. However, it is referred to in the palabras antiguas. The Spanish translation seems to imply that the k'amal b'e brought this monetary gift (called the *b'inb'al*, equivalent to about two days' wages then) to the bride's parents. Manuela and Andrés then had a normal civil and church wedding, as described above. They lived with Andrés's parents until both his parents died, by which time Manuela had given birth to several children.

Not surprisingly, Manuela felt that the biggest change in weddings today was that couples usually knew each other before marrying and that courtship involved less secrecy. Also, newlyweds today usually live with the groom's parents only until the birth of their first child or until they can afford to build their own house. She preferred the old system because parents had more influence and control over the new relationship as they fostered the young couples along, helping them learn to compromise and cooperate. Manuela was the only informant I encountered who believed love was not necessary for a happy marriage. She simply trusted her judgment of Andrés's good character from the beginning. She considers their marriage a successful and happy one.

Marta, Age Forty—A Transitional Period Story

Marta's "love story" came out casually while she knelt by my bedside and showed me a basket-weaving project from one of the women's development group activities. A mother of four, Marta was a happy, energetic woman, actively involved in her community. Her marriage stemmed from a courtship of the transitional era, when marriages were not arranged, but secrecy still played a key role. Her husband, Tomás, first contacted her by means of a letter carried by her cousin. At first, the letters startled and frightened Marta because she did not know Tomás at all and did not want to talk to him. Slowly her feelings changed and the couple secretly met in brief encounters until they eventually arranged, by letter, a secret date for the karelaq'aaj. The morning after the karelaq'aaj, Tomás petitioned Marta's parents himself, with bad consequences. Her father's intense anger convinced Marta to hide at a friend's house for a week while he calmed down. They did not dare ask permission again for another five weeks, after which her father finally consented. Their house wedding was held on a Friday, the civil wedding on Saturday, and the church wedding on Sunday.

Irma, circa Age Forty-five—A Transitional Period Story

In the story of her marriage, Irma underscored the secrecy of her entire courtship. For four years she wrote letters, delivered by a trusted friend, and dared to speak with her husband-to-be only during chance encounters that lasted but one or two minutes each. Finally, her husband-to-be arranged a

secret meeting and told her, "*vamos a casarnos*" (Let's get married). Shortly
afterward Irma's future mother-in-law approached her in the street and asked
if she indeed planned to marry her son, to which Irma said yes. Her
prospective mother-in-law set to work preparing the clothes that Irma would
receive upon entering her new household. Irma described the night she flung
the door open with furtive enthusiasm and ran away while her parents slept.
She and her husband hid at his aunt's house because they feared her parents
would come searching for her. The next morning, his parents, accompanied
by a k'amal b'e, began the petitioning process which consisted of two visits
a day for ten days. Their house wedding took place in November and the
church wedding in December. The couple did not have a civil wedding
because it was not considered necessary at the time.

Laura, Age Twenty-three—A Recent Period Story

Laura is the mother of two young children. She and her husband,
Roberto, live in a brand-new house with tile floors, glass windows, a gas-
burning stove, large wooden doors with metal locks, and a porcelain flush
toilet. In Ixtahuacán, such furnishings indicate substantial financial security.
Laura first met her husband in the street when she was thirteen and he was
fifteen. They immediately fell in love, and for a month their courtship
remained covert. They met secretly in the cemetery or any other place away
from inquisitive eyes and telling tongues. Before long, Roberto gathered
enough courage to ask Laura's father for permission to speak with her openly.
Her father was infuriated and ordered him to leave the house, but he also told
Roberto to come back the next day for an answer. Roberto did as he was
told and was given permission to "date" Laura openly. After that, a normal
outing for Laura and Roberto lasted for thirty minutes to an hour and consisted mostly of simple walks and long talks together. Occasionally they
would visit each others' houses. After courting for two years, Roberto went
to Guatemala City to work while she went to Huehuetenango to study. They
never wrote letters but kept in contact by telephone. After two more years
of courtship, Roberto finally proposed to Laura, who waited a month before
answering yes.

Their use of the k'amal b'e only lasted for two visits, but Roberto's
parents continued to visit her parents about ten more times while they planned
the wedding. Laura remembers that during the house wedding all of her
relatives instructed Roberto to provide for her and not to let her suffer. They
also told her that she would need to wash, cook, clean, and care for the

children. That same day Laura and Roberto met at the municipal hall for the civil wedding, and the church wedding took place the following day.

Catalina, Age Twenty-one—A Recent Period Story

Catalina's story most closely resembles the Western scenario of courtship. Catalina and Miguel first met in school when she was fourteen and he was about sixteen. At the time, Miguel already had a girlfriend, but he broke off the relationship a month after meeting Catalina. Catalina admits to fighting a lot with Miguel in the beginning. Catalina had to go to Huehuetenango to repeat her last two years of school, and when she returned, she found Miguel dating another girl. This ended the relationship, but it resumed again shortly afterward. In fact, they broke things off four times before marrying. Finally, after they had dated for a solid year without fighting, they decided to marry.

Although this bumpy love story sounds familiar to members of Western culture and seems "modern" compared with more traditional courtships, their own engagement contains many traditional elements, such as complete secrecy in order to avoid punishment. Catalina also participated in the karelaq'aaj by running away in the night to Miguel's house, and the next day his parents began the petitioning process, though without a k'amal b'e on the initial visit. However, for the next twenty visits they did employ a k'amal b'e. Catalina married during Holy Week, and all three ceremonies took place within three consecutive days.

FACTORS LEADING TO CHANGE IN COURTSHIP AND MARRIAGE

Among the factors leading to changes in courtship and marriage, the most salient are material and economic change, external influences, and economic uncertainty.

Material and Economic Change

General changes in community life have impacted the courtship and marriage process. The introduction of plumbing some twenty to thirty years ago was one of these. With a water faucet in almost every household's courtyard, women no longer needed to gather at the rivers or public fountains. This eliminated an opportunity for young men to observe or associate with eligible young women. Forced to invent other ways of getting to know each other, young couples relied more heavily on secretly arranged meetings.

The transition from an agriculture-based economy to a market-based economy has also brought change to courtship and marriage. Children, once required to spend most of their time helping in the fields, now attend school, where they have the opportunity to interact with the opposite sex. Post-marital residence has also been affected by the cash economy. Those who depend solely on cash income instead of agriculture to sustain their families are still a minority, yet more men are leaving the village in search of work. Several men and women left Ixtahuacán to become teachers in other towns. My host father, for example, left several times during my stay to work on the coast and did not return for two to three days. The new highway has made traveling in search of work more feasible. This will increasingly disrupt the traditional pattern of living with the groom's parents following marriage.

External Influences

An additional source of change stems from outside influences and their infiltration into indigenous courtship habits. Radio, television, and movies from Mexico and elsewhere have impacted gender roles and expectations of how courting should take place. This infusion of new social standards from Western media has clashed with existing traditions and created a unique blend of media-inspired practices and village-based customs. Couples are in an awkward predicament as they try to determine if they can still rely on the compromiso, or commitment, as the basis of their marriage. The clash between agricultural and cash economies makes it difficult for couples to rely on a solid economic agreement to hold marriages together. What will become the new basis for the institution of marriage, when traditional duties and responsibilities no longer provide the sure foundation that they did in the past? Is it possible that the Western idea of romantic love will replace the fundamentally economic elements of marriage in Ixtahuacán? Western romance has not only become a part of the current wedding trends, but continues to weaken and destabilize the foundations of the compromiso and other traditions.

While economics was the basis for most marriages belonging to the middle-aged and older generations, young wives reported that love, respect, and understanding were the basis of their marital relationships. Thus, even if a young couple can not rely on the traditional compromiso to hold the relationship together, at least they may stay together because they love each other. The weakening of compromiso may not be complete, though; many believe it is still crucial to maintain elements of the compromiso. Upholding respective duties to home, work, and family still acts as a glue. However, as love plays a more vital role, we may see changes in the perception of the marriage relationship and in the implementation of wedding rituals, while couples maintain some traditional values and expectations.

Government intrusion and other outside influences contributed to the changing structure and basis of marriage. José María commented on the influence of government in the dwindling use of the k'amal b'e. He cited the mayor's concern about forced or arranged marriages. The reduced number of visits made to the bride's parents by the k'amal b'e, he believed, was attributable to a direct attempt by the government to focus on the couple's love for each other rather than on the traditional format of marriage. José did not like this development and believed it pulled people away from their ancestors.

Increased contact with Ladino points of view also affects the developing notion of love in marriage. One informant believed Ladino couples shared a greater bond of love because they went on a honeymoon after their wedding. Most informants, however, felt they had too little experience with Ladinos to know for certain. Many women believed Ladino weddings consisted of a small gathering before a lawyer or a judge, where they would simply sign a piece of paper to make the union official.

Economic Uncertainty

Members of the Ixtahuacán community have repeatedly emphasized that a marriage is a compromiso—a promise, a commitment, an obligation. Spouses are expected to uphold their end of the bargain by fulfilling their respective duties. In this scheme of things, men are the bread winners and work diligently in the fields to provide material goods for the family. Women then use these goods to wash, cook, clean, and tend children in the home. Their duties are complementary and it is difficult for one gender to survive in the community without the other.

This philosophy became evident in the numerous discourses given during the wedding ceremonies concerning a man's responsibility to provide for his family and a woman's responsibility to care for home and children. In earlier times these basic elements of duty and responsibility formed the foundation of the compromiso. Manuela, who experienced an arranged marriage, believed that love was not essential for marriage and that what mattered was that a husband be morally responsible, a good worker, and an adequate provider. For her, that commitment sufficiently engendered a successful marriage and sustained it for many years.

Today, remnants of that philosophy exist. Yet I also sensed fear that a woman could no longer rely on the compromiso because a man could not be relied on to fulfill his responsibility to provide for the family, whether because of bad character, disability, lack of land, or unemployment.

Financial security is a delicate subject in this community. The young women who offered an explanation for the persistence of parental anger said that their parents wanted them to finish their education before marrying. Parents might also object to the match if the young man was known to drink too much or be a poor worker. These problems posed major concerns to parents because, after marrying, a husband had the right to forbid his wife to work or study outside the home and had almost complete control over the family's, and therefore their daughter's, financial well-being.

As in many societies, an Ixtahuaquense man's work and his ability to provide for his family defined who he was. However, the reality of the struggling economy in Ixtahuacán has forced many men to recognize that no matter how hard they work in the milpa, their efforts still may not be enough to support their families. Thus, in an effort to contribute to the family's income, many women have taken up weaving petates or huipiles to sell in the market. This infringement on the male world may cause men to question their current social role and usefulness within the home and community. According to my interviews, most women still want to believe their husbands will always take care of them; they want to believe in the compromiso. Yet, the economic uncertainty of today weakened the reliability of the commitment implicit in el compromiso.

PARENTAL ANGER

It would appear that secret courtships and parental anger have remained constant across each era of the marriage and courtship process. This apparently age-old tradition of fierce anger and opposition to marriage seems ironic. Can it be that parents have violent objections to the idea of their daughter leaving home and marrying an eligible young man? What is it that makes Ixtahuacán parents of three generations so uneasy and so unwilling to accept a young man's proposal as a natural and exciting part of their daughter's life?

Men and women alike would shrug their shoulders and offer no satisfactory response. It appears that some parents' anger stems from a cultural expectation that they must demonstrate strong emotion at the prospect of marrying off their daughter. Imagine the community's reaction to a marriage not received by the parents in the traditional way: that is, the parents accepting a marriage proposal without protest. Would this imply less-than-pure reasons for the marriage? Perhaps the couple had to marry due to an unexpected pregnancy. Or perhaps it would connote parental negligence and indifference. Imagine the feelings of a young girl whose parents showed no sign of emotional upset at the thought of her leaving the home. Would it mean that her parents would not miss her or that they were anxious for her to leave?[9]

I sensed a strong feeling of family unity in Ixtahuacán. Each family member was a valued participant in daily life. Anger may represent a family's affection for their daughter, who must inevitably be lost to her husband's family when she takes on the responsibility of caring for her husband's family. As indicated by the good-byes that are sometimes said at the end of the church wedding, a daughter will never see her family in the same way after she is married. Although she may only live across the village, she loses her original place within the family unit.

My host family's newlywed daughter, Juana, lived a five-minute walk from her parents' house, but she only visited them three times during my two-month stay. When she did visit she participated in the household duties less than her two unmarried sisters. She took the role of a guest, laughing and talking with her hosts and helping when appropriate, but not initiating any work herself. A sense of love and friendship existed between Juana and her family, but her duties now lay in her husband's household. Her position in her parents' household had become that of an outsider coming to visit, rather than an insider expected to work. In short, parental anger may express the multi-faceted change of a daughter's relationship with her parents.

Parents may also be concerned, anxious, and therefore angry about the changing nature of courtship and marriage because marriage no longer implies firm economic agreements and obligations. Parents have no guarantee that their daughter will be taken care of. As a result of the evaporating compromiso, perhaps parents also feel some loss of respect and control because they no longer have the cultural authority to arrange their children's marriages. They cannot choose the person who will care for their daughter, thus heightening their uneasy concern for her long-term well-being.

Yet, parental anger was traditional, expected of parents in the pre-change conditions of peasant life. So its explanation must also be rooted in the general conditions of marriage in peasant indigenous society. Here one sees the value of Hawkins's analysis of responsibility and control over female sexuality and over familial assets. Respectable families must carefully guard their daughters' sexuality if the family is to maintain its social status. Anger is the proper response to the loss of control resulting from courtship (Hawkins 1984:245–66).

CONCLUSION

In light of these changing views of men's and women's marital roles, it should not be surprising that married women offer the following advice to future brides. I quote or closely paraphrase in each case, for these women's words give us a hint of the rush toward change. However, young people's words are freer to change than their behavior, for they must also reckon with the power embedded in parental and grandparental generations.

Irma, circa Age Forty-five

Young women today should begin early to understand exactly what it means to be married and all the responsibility it involves. Irma felt very unprepared this way. She encouraged her thirteen-year-old daughter to wait until age thirty or thirty-five before marrying. By this time she will have finished an education and will be prepared to support a family.

Laura, Age Twenty-three

Laura advises youth to "marry someone that you really love and who you are sure loves you, too. Love is essential for a happy marriage. It is necessary that a husband work, too, in order to provide the family with food and clothing. But it is more important to love each other than to work."

Catarina, circa Age Twenty-eight

As the mother of three young boys, Catarina advises young women to get an education and prepare to support a family someday. Love is necessary for a happy marriage, but if for some reason a husband decides to stop working, it is acceptable to leave him and look for a man who will work. This is particularly true for women with small children. However, Catarina adds that she does not advocate divorce and believes it is utterly impossible after a church wedding. Catarina is currently attending school to become a teacher like her husband.

Catalina, Age Twenty-one

Women should definitely wait until at least age twenty before marrying. By then they should have finished studying and have a job. Women need to be mature and understand what they are getting into before they marry. Love is necessary to prevent a couple from fighting.

Manuela, Age Sixty-six

Manuela believes women should marry between the ages of eighteen and twenty and remember to care for the home. Love is not essential for a successful marriage.

Much of the advice proffered above could have come from an average North American woman involved in the feminist movement. In some measure, Ixtahuacán is experiencing its own version of feminism as it relates to courtship, marriage, and the economy. Yet, I can in no way agree to the proposition that Ixtahuaquenses are consciously forsaking their heritage. To the contrary, I had the opportunity to attend a Maya New Year ceremony, reinstituted after years of lapse by the blossoming local Maya resurgence movement. Both young men and young women actively participated in the ceremony with obvious cultural pride. Members of the community often speak of their ancestors and the way things used to be.

Even though courtship and marriage practices may be changing rapidly, the community is not anxious to forget its past. As the heart of the home and the cultivator of future generations, marriage forms the seedbed for social change as well as social continuity. Young people today are confronted with the option of clinging to tradition, leaping into change, or doing a precarious balancing act. Whatever changes sweep through Ixtahuacán, however, I believe that echoes of the past will remain within earshot, at least for a while.

NOTES

1. See Morgan, ch. 2, this volume; Mendelson (1965).

2. See Hawkins (1984:245–48, 253–56) for comparative material.

3. This material relates to issues of rape and coercion of women discussed in Thompson and Hanamaikai, ch. 4, this volume.

4. In addition to waning interest in the palabras antiguas (*tz'onob'al tziij*), the profession has also been affected by the breakdown of the Catholic cofradía system, which distributes religious responsibilities throughout the community. Very recently, the number of cofradías in Santa Catarina has decreased from five to two. The cofradía served as a school of sorts, where aspiring young men learned the palabras antiguas from a seasoned k'amal b'e. José explained that his motives for entering the profession and endeavoring to learn the old words stemmed from a dream he experienced as a young man. He dreamed that all of the dead k'amal b'es and many of his ancestors stood on a riverbank calling to him, asking him to lead a different sort of life and become a k'amal b'e. José responded to the dream and eventually recited the words in the cofradía, as part of the *probación*, or test. Surrounded by current k'amal b'es and the holy saints, José and the other students gathered in the cofradía to recite the words one by one in a trial-like setting. The participant giving the best recitation was chosen, and the people of the community were then free to solicit his services as a k'amal b'e. José mentioned a ceremony that accompanied this process but omitted the details.

5. Ajpacajá Tum (2001) has transcribed and translated the palabras antiguas of the marriage k'amal b'e.

6. Chuchqajaw does not refer to a specific office or position. It is a respectful title, similar to the words *Don* and *Doña* in Spanish. However, if you ask someone to point to the chuchqajaw at a wedding ceremony, he or she will point to the bride's father.

7. The word *la*, loosely translated, means "we have respect for you." They will also use a different voice inflection with members of the other family. Instead of ending their sentences in a downward or flat tone of voice (ordinary usage), they carry their voices up slightly (respectful usage).

8. No church wedding took place during my stay in Ixtahuacán. This material is based on informants' idealized descriptions.

9. See also Hawkins (1984:245–48), who treats the matter of courtship and parental anger extensively.

About the Lead Author: *Upon returning from Guatemala in August of 1995, I resumed my studies at Brigham Young University and graduated in fall 1997 with a BA in Spanish and Social Studies Teaching and minors in Sociology and Family Science. I accepted a marketing position with a local Utah company, Nuskin International, and upon leaving my employment in 2002, I opened a furniture company in San Francisco, California. I recently relocated to Provo, Utah, where I manage the competitive intelligence department of a Utah-based company. I plan on attending law school in the fall of 2005.*

Reflections on the 1995 Field experience: *I consider my experience working with Heather Hanamaikai, the justice of the peace, and the people of Nahualá as the high point of my adult experience. The single greatest effect it has had on my life is simply a remembrance of all the laughs and expressions of love that were shared between me, the K'iche' people I knew, and the other students in the program.*

I gained a tremendous amount of respect for my research partner, Heather Hanamaikai, and hold her in the highest regard both as an astute and passionate social scientist and as a dear friend. In my memories of Guatemala, what stands out are the people that we lived with, whom we loved and who seemed to love us in return.

The study itself was a window that exposed some salient cultural differences. Living with the people and sharing with them, however, showed me that we have much more in common than I would ever have believed. These relationships have had a profound effect on my personal life and have enriched my understanding of other people and cultures beyond my own.

CHAPTER 4

"ALL MEN ARE LIKE THAT"
Gender Roles and the Sociocultural Context
of a Rape in Nahualá

Ryan Thompson and Heather Hanamaikai

On our first day in Nahualá's largest public school, we visited with the teachers and introduced ourselves. We briefly explained our background as social work students and asked the teachers what sort of disciplinary problems they had in the classes, as the school's director had asked us to. The fifth grade teacher, whose students consisted mostly of fifteen-year-olds, informed us in a rather matter-of-fact way that one of his students had been raped two weeks earlier and this was her first day back at school. He told us that her father had beaten her because she had been raped and had prohibited her return to school. The teacher said this student had previously been very social and outgoing, but was now quiet and did not participate in class. Then he asked us if we would speak with her and, because we were social workers, help her to readjust to school and life or make whatever adjustment she needed. Ryan was taken aback and his first reaction was to explain how unqualified we were. Heather, by contrast, very much wanted to speak with the young woman (who we will call Juana), so we did.

The teacher had Juana wait in the classroom while he took the rest of the class to recess. We tried to be friendly, speaking about trivial things to break the ice and make her feel comfortable. We decided that rather than hold a "pseudo-counseling" session, we would just try to make her feel better about herself. We spoke for a while and then Juana decided to open up. "I have a problem," she offered tentatively. Juana told us that she and her friend had been walking home and took a different route, up by the pine-forested communal land just above Nahualá center's highest houses. Three young men who were up there had called to them and then chased them, eventually catching and raping them. Juana said her father had been angry with her and, as a result, had forbidden her to return to school. She was only fifteen years old and her friend, Jéssica, was fourteen. The three boys were in their early twenties, she said, and she gave us their names. Juana told us that the neighbors of the boys said they [the boys] were thieves, one of the worst accusations one can make in Nahualá.

We spoke with Juana for about forty-five minutes. After we gave her a final pep talk, she smiled and seemed able to go on with life. In fact, we were surprised at how well she responded to our many probing questions, for we had asked about her parents, names of the people involved, where and how the rape had happened, and how she was feeling about it now. We concluded by asking if we could help her in any way. She responded, "Help us so that the men go to jail." We were speechless. What had happened to the idea of neutral observer championed by academic anthropology?

Later that afternoon, we saw Nahualá's justice of the peace on the street and mentioned to him what had happened. He knew of the rape and had tried to help the girls, but they did not give him any information, and he said that it was too late to do much about it. He also noted that it was very common for girls here to provoke rape and he assumed that is what had occurred. We entered his office the following day and asked him to provide his point of view of the events.

The two girls had visited his office with their mothers and explained what had happened. He asked them for names of witnesses, but they gave none. He sent them to the health center to get proof that a rape had taken place. The girls left but returned to the justice of the peace the following day without having filled out the medical papers. They had not gone to the clinic. The following day he sent them to have a gynecological exam in the hospital of Sololá. He said that one of the girls was quite upset, while the other laughed and giggled. The justice of the peace felt that either they had not been raped, or if they had, they had provoked it. Without an examination, the justice of the peace could do nothing more about the incident and therefore had let it drop.

We began searching around the area where the rape had occurred to speak with anyone we could about it. We became good friends with Isabella, Juana's neighbor. Through the eyes of Isabella and her mother, María, we learned more about how the common person may feel about the social issue of rape. They related their perspectives on what had occurred. They said the girls had been on their way home and went up by the radio tower in the pines, where the girls saw three boys and began watching them. They said the girls whistled and called to the boys (which is an act of a prostitute in K'iche' culture), who began chasing the girls and eventually caught them. "*Las bajaron a un barranco*" (they took them down into a ravine). The girls shouted, but no one heard because there were no houses around. The girls then ran home shouting and told their mothers what had happened. They then went to the hospital and, since the incident, the girls had not menstruated. We do not know how these members of the community knew all that; they said everyone knew.

We asked who was to blame: whether the boys had the right to do what they did, and whether the girls deserved it because they were said to have provoked it. Isabella and María responded that it was "a very terrible thing," that Juana and Jéssica "*tienen la culpa*" (are at fault), but the boys did not have the right to do it, and that the girls did not deserve it. Then they said that rape is not a common occurrence in Nahualá, a clear contradiction with the perspective of the justice of the peace.

We also asked them what would happen to the boys. They responded, "Nothing will happen." We asked why the victims were judged negatively. María and Isabella replied, "because their rights were violated and they are different from how they were before." María and Isabella concluded that Juana and Jéssica would not marry, and if they did, they would have problems. Yet, the boys could still marry, though their families were shamed. This comment also differed from what the justice of the peace had said. María and Isabella said that they felt the boys should be punished, though both parties (the rapists and the victims) were equally guilty.

After the interview, Isabella turned to Ryan and said, "Now that we have talked about this, hopefully you will not do the same thing." Ryan, greatly shocked, asked why they thought he would do that. Both women responded without hesitation, "All men are like that," suggesting that all men would do the same if a girl whistled at them.

Ryan protested that what they asserted was not always the case. After all, he had been whistled at before and had never had the urge to chase after the girl. But then again, he could only speak for himself because, in the world these girls live in, that may be their reality. Perhaps men really do behave in that way here. Nahualá is a patrifocal society where the social dynamics place the man in the center of the system. A male is punished less than a female for the same offenses, so it would make sense that a man would be able to get away with more. Perhaps the women with whom we spoke were merely stating a fact of life, part of their paradigm for viewing reality. Maybe for them, all men really were like that.

What would account for such behavior? What would account for such beliefs and expectations regarding the conditions of sexual assault? Culture, lived daily, comes as a multitude of incidental jigsaw pieces. Could we construct a picture of the expectation and reality of rape in this community from the limited number of incidents we would encounter? The answer is yes, in part. We will provide the outlines of an interpretation, though not as fully as we would have liked. Here are the pieces of the puzzle we encountered during our stay, and our interpretation of the picture that emerged.

THE DISJUNCTION BETWEEN CULTURE AND LAW

As we observed human interaction in Nahualá, we consulted frequently with the "Judge," the justice of the peace, regarding social issues.[1] He was a K'iche' from Totonicapán who embraced the customs and traditions of his people and had an implicit understanding of them, yet loved justice and respected the law. Unfortunately, custom and law were often in conflict. He did not agree with a number of laws because they were discriminatory and promoted elitism. For example, in 1995, most Guatemalan legislation treated all Guatemalans as Ladinos, without giving thought to cultural characteristics of the Indian community. The justice of the peace, however, related to both the Indian point of view and the supposedly universal perspective offered by the law. So, he continued looking for a way in which both might be embraced, and he keenly recognized the disjunction between national law and the law-like attributes of local Indian custom.

The justice of the peace further bridged the gap between law and culture and helped overcome the distrust of authority prevalent in indigenous communities by acting as a counselor, as would a village *principal*. Because there were no formal institutions to offer aid or guidance in the event of marital or familial difficulties, Nahualenses went to this justice of the peace (but not to previous Ladino justices of the peace) with every problem imaginable. He dealt with the people who came to him by being casual, relaxed, and close, rather than formal and distant. He manifested a kind demeanor. Rather than separate himself by sitting behind his desk, he chose to sit beside the people on a couch in his office or casually lean against the wall. He did this intentionally to help the people feel comfortable.

An astute observer of human nature and culture, the justice of the peace used what he called "natural psychology" so as to bridge the gap between local culture and national law. For him, natural psychology consisted of using a people's strong belief system to bring law and custom together with a humane result. For example, he would say to those who came before him, "You can tell me anything, but God will know the truth and He will deal with you." Many then told him everything, truthfully, for fear of being punished by a higher power. Thus, while the people's traditions and customs were at times in conflict with the legal system, his knowledge of their psycho-social alignment helped him attain his goals with regard to the law. Yet, in this case of rape, even the justice of the peace could not overcome the people's aversion to the law—with its required sexual examinations— in a matter so private as women's bodies.

We asked the justice of the peace if what the girls and their parents did had hindered the legal system, or if the legal system was already hobbled. He replied that the girls had obstructed the legal system by not getting gynecological examinations and by not pressing their case. We felt his comments to be inadequate, because the manner in which the girls acted paralleled behavior often reported for rape victims in the United States; reaction to rape, gender, and hierarchy may well go beyond culture.

The justice of the peace's perspective on the incident showed a concern for the girls' welfare. He saw the rape as a great injustice; yet he believed that they had probably provoked the crime by whistling at the boys. His main concern was for them to act quickly and inform him of the details. But these rape victims did not cooperate. Surely they were traumatized by the incident. Just as surely, the legally necessary response to the rape would have brought them too close to the system of authority they distrusted and would subject them to the cultural indignity of a sexual examination by a Ladino man. Although the justice of the peace tried to help, in this case he could not bypass the cultural issues the alleged victims faced. Then, with the passage of time, his hands were tied.

PATRIFOCAL EMPHASIS

In Nahualá, men are the center of a male-oriented or patrifocal society. The problem, however, is that patrifocality comes at the expense of women. The justice of the peace and others observed that Nahualá is a closed corporate community (Wolf 1957), its people conservative, self-isolating, rejecting of the outside world, and focused on the community and the management of the community's jointly held assets. Yet they seemed to be quite libertarian in how they viewed rape and other injustices, especially offenses toward women.

The laissez-faire approach gives license to abuse and constitutes a kind of discrimination against women. The justice of the peace and the school director both advocated the idea that women caused many of their own problems, and, in this regard, they agreed with most other men with whom we talked.

Gender role differences also promoted the subordination of women. Women throughout the community were frequently observed sitting on dirt floors and serving the men, who sat on chairs. Men—including pre-adolescent boys—often ate first and ate more (or even all) of the best foods, including meat, if there was any at the meal. When we told our families that many of the male students in our group knew how to cook and did so frequently, many laughed. A ten-year-old boy even made a joke about it, asking Ryan to retrieve a tortilla for him. Women's role is seen as serving the needs of men. By the same token, women's sexuality is thus literally to be "taken" for the service of men, exposing women to a greater risk of rape.

Other indications of male orientation include such things as the male prerogative in courtship (as in many societies), a man's sense of ownership over his wife, and a woman's extreme economic dependence on a man. To the degree that woman's role is seen as serving the needs of men, women's sexuality may be appropriated with little thought or restraint.

THE SEXUAL INITIATION OF COMMON-LAW UNION

Another factor that undermines the community's response to rape is that members of the community may view a woman's violation as an initial step in the process of marriage. Even the women we interviewed saw it as the girls' fault. Juana said what happened to her was very bad and should not happen, but the symbolic confusion with robo (karelaq'aaj, robbery), the first step in marriage, relativized people's attitudes.[2]

We asked Rufino, a seventeen-year-old husband, how one gets married in Nahualá. One merely hangs out at the market, he said, and looks for a girl who "is suitable for you." When a boy sees a woman who suits him, he will proceed with the courtship by talking with her. Indeed, the K'iche' word for speaking together implies sexual involvement among the K'iche'. To speak to someone of the opposite sex can connote sexual and marital availability; to say a boy and a girl spoke to each other can imply they had sexual intercourse. Hence, the self-justifying contradictions about who spoke to or whistled at whom in discussions of the rape incident.

According to Rufino, the standard or traditional procedure for marriage is for a boy to meet the girl, have sex with her, and then take her home to become his wife. This process, even with the woman's consent, is called karelaq'aaj (stealing a woman). This is what Rufino told us he did, claiming that it is expected that the girl will go along with this type of marriage ritual. In some instances, the marriage begins with sexual intercourse forced on the woman—which is, in fact, a rape.

This is not just according to our ethnocentric perspective. When we asked the justice of the peace how people in Nahualá normally react to cases of rape, he responded that people are used to it because often the youth is just trying to "get married" to the young lady. "It's normal." As a result, the woman, rendered unable to find another accepting partner after having sex, becomes solely dependent on the boy who "steals" her. It should be noted that this customary procedure for initiating a domestic relationship results only in a common-law union, a structural position of considerable disadvantage to the woman.

In Guatemalan law, common-law union makes it easy for a man to abandon a woman and assume little further responsibility. On several occasions, we witnessed women going to the justice of the peace to seek legal recourse when their husbands had abandoned them and their children. The justice of the peace repeatedly explained that he could do nothing, because the couple was not legally married. In some cases, however, he offered to call the man in and speak with him in an attempt to help the situation and perhaps get some money for the woman.

The justice of the peace strives to have as many couples as possible legally married to insure the future rights of the women. In his periodic addresses from Nahualá's radio station, he encourages young couples to get their marriage licenses. In private, he said that legal marriage would "serve the woman in the future when her husband leaves her," so that she can take legal action against him. It is noticeable that he said "when" and not "if" the woman is abandoned. The presumption is that women will be left, and that threat helps keep women in their place.

GENDER BIAS IN NATIONAL LAW

Another indicator of a male-oriented society is that certain laws favor the man. The justice of the peace pointed out that the law on adultery is among the most blatant of these and that there are too few women legislators to help correct the issue. Adultery laws are biased in that the definition of adultery reads differently for males than for females. For males, adultery is sexual intercourse with one who is not your spouse, *knowing* that she is married. In Spanish, the law states, "*quien yace con ella sabiendo que es casada*"—he who lies with her knowing she is married. The male brought to court simply states he did not know the woman was married, which gets him off the hook. By contrast, the woman is bound by the statement "she that lies with a man that is not her husband." The woman who commits adultery goes to prison for six months to two years, while the man does not go to prison.

The law reflects a cultural presumption that blames the woman. The justice of the peace told us of an incident of a man who returned home and found another man with his wife. The husband promptly called in nearby members of the community to do what they deemed as their duty. The man was allowed to escape, but the woman was tied to the bed and punished in the traditional fashion of having chile peppers inserted in her vagina. The woman was close to death when she finally received medical attention. Although some may argue that the difference between men and women before the law is a cultural idiosyncrasy, we would argue that the difference sustains a gender hierarchy that causes ripple effects in all facets of society. Indeed, the cultural presumption that women are at fault in adultery is one of the most demeaning aspects of Guatemalan gender bias and bears on the way the rape case was handled by all the parties involved.

We asked the justice of the peace how honor and shame relate to the individuals involved in the rape. "They always put the weight/responsibility on women; they are chauvinists," he said. He felt the boys' parents would "justify the violent attitude of the male." In other words, there is no loss of honor to the boys or their families, and the shame is felt only by the girls— thus the punishment of being hit and restricted from going to school. Although the justice of the peace admitted that regardless of what really happened, the boys would be considered in the right; he recognized the sad and unjust reality for the women. He spoke matter-of-factly: "It happens all the time, in the forests, the cornfields, and the lands." He also said that incidents of rape and marriage (the two go hand in hand) increase during the beginning of the rainy season because the milpa (corn) is high and hides the crime.

We spoke with two K'iche' nurses from another town about the dynamics surrounding the rape. The older nurse simply said that it probably was the girls' fault and that it's one of the ways girls get attention here. She gave the example of girls enjoying being "touched [felt up]" on the bus. She said the girls probably did enjoy the whole ordeal, and the claim that they did not like it was a ploy to get attention. The nurses viewed the rape not as a social assault with psychological repercussions, but as something common, to which girls actively consent, and perhaps even enjoy.

EXPRESSIONS OF BIAS

Other indicators of gender bias include literacy rates and public access, drunkenness, divorce and separation, and other social mannerisms which are different between men and women. Men in Nahualá are likely to speak more Spanish, have more education, and experience more social interaction with the outside world than women. Some have told us that women can speak Spanish like men can, but are embarrassed to do so. If so, why are they embarrassed and the men not? What sort of socialization have they received that would cause them to behave differently from the men?

Public drunkenness is common among the K'iche' Mayas, yet in the time we spent in Nahualá, we never saw even one drunken woman. According to the justice of the peace, a woman will generally drink in private, and in public only when invited by her husband. Whatever the theory that explains alcohol abuse—poverty, inability to meet obligations, or despair—surely the women suffer from similar social and psychological stresses that might be expected to drive them to drink. Yet it was only the men who swayed through the streets in their sloshing, often belligerent way—never the women. The difference in public drunkenness indicates a difference in what men and women are socially allowed to do. Disorderliness, failure to sustain one's family, and even violence are excused by drunkenness, and it is the alcohol's fault, not the person's fault. The implied license for misconduct, culturally more available to men, sets up the context for rape.[3]

Finally, we noticed other social idiosyncracies wherein women play a role subservient to men. We make this statement not because our "American mentality" is imposing our culture on them but because these ideas were expressed by some women in the community. Some signs of subservience include the women sitting on the floor in the Catholic church while the men stand or sit on benches, women feeding men first and the best food, and women performing all domestic work. While women often accompany their husbands in the search for wood and even work with them in the fields, some women note that they get little help in the household and would prefer that "men help out with domestic duties rather than drinking or playing their afternoon soccer games."

We arranged to meet with the parents of Juana and Jéssica. Juana's father was dignified; he sat down with us and admitted not knowing much of the situation. He said this had been the first problem of his life, and when we asked very politely how he felt about and reacted to it, he said he was "more or less angry" and had given her "a hit and a belting." Knowing she had committed a "sin," he punished his daughter, although he did say that the three boys were the guilty ones.

We asked if there was any shame felt now. After a long pause he said, "Perhaps there is not." In the case of rape, the resolution seems to be to punish and blame the woman, and then the problem goes away. The father was little concerned about the rape and changed the subject to the predicament of his son, because they had paid a *coyote* (illegal guide) to take their son to the United States, but the coyote had been put in jail before making the journey. He wanted to know what we could do to retrieve his money.

Juana's fifth grade teacher exhibited another pragmatic version of "life must go on." He viewed her condition as one that she should simply get over. Other things mattered more. The director of the school had a similar response. However, after we shared with him our own feelings about the rape, his attitude seemed to change. We said, "People always blame the women, but no matter what, nothing justifies being raped, no type of supposed provocation." He smiled and said, "Yes, women are blamed more than men, and rape is not justified." Though the director's response was interesting, through the whole ordeal, the school leaders were more interested in having the girls return to normal than in changing the conditions that expose women to violence.

SILENT ANGER

Although Juana's mother was also at home during our interview with Juana's father, she did not speak because the father spoke. We deliberately went to Jéssica's house when the father was not home so we could speak with her mother, alone. Jéssica's mother seemed interested that we wanted to find out how she felt about the rape. She said that at first she was "very angry, but now, not so much." As we spoke with her, we could see her demeanor change from calm to emotionally charged. She said it was the boys' fault and that they should go to jail. We asked Jéssica and her mother for their version of what happened. "Two of the boys carried Jéssica away into a barranco and hit her and pulled her hair and spit on her, saying, 'I'm going to take away your life now.'" Jéssica and her mother told us that the girls had not called or whistled at the boys; it was the other way around: "the boys said bad things to us."

Jéssica's mother became progressively more angry and emotional during the interview and said she wanted someone to kill the boys. She also said she wanted justice. The two mothers and daughters had spent almost four hundred quetzales traveling to Sololá, to the justice of the peace, and the hospital. Juana and Jéssica's families were quite poor, and it was sad to see that Nahualense society apparently does not allow a victim to seek retribution or compensation for an injustice. Rather, it seems to close its doors to them, making their lives that much more difficult.

During the interview with Jéssica's mother, we observed a marked difference between her perspective and that of Juana's father. Having the mother talk about what had happened was like going into a room that had been off limits, because no one had ever spoken to the mother about her daughter's rape. As we left, Jéssica's mother rushed inside and returned with some small, blackened bananas for us, a token of her gratitude. We were grateful she had opened that window into the mind of a people who, in many ways, are a silent majority.

CONCLUSION

We tried to avoid having our American attitudes and prejudices dictate our reactions to this culture. Though not entirely possible, we sought a detached perspective. One of the first facts we were taught about this town, both by our professors and by the residents themselves, is that Nahualá and its people, as a general group, were tightly knit—a closed community—and that we probably would not get much information from them. We realized, however, that the rape, while embedded in macro-level social and cultural phenomena, was also made up of micro-level interactions.

Thus, one day, we walked among the houses where the rapists lived, looking for someone to talk to about the incident. Not realizing that most of the people in this area were related, we soon found ourselves surrounded by a number of teenage girls. We chatted briefly, and we subtly indicated that we were studying a "bad situation" that had occurred there a few weeks earlier. Without saying the word "rape" to them, we described in a round-about manner what had happened. All denied knowing what had taken place. We wandered up the side of the mountain, through the trees, to the general area of the crime and were quickly accompanied by a few of the girls with whom we had spoken. They knew exactly what we were doing and all about the rape. They asked us, "Who are you helping, the boys or the girls?" We took a guess and said, "the girls." They pointed out the houses of the boys and indicated that everyone knew about the rape. Before we could interview further, they were startled at seeing the sister and friend of one of the boys coming up to "investigate" us. We calmed them down, and they said they would talk to us later. We proceeded to talk about the trees and other small talk, and went on our way.

Thus, the very neighbors of these boys were willing to speak to us about the rape and forego community closedness, demonstrating their individual autonomy. Although we feared people might not open up to us on such a socially stigmatized matter, on an individual level it seemed that they wanted to, and perhaps needed to. This was demonstrated time and time again, especially when we were speaking to the women. The anthropological assumption that Indian communities are closed may not be as accurate as we think. Perhaps the Nahualense women opened up to us as a natural reaction to their suppression by authority figures, or perhaps by virtue of our foreignness. Maybe they experienced a sense of anonymity that facilitated their being open with us. Or perhaps we were simply nice, manipulative, or charming. We feel, however, that the explanation that makes most sense is that people, though part of a group, vary as individuals. Although there are salient commonalities within their culture, beneath those commonalities lie many individual differences and personal idiosyncrasies as well as universal senses of humanity that rise above cultural locality. Though there are gender-related traits and expectations imposed on women, some Nahualenses feel themselves victims of these same social norms and characteristics. In our opinion, many women want to burst the constraints of gender expectation, to be acknowledged, and to be heard. Through this study, we discovered that many Maya women no longer wish to remain a silent majority.

NOTES

1. Editors' note: In 1996, the justice of the peace—one of the few K'iche'-speaking justices in Guatemala—was hired by the United Nations to assist

in their efforts to better accommodate Maya customary practices with the tenants of national law and strengthen the legal position of the Indian community as called for by the Peace Accords. A Ladino later replaced him.

2. See Araneda's discussion of karelaq'aaj, ch. 3, this volume.

3. See Eber (1995) in this regard.

About the author: *I graduated from Brigham Young University in 1996 with a degree in Latin American Studies and with additional studies in art history and ancient New World societies. With our four children, my husband and I have explored many different parts of the United States, and we currently live near Annapolis, Maryland. I am thoroughly enjoying this stage of my life and am challenged to learn and grow every day in unexpected ways.*

Reflections on the 1995 field experience: *The time I spent in Nahualá significantly changed my perspective on the world. I learned that the experience of women in Nahualá was, on the surface, far removed from my own. Over time, I came to appreciate that we shared much in common, and that their culture expressed these common traits in a unique and beautiful way. The women I met, like me, cared deeply for their families and homes. They formed intricate relationships with the other women in their lives. They were generous and quick to laugh. Most of all, I was impressed by their strength. Their lives were often marked by the sorrow of losing children and by the endless physical labor required to provide for their families. Yet they were not defined by their problems, but by the character, humor, and resourcefulness with which they faced life. They were part of a tightly-knit community with a wealth of knowledge and wisdom. I am grateful for the time I spent with them and for all that they taught me. Most of all, I am grateful for their friendship.*

CHAPTER 5

"BECAUSE WE WEAVE TOGETHER"
Women, Work, and Dominance in a Nahualá Extended Family

Rebekah A. Semus

Gender and work dominated and defined life for women in Nahualá. The deep lines and wrinkles that creased their faces from an early age told the story. The average age at which women married was fifteen or sixteen, although a significant number married even younger, some as early as thirteen. Usually they began bearing children right after marriage. Children under the age of five accounted for 58 percent of the deaths in Nahualá (Michael Jones, personal communication). Women often bore ten to fifteen children, which increased their chances of having enough children grow to adulthood to care for them in their old age. Because of the high infant mortality rate, large age gaps between surviving children were common, especially as women often bore children until menopause.

GENDER, AGE, AND DOMINANCE IN FAMILY AND CULTURAL CONTEXT

In most households, caring for children was solely the woman's responsibility. However, this task was one among many and could not interfere with other activities. A mother would strap her infant or toddler to her back in a shawl, called a *peraje*, and proceed with her other chores. Older children were usually unsupervised and left to play outside with other children, perhaps cousins who lived close by.

Women rose before the sun, usually around 5:30, to begin preparing the morning meal. They lit a fire in the wood-burning stove or on the floor. They formed corn tortillas by hand, slapping the dough rhythmically from hand to hand. Women also prepared other foods if they could afford them; black beans, eggs, and a spinach-like plant called *hierba* were other common components of a meal. A family's diet typically did not vary significantly for lunch or dinner. After the family ate, the women straightened and cleaned, washed the clothes if necessary, or went to the market. Time not consumed with these tasks was spent weaving.

These activities stood as clear role expectations that defined the existence of women. Shortly after we arrived in Nahualá, one student found this out forcefully as he spoke with a Nahualense who was curious about life in the United States. The man asked, "How do they [women] make tortillas there?" Jon said, "They buy them." The man then asked, "How do they wash clothes?" Jon answered, "With a machine." Perplexed, the man wondered, "Then what do you need women for?"

Roles within the marriage and family were firmly molded by the indigenous tradition, which promoted the subordination of women. Many women were illiterate and spoke little if any Spanish, speaking only K'iche'. This hindered their participation in life outside the village, and sometimes limited their activity or economic opportunity even in the village. In contrast, most men had at least a rudimentary mastery of Spanish, which allowed them to participate more freely in public affairs inside and outside of Nahualá.

Men expected strict obedience and compliance from their wives. Upon discovering that I was married and that my husband had not come to Guatemala with me, the women I spoke with appeared shocked and frequently laughed. I received comments such as "If I were to take a trip like that my husband would not want me when I came back," or "He gave you permission to come?" On one occasion, one of my roommates planned a trip to Sololá with our host mother, Rosa. The trip entailed a simple forty-five-minute bus ride but was almost called off when Pedro, Rosa's husband, would not give his permission for her to go.

A woman was expected to learn how her husband wanted things done and conform to his desires. Rosa said that when the laundry was dry and folded, her husband expected his clothes to be on top. This example, though seemingly minor, indicated a man's dominant position in family relationships. In some households, there were only enough chairs in the kitchen for the men and boys. The women and girls sat on the floor.

Whatever their main occupation, whether they worked long hours in the fields or spent much of their day at home, men did not, with rare exceptions, contribute to the housework. A seventeen-year-old girl said that her father remarked, "I do not do things like that [housework]. That's why I got married:

to have a woman to do those things for me." A twenty-five-year-old married woman said, "There are few men who place their women in a high position." When the male students in our group offered to help their host families with the dishes, they were met with laughter and confusion.

Gender separation—especially among the elderly—is further inscribed in the behavioral patterns that avoided the emotional or physical demonstration of affection between husbands and wives. Married couples rarely walked together in the streets, and they certainly never engaged in any form of physical contact in public. I did not observe any display of affection between husbands and wives in any of the homes. Rosa's cousin Aurelia told me that her parents had never kissed in their lives, and that her mother did not even know how to kiss. Rosa admitted that she and her husband occasionally kissed in private, but never in front of their children or anyone else. Similarly, Nahualense parents did not show affection for children who were past the toddler stage. However, the women gave no evidence that the absence of public physical contact detracted from their lives. In fact, Rosa said that to kiss in front of the children encourages them to play in inappropriate ways and leads them to engage in sexually deviant behavior. These reports were in sharp contrast with the Ladino culture, in which public displays of affection were commonplace, even among virtual strangers.

Male dominance in Nahualense society extended beyond familial relationships. In some churches, men sat on benches while women sat on the floor. The law exhibited bias against women (see Thompson and Hanamaikai, ch. 4, this volume). Boys were given preference in regard to education as well. Although more girls attended school in 1995 than in the past, they were still outnumbered by boys. Men and women in Nahualá shared the belief that formal education was not important for women. Aurelia, who completed sixth grade, said she had no desire to continue her schooling because, "*No me sirve para nada*" (It is not at all useful for me).

Textile Weaving

Women contributed to the family economy primarily through weaving; few girls reached marriage without mastering this skill. Most handwoven clothes were worn by women.

Each village had a distinct series of patterns and colors unique to that community's women. The traditional costume emphasized the establishment of one's identity as a member of the community. However, the key elements could be manipulated to give distinctiveness to each weaver's work while still maintaining the identity of the community pattern. The individual variations of each weaver were generally subtle enough to be recognized only by one with an experienced eye. However, the traditional pattern of their huipiles has begun to vary as Nahualenses have come into contact with other communities. Today, some women wear machine-made blouses with machine-embroidered flowers. Others buy commercially made cloth and sew it into a huipil. The majority of women, however, still handweave the cloth for their huipiles.

Weavers contributed to the family economy by producing clothing to wear or to sell. Textiles were sold to other members of the community for their own use or to resell. Almost always, the weaver or another family member wore the textiles before they were sold. The money was then used to buy materials to weave another textile, hopefully with a small profit for the woman's time invested.

THE HIERARCHY OF WEAVERS AND SELLERS

Women in Nahualá managed textile production in five basic modes of production related to their economic status. At the lowest economic level, the weaver sold her textiles to another person who then used or resold them. These weavers generally needed money so urgently that they sold at wholesale prices, knowing that their weavings would be resold at a higher price. The businesswomen who resold the textiles always paid the lowest possible price to ensure a maximum profit margin. Often, weavers who sold to other dealers wore plainer, older, clothing because their economic needs forced them to sell their better or more recently woven clothing.

The second tier included women who wove only for their own family's use. With many women or girls in the family to clothe, or because old age or infirmity hindered the speed at which they could weave, they produced no surplus.

In the third tier, women wove both to meet their own needs and to sell directly to other women, family, or friends for the buyer's own use. Because there was no intermediary in these transactions, both buyer and seller benefited. Their economic circumstances were secure enough that they could wait until someone offered a fair price for their goods. Still, they lacked either the capital to invest in resale or the ability to speak Spanish well enough to expand their markets.

In the fourth tier, women bought textiles for their personal use, not for resale. For them, cash was easier to come by than time, indicating that they had a relatively secure income. Members of this group may also be in the fifth group, because the *negociantes*, the businesswomen who bought and resold textiles, usually did not have time to weave for themselves.

The fifth level, the wealthiest group, consisted of women who bought from the weavers and sold to foreigners. They kept a watchful eye out for potential buyers and competed vigorously when tourists arrived in town. Most of the women also traveled to tourist centers such as Sololá, Panajachel, Chichicastenango, and Antigua to sell their goods. Most could speak and understand enough Spanish to negotiate with tourists. Usually with little education, and sometimes unable to weave, they were shrewd businesswomen who had the capital to invest in the textiles and possibly hold them for long periods of time. They were often resented by women in less prosperous circumstances.

WEAVING AND FAMILY RELATIONSHIPS

The extended family of the household with whom I lived provided a great deal of insight into how the cottage industry of weaving could be a binding force within the family and yet, ironically, cause discord, jealousy, and power struggles. The delicate relationship based on economic necessity, however, virtually assured that peace would be restored if a breach occurred.

I lived with Rosa for two months. She was twenty-three, had married at fourteen, and had three children. Rosa barely knew how to weave simple designs and was illiterate. Nonetheless, she was a successful negociante.

Rosa's mother, Juana, looked weathered and much older than Rosa, though Juana was not exactly sure of her age. Juana, too, was illiterate and had married at the age of fourteen. She had borne ten children, six of whom survived past early childhood. Juana lived across the street from her daughter Rosa. I received conflicting information about Juana's ability to weave. Juana claims that she used to weave most of what she sells but has not woven since her foot was run over by an automobile a few years ago. The accident is a verifiable fact, and would indeed impede her ability to weave, because women weave kneeling with their buttocks resting on their feet. However, whether or not she wove before the accident is uncertain. Other family members claimed that she did not know how to weave at all.

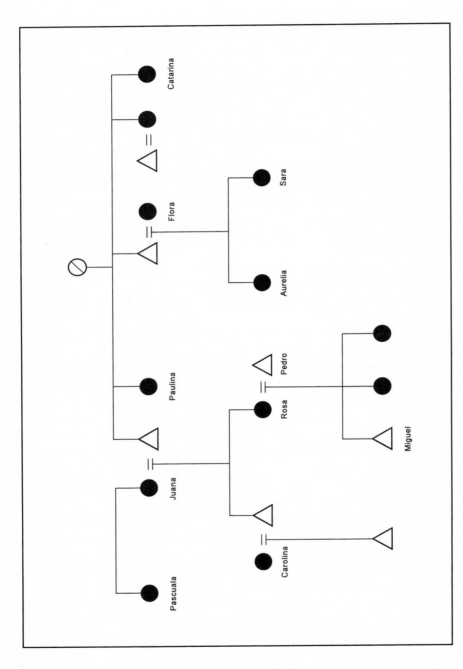

Kinship diagram of Rosa's family.

Juana's niche in the family business was based on her success as a negociante, drawing on years of experience.

Flora, one of Juana's sisters-in-law, also was illiterate, but, unlike Rosa
and Juana, she spoke no Spanish. Flora lived across the street from Juana,
adjacent to Rosa. Flora had given birth to thirteen children, seven of whom
survived. Her family was extremely poor; they lived in a small adobe house
and cooked over an open fire on the dirt floor. Flora and her daughter, Aurelia,
spent much of their time together weaving. Aurelia was seventeen and had
completed the sixth grade. Consequently, she spoke relatively fluent Spanish.
Aurelia was a skilled weaver and wove clothing for both herself and her
younger sister. In addition, she sold to other women. Sara, Aurelia's eight-
year-old sister, was already learning to weave by observation and imitation.
Juana's sister, Pascuala, was also illiterate. She made huipiles for her family's
use and occasionally sold her weavings if the family needed money. However,
she claimed that when the economy was better than it currently was, she
bought from others and resold.

Paulina, Rosa's father's sister, was about forty-two and illiterate. She
spoke enough Spanish to handle her business dealings. Our interviews were
conducted mostly with Rosa's translation, although Paulina usually understood the questions and just needed some help articulating her answers. She
resold handwoven textiles to outsiders. Although the tourist market was slow
then, Paulina traveled extensively to the coast for her business dealings, and
(according to the other women in the family) to meet with her lovers.

Carolina was the wife of Juana's oldest son. Carolina spoke Spanish
very well and could read and write. She claimed she could weave, but due
to her eight-month-old son and her household responsibilities, she was not
currently weaving. She bought her clothing directly from other weavers.
Other women I observed, such as Flora, wove their own clothing in spite of
numerous responsibilities. Therefore, Carolina's choice reflected a certain
degree of financial security.

Rosa and her mother had a close relationship. They visited each other
several times a day and their mannerisms mirrored each other. Rosa's business
dealings were more active at that point than those of her mother. Aurelia
refused to sell to Rosa and Juana because, she said, they paid unfairly low
prices and resold at unfairly high prices.

Rosa and Juana held powerful positions in their family within the
economic system created by weaving, buying, and reselling and this affected
their relationships with the other women in their extended family. Aurelia
deeply resented her economically inferior position although she was educated

and a skilled weaver. Rosa, in turn, felt threatened by Aurelia's education and skills, but ultimately retained the more powerful position. However, both had to maintain a superficial level of normalcy to keep the economic relationships intact. Therefore, the expression of any negative feelings took the form of private gossip and backbiting as opposed to direct conflict.

Aurelia was extremely jealous of Juana and Rosa because, though they had received little formal education and did not weave, they were much better off financially. As a result, Aurelia took great pleasure in pointing out their shortcomings behind their backs. She was careful, however, to maintain good relations with them and not to offend them. Her fear of angering them indicated an imbalance of power in the relationship. For example, Aurelia spoke at great length one day about Rosa and her family. She began by calling Rosa's children "*malcriados*" (brats). When I remarked that Rosa's seven-year-old son, Miguel, was deaf, and therefore might have difficulty learning appropriate behavior, she replied that it did not matter. She said it was the mother's responsibility to teach the children correct behavior. She also claimed that everyone in Rosa's family was dirty, and that consequently they all had lice, which, she said, was shameful. By contrast, Aurelia claimed her own family washed their hair every day, and that was why they did not get lice. Aurelia often made other such petty criticisms of Rosa's family.

Aurelia also talked about money issues and said that Rosa was "*mala gente*" (a bad person) for paying such low prices for the weavings. She called Rosa "lazy" and a "malcriada." Indeed, Aurelia could not understand how Rosa got such a good husband because most girls who behaved that way married men who beat them. She said that Rosa was so lazy, her husband had to do the cooking and care for the children, which results in shame for the woman.

Aurelia called Rosa's mother, Juana, "mala gente," too. She said that Juana stole five thousand quetzales, probably close to a year's income for Aurelia's family, from Aurelia's mother, Flora. Aurelia said that the grandmother gave a large sum of money to Juana to keep safe for her. When the grandmother died, the money was supposed to be distributed evenly among the five siblings, including Juana's husband and Aurelia's father. Juana allegedly kept the money and never said anything to the other siblings. Catarina, another of Juana's sisters, came over to Aurelia's house one day when I was visiting and Aurelia told me later that Catarina, too, is stingy. She said that Catarina once asked her to make a huipil and then paid her practically nothing for it.

Aurelia claimed that Rosa can barely weave (which Rosa admits), and that Juana cannot weave at all, which both Rosa and Juana deny. Aurelia and Flora both said that they have never seen Juana weave once. Aurelia takes great satisfaction in the fact that Juana and Rosa do not weave. She said it is "shameful" not to know how to weave. One afternoon while I was weaving with Aurelia, Rosa and Juana came by at different times. Both times Aurelia leaned over and whispered, "When I ask you if weaving is difficult, say loudly that it is not. Make sure they hear you." After Juana left, Aurelia said, "You should have asked her to help you out," laughing sarcastically.

Aurelia said she had agreed, at Rosa's request, to teach Rosa to weave. I asked Aurelia if she was really going to do it, and she said, "No, of course not." Then she modified that and said, "Well, if I have time." Rosa, in turn, frequently expressed disdain for Aurelia and Flora, usually by criticizing their economic circumstances. She made fun of their clothing because it was simpler than her own. She also claimed that they could not be trusted.

Rivalry among Weavers

I was interested in purchasing some weavings. Rosa had many textiles, but her prices were high, so I spoke with Aurelia, too, about buying weavings. Aurelia offered to sell a corte for thirty-five quetzales. She also tried to find a certain red huipil but did not have any success. When Rosa tried to sell me a corte for sixty-five quetzales, I told her I would have to think about it because Aurelia had offered one for thirty-five. Rosa lowered her price to fifty quetzales and went on at length about how it was high quality, worth the money, and Aurelia's was probably poor quality. Because Aurelia could not find a red huipil, I had asked Rosa to help me find one. The next morning, however, Aurelia found a red huipil. That afternoon, Rosa came over to Aurelia's house while I was there, and she saw several cortes sitting on the bed. They were the cortes Aurelia had shown me, including one nicer than the one I was looking at from Rosa, but this one was forty quetzales. Rosa became suspicious and questioned why the cortes were there; she warned Aurelia not to dare sell me a corte because I was buying one from her, and a huipil, too. This incident further revealed that Rosa was aware of, and exploited, the power imbalance. That imbalance gave her the leverage to make such threats. Aurelia, however, did not feel that the situation would always remain this way; she believed her education and skills would help her get ahead.

Paulina was recently involved with another man. When his wife found out, the two women fought and Paulina lost. Aurelia reported that some of her hair was pulled out and her clothes were ripped off in front of a large crowd. Rosa, Aurelia, and Flora appeared to find the event comical, laughing as they related the story. I would have expected them either to be angry with Paulina or to be sympathetic with her. One possible explanation is that they felt justice had been served. However, that did not account completely for their reaction. Once again, the economic interdependence of the family forced them to keep working relations with each other, but the derision and backbiting provided an acceptable outlet for their feelings.

Carolina, having married into the family recently, had not yet been drawn completely into the network. She lived with Juana and this gave more material to the gossip mill for those who were inclined to dislike Juana. The stereotype of the cruel and demanding mother-in-law seemed to be common in Nahualá, because I heard stories in the community of Juana ordering her son to beat Carolina, and other such accounts for which I found no basis.

Conclusion

Although women wove alone most of the time, the economic relationships created through weaving became a binding force, for better or worse. The economics of weaving dependence produced strong emotions and dominated the relationships of women with one another. The contradictions between age, weaving skill, the ability to speak Spanish, kinship status, and economic position produced highly ambivalent emotions. Yet economic necessity dominated and forced these women to hide their feelings in the interest of marketing their weavings. Weaving not only bound women to their community through the manifest style of what they wore; it also bound women to each other in stable micro-enterprises that transcended kinship and household. As Aurelia told me, "When you leave, we will miss you, because we weave together."

About the author: *I graduated from Brigham Young University in 1996 with a degree in elementary education. Immediately following graduation, I taught first grade in the Provo School District in Provo, Utah. After my first year of teaching, my husband and I accompanied the principal of my school to Mexico, where we participated in various humanitarian aid projects, including work in orphanages and schools. In my third year of teaching I was asked to be one of a few teachers to teach a 200-day calendar and evaluate the benefits of that schedule as opposed to a traditional 180-day school year. I was also asked to assist BYU professors in observing and evaluating students who were studying to become educators. I left my teaching career in 1999 to be a homemaker and mother, and I now volunteer in my son's school. I currently reside in Auburn, Washington, with my husband and three children.*

Reflections on the 1995 field experience: *Studying in Guatemala was my first experience abroad. Upon arriving in Nahualá, I felt intimidated and uneasy. I stood in the center of town wondering what I had gotten myself into. Was I adequately prepared to live and participate in a community that was so foreign to me? As I settled into my new surroundings, I adjusted quickly and, to my surprise, almost effortlessly. My eyes were opened to a new culture, land, and people. I learned to see past our differences and delight in the many similarities we share as human beings. I also gained a greater appreciation for the luxuries of life so many of us enjoy. The field experience taught me to reach beyond my comfort zone, to expand my ideals and ways of thinking. My time in Guatemala ended much too soon, but I returned home enlightened and enriched.*

CHAPTER 6

"SIT PROPERLY"
Elementary Education in Nahualá

Tara Seely Hatch

More than fifty students crowded together, peering through the tall chain link gate. Hundreds of deep brown eyes gazed at a spectacle that stood outside the schoolyard. I was the spectacle: a blonde-haired, blue-eyed woman who seemed vastly different from themselves. Standing in the dusty dirt road on the other side of the gate, I looked at a sight that was as foreign to me as I was to them. My project was to observe in the classrooms, interview teachers, and try to gain insights into education in Nahualá. Anxious to begin my project, I longed to pass through the chain link gate, which remained locked during recess. Feeling awkward, I asked my audience of students if I could come in. Expressionless faces stared silently, and not one dared respond. After questioning at least five times, I finally resolved to return at a later time.

Making his way through a maze of students, the director approached me with a warm and friendly welcome. School had let out, the gate was unlocked, and many students roamed the school yard. Desiring to get a good look at the stranger, students surrounded me. Erasmo, the director, invited me to chat with the students and return the following morning to begin my study. Hoping to build a trusting relationship with the students, I attempted to speak with some of the many who flocked around me, and I was disappointed that not one student would speak. Paxixil, the school was called, sharing the name of the small rural hamlet in which its students lived. Weeks would pass before the students of Paxixil became accustomed to my presence.

Throughout the next two months, I experienced the culture of the Maya-K'iche' Indians living in Paxixil. Entering with an American idealistic view, I was initially shocked by what I observed in the education system. It seemed insufficient in many areas; I later learned, however, that for this Guatemalan society and culture, the education system is serving its purpose.

Physical Facilities

Eight small classrooms formed an L-shaped row, the main body of the school building. Kindergarten and first grade had two classrooms each, and third through sixth grade had one each. Third graders met in a portion of a private house located approximately seventy-five meters away from the main school structure. Each classroom door opened toward a cement playing field that was fenced by six-foot-tall cinder block walls. Basketball and soccer were the two most popular games on the rugged court. Although the school was equipped with lights, electricity was rarely used because school funds were so limited. Thus, classrooms were dark, functioning solely on the sunlight seeping through the windows. A tin roof, thin metal doors, and barred windows characterized the school's construction. Floors and walls seemed to attract dirt rapidly.

In the corner of the yard, wooden shacks with scanty doors functioned as the school bathrooms. A faucet for washing hands was located outside the rustic stalls. The toilet facilities were provided, but never used. Perhaps accessibility or even laziness caused the students to seek out other resources. When recess was over and the gate opened, boys and girls ran outside the schoolyard. Boys formed a line along the school's cinder block wall to urinate; girls ran down a small hill into a cornfield. Whatever the reason, this method of relieving bladders was the expected daily occurrence.

Classrooms were not ideal, but they provided a place for education. Each classroom had different types of desks or tables. Some had tables with benches seating at least two students; others had shabby desks made mostly of thin wood. Chalkboards, used intensively in the Paxixil school, were vital to every classroom, although most chalkboard surfaces were ragged and nearly unreadable. Visibility problems plagued many students, who struggled to see markings on a rough writing surface that leaned against the wall. Fortunate students enjoyed a smoother surface mounted on the wall. Students and teachers made do with what was available.[1]

Materials and Resources

Classroom learning materials were similarly limited, providing only one textbook per subject, per class. Teachers consequently dictated text information and students filled their notebooks with these writings. Students had two notebooks for math and a few other subjects—one for writing notes and the other for completing exercises. Most students in grades two through six carried five to seven of these paper notebooks. Pre-primary and first grades did very little writing.

Each student wrote with at least two different-colored pens: one color for writing and the other for highlighting important points. The younger students in kindergarten through second grade used pencils. Beyond those grades, students did all work in pen, including mathematics. Correcting mistakes neatly was nearly impossible, which sometimes led to messy, illegible notebooks. Along with their notebooks and pens, students were required, one day each week, to bring wood to school for the fire to heat water for their powdered milk snack, or *refacción*. Each morning dozens of little schoolchildren could be seen carrying two or three pieces of wood. After recess every day, students were provided one biscuit-like cookie and a small cup of hot milk, heated by the wood they brought to school.

STAFFING

Students were assigned *limpieza* (classroom cleaning) on rotation, one day a week, because schools did not have janitors. Numerous brooms and mops were stashed in the corner of each classroom. On their assigned day, students cleaned the classroom after school was out. Every now and then, teachers had the students scrub their tables or desks using wet corn husks.

Children served easily as janitors because they were accustomed to hard work. However, the school had other vacancies in personnel that the children could not fill. When asked, "What do the children do when a teacher can not come to school?" Miguel, a fifth grade teacher, replied, "They stay home," because there were no substitute teachers to cover classes. My little friend, Diego, was not in school. When asked why, Diego responded, "There is no class." "Why is there no class?" I asked. "Because my teacher went to Quezaltenango" for the day. Similarly, when I went to observe the fifth grade one day, the room was completely unoccupied. I was later informed that the teacher had gone out of town for an education meeting. The fifth grade teacher doubled as the director of the school, further evidence of the shortage of personnel.

Physical education, music, art, and other "extra" classes were all taught by the regular classroom teachers. There were no specialists for any subjects or aides to give special help for slower learners. The schools were not equipped with services, such as a resource room or special education, so students with special needs made do as best they could.

One-on-one assistance was difficult to give in a classroom of forty or more students. It was also difficult to be fully aware of every student and his or her individual needs. For example, one boy was chosen to read a chart in front of the class. The chart displayed the letter *F* combined with every vowel, plus sixteen words with *F*s, and two sentences. The students in the classroom had spent an hour learning the chart, but this student was highly unsuccessful. The young boy was criticized harshly for his failure and told that he needed to pay better attention. Humiliated in front of his classmates, the boy was sent back to his desk. I sat quietly in the back of the room feeling sorry for this struggling student. Having observed the entire lesson, I did not feel the boy's lack of success was due to inattentiveness. He had watched, listened, and participated. Perhaps a little extra help was what he needed, rather than criticism. Moreover, having never seen a student wearing glasses, I thought it likely that hearing and sight problems also might go unnoticed.

TEACHER PREPARATION AND PAY

Teachers in the elementary schools studied thirteen years to become a teacher. Beginning with *pre-primaria*, which is equivalent to kindergarten in the United States, elementary education ends with *sexto grado*, or the sixth grade. Those students who continued their educations attended básico (junior high school) for three years. The final three years were completed in *magisterio*, the high school track focused on becoming a teacher.

Teachers were paid monthly. Salary levels, of which there were six, were determined by number of years of teaching experience. Beginning in level A, a teacher made 700 quetzales per month for the first five years. Each five years of service triggered an advancement in level and an increment in pay of 140 quetzales more than the previous level. Thus level B teachers earned 840 quetzales a month; level C earned 980 quetzales; level D earned 1,120 quetzales; level E earned 1,260 quetzales; and the final level, F, earned 1,400 quetzales per month. With an exchange rate of approximately 5.60 quetzales per US$1, a teacher in level A made about $125 in one month and increased about $25 per month with each five years of seniority. The two second grade teachers in the Paxixil school said the salary was insufficient. One said it required every penny to cover a family's costs for food and clothing.

SCHEDULE AND CURRICULUM

Erasmo, the school director, held the key that opened the schoolyard gate. Peddling his ten-speed bicycle up a bumpy dirt road, Erasmo arrived at the school's entrance at 7:30 A.M. Some of the students and teachers stood outside awaiting his arrival. School was scheduled to begin at 7:30, but Erasmo was not the only person running late; many of the teachers had yet to arrive. Rarely, if ever, did classes begin on time. The daily welcome, *"Buenos días, profesor,"* was usually heard anywhere from 7:45 to 8:00 A.M. The school day ended at 12:20 P.M. When it was their day for limpieza, students left school at 12:30 P.M.

A curriculum of varying subjects allowed for a well-rounded education. Every second Monday of the month, one class had the responsibility of putting together a civic program or assembly for the rest of the school. All students gathered outside to watch songs, dances, and speeches, all pertaining to patriotism. The schedule was explicitly outlined but was not rigidly followed. Many lessons extended beyond the designated forty-five-minute time frame per class period.

Also common were days when school was not held. One week, for example, school was out one and a half days of the regular five. Beginning on Wednesday, students were released at 10:00 A.M. to celebrate the intro-duction of lights and electric power to the hamlet, with music, food, programs, and festivities, because electricity was still very new to Nahualá. The fiesta, provided for the entire cantón, was held at the school. Men, women, and children attended the fiesta that lasted long into the night. Needless to say, school did not begin on time Thursday morning. On Friday, school was out for a *día del campo* (field day). Students arrived at school at the normal time, ready for work in the field, wearing their sombreros and carrying their machetes.[2]

The following week, classes were out three days of the scheduled five. On Monday, the teachers were required to attend a regional meeting for all teachers in the area. Tuesday and Wednesday proceeded normally, but Thursday and Friday were again free days for students. The teachers and students who could afford the trip made an excursion to Antigua, Guatemala. Those students unable to attend simply stayed home and, most likely, worked for their families. Thus, out of ten school days, only five and a half were actually spent in classes.

TEACHING METHODS

Screaming as loudly as possible, students repeated everything said to them. I needed my umbrella on *F* day, when the students practiced the *F* sound, because spit was projected in every direction. United in chorus, voices echoed loudly against concrete walls as the students shouted back what the teacher said. Choral repetition was lessened in the upper grades but still occurred. Kindergarten and first grade students did very little writing. These students learned by listening and repeating.

Because textbooks were so few, students wrote their own. Pictures, texts—everything—were copied from the board or written by dictation in the notebook designated for that subject. For example, when fourth graders were studying natural sciences, they had a day when the subject was the sense of taste. The teacher drew pictures of the tongue on the board, displaying taste buds for bitter, sweet, and so forth. Text relating to each picture was also written on the board. The job of the students was to copy, word-for-word, line-for-line, picture-for-picture, what the teacher put on the board. As students became more proficient in Spanish, teachers did not write as much on the board, but rather, dictated the text to the students. Whether content was written or dictated, the process of copying their own textbooks occupied hours of daily class time.

A bottom-up theoretical style of learning was practiced in all lessons: students learned a step at a time, starting from the most elemental concept. Learning the letter *B*, for example, involved first learning the shape, then learning the sound, then combining the letter with vowels. The letter was then put in words and finally in sentences. All lessons of all subjects were taught in this manner. Students were not shown how to solve math problems; they were simply told the answers and instructed to copy the given information directly into their notebooks. Discovery learning, deductive/inductive learning, and active learning were as rare as textbooks. Student participation and interaction did not play a big part in the learning process except on field days. When teachers asked questions, students were required to repeat verbatim what had been told to them.

Indeed, teachers spent much time writing assignments on the board. Students were instructed to "sit properly" and watch while the teacher wrote.

Once assignments were given, more time was spent working on the assignment. Upon completion, all assignments were graded in class. During grading time, students socialized or harassed one another, often resulting in chaos. A fifth grade experience exemplifies the issues. First, fifteen minutes were used in dictation of one math problem, a story problem involving addition of fourteen three-digit numbers. Students were then given time to complete the assigned work. Each assignment was corrected, and then the problem was done together as a class. The entire process took an hour and a half.

Students were not assigned a designated seat. They sat where they wanted, perhaps in a different seat every day. Distinct separation of boys and girls was evident in students' choice of where to sit. Especially as the students grew older, it was rare to see a mix of sexes.

Criticism was commonly used as a disciplinary tool in every classroom. Girls tended to be shy and were sometimes harshly criticized by teachers as a result. In a class that had only one book with nearly seventy students studying from it, Alicia was chosen to read a short paragraph to the rest of her classmates. Acting like most other girls in the class would, Alicia approached the front of the class, her hand covering her mouth and dragging her feet. Timidly taking the book, she began reading in barely audible whispers. With every word the teacher turned to the class and said, "Can you hear her?" The unified response repeatedly rang, "No." Unable to find the courage to raise her voice, Alicia was asked to step aside. Víctor was asked to read to show Alicia the correct volume for oral reading. Once sufficiently humiliated, Alicia was told to return to her seat. Though praised for his loud voice, Víctor was harshly criticized for his lack of fluency. Raúl, the third reader, was both loud and fluent. He was therefore praised and applauded by his fellow students. A number of students read and upon completion received a rating from the class. In this school, criticism was a form of teaching as well as a form of discipline. Rated on a scale of *muy bien* (very good), *regular* (average), or *mal* (poor), only the "muy bien" received applause. Only one female student earned applause.

EVALUATION

As previously mentioned, assignments were corrected or graded in class upon completion. When homework was assigned, it also was graded in class, first thing in the morning. Each assignment was marked with a percentage.

At the end of every two months, every school and every grade had test week which involved taking tests in every subject of study.

I saw two types of review or preparation for the bimonthly test week. During the preparation of third graders for the natural science test, the teacher dictated a sentence about the circulatory and respiratory systems, including an underlined blank that would be filled by a vocabulary word. The students wrote the sentence in their notebooks and the teacher told the students which word should fill the blank. Later, the test would be worded exactly as the review was dictated, and the students would simply fill in the blanks from a list of words.

In a fourth grade class, students were given an hour to read their notes and share information with each other. In a two-month period, a majority of students had missed at least one day of class, and therefore of text, that they had to catch up on. At the end of the "study session," the teacher held a formal review that proved unsuccessful. Row by row, the students were placed in front of the room to answer questions from their texts. Unable to answer most of the review questions, the students were reprimanded for their lack of success. The teacher dismissed them with a warning and a reminder to study and be prepared for the test scheduled the following day.

During test week, teachers graded the *cuadernos* (notebooks), which included notes and homework, and gave a signature of approval or completion to each notebook. When tests were completed, the director gave the parents a *tarjeta de calificación*, a report card.

DISCIPLINE

The young third grade boy cupped his hands around his mouth, making a perfect whistle. Blowing forcefully, the boy created numerous loud, distracting noises. Staring at the teacher, I expected an immediate disciplinary action. Amazed, I saw no reaction from the teacher, who undoubtedly heard and was distracted by this nuisance in the back of the room. No more than a few minutes passed and this same boy began hitting another boy, distracting him from his work. This behavior persisted throughout the morning. Rowdy students were common, but discipline and order were not. I watched a kindergarten teacher literally chase his students in circles while trying to organize a physical education activity. This teacher was controlled by his students, who ignored every command.

After observing the rowdy boy in her classroom, I was anxious to hear Angela's beliefs on discipline. Her discipline system functioned on a point scale. When students took a test, forty of the test points were discipline points. Students who failed to fulfill duties or acted inappropriately lost some of their forty points. Angela also said she would talk to parents if students were out of hand. Angela did not verbally address her rowdy student; perhaps he lost discipline points for his inappropriate behavior. Class time was never wasted for disciplinary action of an individual's misbehavior.

I asked the other teachers about their thoughts and beliefs regarding discipline systems. Emilio, teacher of the first grade, shared with me the *reglamento de la escuela* (school regulations) which had been written jointly by the parents and teachers. Emilio said that discipline was important, and without it the students were not going to learn. The guidelines stated that troublesome students who failed to follow the regulations would be expelled. Emilio said he talked with students individually after class if they were causing problems. He followed the designated rules and expected his students to also.

Mario, a sixth grade teacher, also talked with his students when they got out of hand. When students became restless and uncontrollable, he played games to refocus attention. Bored with the spelling lesson they were being taught, his students were talking instead of listening. Sensing the loss of interest, Mario organized a quick game. After this, he continued the lecture and dictation with better concentration by the students.

As was common in all classes, Catarina, the second grade teacher, required her students to sit properly: "*Siéntense bién.*" This instruction could be heard numerous times every day in every classroom. All teachers required students to sit with both feet on the ground, body facing forward, and good posture. All teachers also required the boys to take off their hats in class. Catarina insisted that her students raise their hands if they had questions and listen when the teacher spoke. When asked about punishment for misbehavior, Catarina said her students might lose privileges or they could get tapped with her ruler.

I observed physical discipline from time to time in the fourth grade classroom. On one occasion, the teacher hit a student on the side of his head with her hand when he was inattentive. On another occasion, a student who was staring out the window instead of being "on task" received two smacks on the head with a teacher's notebook. The teacher did not hit the students forcefully; nevertheless, she was not afraid to raise her hand to their heads. Though classrooms seemed chaotic at times, each teacher claimed to value a disciplined group and had his or her own ideas for a discipline system.

FURTHER PROBLEMS IN THE SYSTEM

Inadequate buildings, overcrowded classrooms, limited books and materials, insufficient pay, and lack of discipline were all serious problems, but certainly not the only problems.

Bilingual Issues

Perhaps even more important than the shortage of resources, Nahualá's teachers had to deal with the impact of language on learning. Every child born in this area grows up speaking K'iche' in the home. Not until a child enters school does he or she begin to learn Spanish, the national language.

Language instruction varied greatly from grade level to grade level. Kindergarten students were taught completely in K'iche'. They learned a few words in Spanish, beginning the slow transition of languages. Writing and reading were taught only in K'iche' until Spanish was better understood. Although it differed for each class, K'iche' instruction usually ended by the third grade. Fourth graders learned solely in Spanish. When students spoke with one another, however, they spoke in K'iche'. With dictation as the main form of learning, many students struggled to hear and record correctly the information given in a language they did not know well. Battling a language barrier, students found processing and expressing ideas doubly difficult and frustrating.

Basic education has not always been available in Nahualá, and many parents did not attend school. As a result, many adults (especially women) never learned Spanish. To be sure, speaking K'iche' preserves the traditional Mayan language; however, Spanish was necessary for communication with people outside of the K'iche'-speaking population. José, age fifty, provided his story. He completed school through the first grade and then discontinued his education to work in the fields with his father. Later in life, when he moved to Guatemala City, he was unable to communicate because he knew very little Spanish. He struggled with frustration as he slowly began to learn the Spanish language, which he had to learn "little by little." A vendor of "*cosas típicas*" (indigenous crafts), he needed Spanish to communicate with his customers. Struggling to speak the Spanish language, he also struggled to make a living.

Bilingual teaching was both difficult and frustrating. Hours were spent teaching fundamental concepts and language tools in not one language but two. While conducting a language lesson, a first grade teacher read his class a story in Spanish. The story was short, only one paragraph. After reading the story, the teacher discussed it with his class. When finished with a slow explicit discussion, he read the story two more times. Once this was completed, he had to back up and retell the story in K'iche'. The explicit discussion was also retold in the native language to ensure comprehension. Because the lesson was taught twice, twice the time was spent. Such is the difficult job of a bilingual educator. Lilia, a third and fourth grade teacher, said that teachers experienced a great deal of frustration. She said that teachers ended up screaming at the students, trying to make them understand. She felt frustrated that the students did not understand her instructions and her questions. She said she knew her students wished to express their knowledge but lacked the language ability to do so. Bilingual education, though essential in the schools, added complication and complexity to an educational system already struggling to help students become active participants in this society.

Teacher Placement Bureaucracy

For teachers just starting out, finding a position was difficult. When one received a diploma from the Ministerio, (National Ministry of Education), the complicated process began. First, a teacher had to gain approval from the cantón in which he/she lived or wished to teach. The parents of the families in that area met to propose names of teachers. The proposal was taken to the municipal mayor and the education supervisor for their signatures of support. Once the proposal was signed, the aspiring teacher took the papers to the departmental division of education, where the education director reviewed papers and applications. The proposed names went to one of four regional administrations. Nahualá belonged to the southwest region, with offices located in Quezaltenango. All papers were reviewed once again and sent to Guatemala City. The final step required the personnel administration in the capital to review the proposal one last time. There, the appointments or placements were selected, and notification was sent out to applicants. Candidates had to pass language proficiency tests that ensured sound knowledge of the Mayan language spoken in the area in which placement was desired. This system is sufficiently thorough and it should work.

Corruption entered in the system, however, and created problems for many people wishing to be employed. Ana related her experience. The required language test was in K'iche'. Ana took the test, scoring eighty-six points, which seemed to be a very good score. Pleased with her results, Ana anxiously awaited a job placement. Her spirits were dampened when she received placement in a school in another town, a three-hour walk from home. While many teachers traveled considerable distances to jobs, Ana could not. Ana had scored higher than most of the other test takers, yet others with lower test scores had been placed in nearby schools.

Distraught, Ana confronted the departmental directors of education and discovered that those with lower scores had paid off the director for nearby placements. Corruption left Ana without placement for four consecutive years, even though her test scores surpassed many of those receiving better placement. Ana longed to aid her family financially. Other jobs were not readily available, and the family did not have the funds to seek jobs in other towns. With two small children, neither Ana nor her husband wanted her to travel to a job every day. Being thus homebound, Ana was left jobless.

In another example of corruption, one of the teachers in the lower grades did not speak K'iche'. She spoke Mam, another of the Mayan languages spoken in Guatemala. Yet the regional education supervisor allowed this teacher placement. Though the educational system was carefully outlined, corruption made finding a teaching job ever more difficult and allowed injustice to seep through.

Student Attendance

When and for how long a child attended school depended greatly on the father of the household. In many cases, children were needed at home to help sustain the family, perhaps by working in the fields or preparing thread for the family weaving business. Whatever the reason, providing a living for families took precedence over formal education. Therefore, many children dropped out, entered late, or did not attend regularly.

Although many children were not in school, enough students attended to create overcrowded classrooms. The Paxixil school had 379 students enrolled. With nine teachers, the average was 42 students per class. Kindergarten and first grade each had two classrooms to accommodate the 90 students in each grade. Second grade accommodated 67 students in one room with one teacher. There were 48 children attending third grade, 33 in fourth grade, 34 in fifth grade, and only 17 in sixth grade.[3]

Because no age is designated for starting school, the students of each grade level display a wide range of ages. The following statistics were taken from the Paxixil school. Most students in kindergarten ranged in age from six to eight years old, with a few students as old as eleven. First graders ranged from seven to eleven years old. Second graders ranged from eight to thirteen years old. Students in the third grade were between nine and fourteen years old. The range for fourth grade was also nine to fourteen, with twelve to fifteen for fifth grade and twelve to eighteen for sixth graders.

By law, students had to attend school through the sixth grade, but the law was not enforced. Manuel, a second grade teacher, believed the level of development of a society determined how well its laws are enforced. He argued that parents in the United States sent their children to school because education was a necessity for survival in society—a characteristic of developed countries. In Guatemala, however, work was often in the home or field and did not require education. Therefore, according to Manuel, one characteristic of an underdeveloped country was that parents did not send their children to school.

Manuel also felt that many parents believed education to be "a waste of time." Manuel worked in a cantón of two hundred to three hundred houses. The enrollment in his school was two hundred students. Knowing that there must be more than one child per house, Manuel expressed disappointment that so many children were absent from school. He described one father who, when asked why he did not send his child to school, replied, "because my child does not want to go." Because Manuel, a schoolteacher, believed education helped society progress, he expressed disgust in this father's attitude. Holding his three-year-old daughter in his arms, Manuel made it abundantly clear that his daughter would attend school whether she wanted to or not.

Nevertheless, many parents desired that their children work in the home to help financially support the family. Diego, age nine, attended first grade at Paxixil. Needing his help to earn sustenance, his family often kept him home to work. One day, I asked Diego why he did not go to school that day. He replied that he had to go to the mountains to find firewood, a necessity for every family. Wood cooked the food, heated the sweatbath, and warmed the family in the kitchen. Finding firewood involved a long hike into the mountains, chopping wood with a machete, and strapping the heavy load on one's back for the long walk home. On another occasion, Diego said he did not go to school that day because he had to *hacer hilo* (prepare thread) because his family earned their living as weavers. By staying home and winding thread on bobbins, Diego assisted in the family business. Families like Diego's were the norm.

Traditional customs and beliefs also affected the way the society accepted and reacted to education. Violeta completed the fifth grade. She was thirteen years old and hoped to continue her education. Her parents, however, had other plans for her. They believed she was old enough to be married. Violeta resisted. She did not wish to be married but wanted to go to school. But she had no say in the situation: Violeta's father found her a husband and she was forced to quit school. At age fourteen, Violeta and her spouse were expecting their first child. The young couple lived and worked in the home of Violeta's father. According to Manuel, this is common circumstance: "People get married early and that is a problem in Guatemala." Clearly, however, many felt that the tradition of early marriage was a sufficient and proper reason to drop out.

CONCLUSION

The teachers and I shared common concerns for the educational system in Nahualá. Many problems existed, and the teachers were not afraid to acknowledge them, but solutions come slowly in a society in which formal education is not highly practical. Whether working in the cornfields, spinning thread, or hiking to the mountains to find wood, the children often had to give subsistence of the family precedence over education. Nevertheless, education continues to increase in importance as Nahualá slowly modernizes and the corn plots, through inheritance, become increasingly small. Although lacking in materials and resources, some children attend school and are provided with a foundation on which they may build. As yet, only a relative few find their way out of the community via education and even fewer come back to use their education as culture mediators. For an agricultural society functioning in traditional customs, the mode of education described here has been adequate. It is not at all clear, however, that the same pattern will serve the emerging needs of future Nahualenses.

NOTES

1. Hillary Goodwin, in "'Silence!' The Education of Indian Children in Santa Catarina Ixtahuacán," describes essentially the same situation in the elementary school in that community. See *http://maya.byu.edu* for the full text.

2. On one día del campo, every student and teacher hiked to the mountains to plant trees all day instead of holding classes. The activity was valuable and the learning vital to the society because the students helped to replenish resources that were essential for living.

3. The Escuela Urbana Mixta, a large school in the center of Nahualá, also accommodated a large number of students with a small number of teachers: 880 students were assigned to only 24 teachers, an average of approximately 37 students per teacher.

About the lead author: I completed my BA in psychology at Brigham Young University in 1996 with a minor in current social issues. I continued my education in BYU's Master of Social Work program, completing the program in 1998 with an emphasis in clinical work. My husband, Caleb, and I moved to the Los Angeles area where I worked in a large residential facility for severely emotionally disturbed boys. I have also worked at a community mental health facility where I supervised a program for severely mentally ill individuals with histories of homelessness and incarceration. I am currently in the third year of a social work doctoral program at the University of Southern California where my research emphasis has been mental health issues of minority groups.

Reflections on the 1995 field experience: The experience of living in Nahualá has led me to want to gain a greater understanding of cultures other than my own. I learned that a certain behavior cannot be completely understood and judged outside the context of one's culture. Though the gender inequity we observed in the classrooms at the school was obvious to us as norteamericanos, we attempted to understand and present cultural factors that contributed to this behavior. This experience, as well as my work with mentally ill individuals, has led me to realize that traditional Western methods of assessment and treatment are not appropriate for many culturally diverse groups. While there may be agreement among cultures that a problem exists, ideas of appropriate remedies may not be generally applicable to all groups.

CHAPTER 7

"GIRLS DON'T TALK"
Education and Gender in Nahualá

Heather Hanamaikai and Ryan Thompson

Girls in Nahualá often faced cultural conflict between a desire for education and a commitment to help with domestic responsibilities. As a result, many girls discontinued their educational careers before reaching the sixth grade. Statistics from 1994 showed that 83 percent of boys graduated from their current grade in school, as opposed to 79 percent of girls. Throughout the pueblo, most men were able to speak Spanish, while it was quite common to encounter women who only spoke K'iche'.

Gender differences and gender dominance were manifest in many ways throughout village life. For example, in both the evangélico (Protestant-Pentecostal) and Catholic churches, men and women strictly segregated themselves in their seating arrangements. In the Mormon chapel, a locally made sign hanging on one of the classroom walls asserted that husbands should not belittle or strike their spouses. The sign responded to a presumption that a man was expected to feel he was the *dueño* (owner) of his spouse. As dueños, men often felt justified in beating their wives, a common practice according to the justice of the peace. He spoke of one man who could not afford the forty-quetzal fine for spousal abuse, so he was sentenced to twenty days in the town jail. He also said that the abused wives often paid the fine or brought daily meals to their husbands in jail.

Gender difference was also manifested in families: males of all ages ate before females, generally ate food of better quality and greater quantity, and sat on chairs or at tables whereas women often sat on the floor. Men also participated in public, political, and community discussions, where women, as a general rule, did not. Symbolic male dominance was also important. The father of the family with whom one of us lived insisted on having his clean clothing folded and stacked on top of the rest of the family's clean clothing.

He was considered a "good husband"—neither abusive nor dominating—by others in the community.

Given these premises and practices, it would be logical to find gender differences and biases reflected in the classroom. We approached teachers with the request that they allow us to conduct classroom observations of gender-related behavior. We conducted these observations for one-hour periods, multiple times, in sixteen different classrooms. During each observation period, we documented the sex of the teacher, the number of behavioral problems, the amount of positive teacher-to-student interaction, the amount of negative teacher-to-student interaction, and the amount of student-to-teacher interaction—all according to the sex of the students and the teachers. In doing so, we hoped to determine whether the societal pattern of male-gender preferential treatment would perpetuate practices favoring males in the classroom.

We hypothesized that if societal male dominance manifested itself in the classroom, a teacher of either sex would likely interact positively with male students more often than with female students. A male-oriented attitude might also cause proportionately more boy than girl students to feel compelled to initiate interaction with teachers. We also sought to observe if the gender of the teacher affected how he or she interacted with either male or female students and how the teacher's gender affected the behavior of the students.

Many of the teachers were not accustomed to having observers in their classrooms and may have felt intimidated by our presence. To avoid making teachers feel obligated to prepare in advance for our visits, we attempted to make our observations at various unannounced hours throughout the school day. This was done in hopes of minimizing any unnatural or rehearsed responses on the part of the teachers.

RESEARCH FINDINGS

Data were collected from sixteen classrooms ranging from grades preprimaria (preschool) to sexto grado (sixth grade). We observed a total of 307 male students and 270 female students in these sixteen classes. A distinct difference was revealed in the amount of positive teacher-to-student interaction, in that 16 percent of girls, as opposed to 45 percent of boys, received positive exchanges. In contrast, 15 percent of girls versus 14 percent of boys received negative interaction.[1] Comparatively little student-to-teacher interaction took place. The figures are instructive: 5 percent of the females and 22 percent of the males initiated exchanges with their respective teachers.[2] Those girls who did initiate interaction usually did so only once during the observation period. With respect to behavioral problems, 17 percent of females and 36 percent of males exhibited behavior which, using admittedly American notions, we judged to be disruptive or problematic in some way.[3]

Male teachers and female teachers were almost identical in the amount of positive interaction they initiated with boy and girl students. Of the total amount of positive interaction given by female teachers, 32 percent was given to girls and 68 percent to boys.[4] Male teachers gave 30 percent of their positive interaction to girls and 70 percent to boys.[5] The gender of the teachers was not found to affect their negative interaction: with female teachers, 64 percent of their negative interactions were with male students, while 36 percent of their negative interactions were with female students.[6] Similarly, among male teachers, 48 percent of their negative interactions were with male students, versus 52 percent with female students.[7]

Slight differences were found in how students interacted with female and male teachers. Girls seemed more apt to participate with female teachers (twenty-one percent) as opposed to male teachers (seventeen percent). Observations of behavioral problems showed that boys' behavior constituted the majority of classroom problems (68 percent of problems experienced by female teachers and 66 percent of problems experienced by male teachers).

CULTURAL INTERPRETATIONS

These findings suggest that societal gender concepts impact the amount of personal attention given to either male or female students. Positive attention was typically given more often to boys than to girls. This could be a reflection of general K'ichd' societal practices, where the needs of males often take precedence over the needs of females. A higher percentage of male students initiated interaction with the teachers, which might also naturally cause the teachers to reciprocate by focusing more of their attention on them. It was apparent that the teachers often felt frustrated when female students refused to respond when called on, much less raise their hands or participate voluntarily in class. In this sense, teachers may have been interacting with those students they felt might benefit more from their attention.

Males were viewed as primary providers in the family and that view may have predisposed teachers to focus more of their attention on boy students in the classroom. Because their role was perceived as more vital, the need to educate young males may also have been felt with more urgency, either on a conscious or subconscious level. In contrast, women's roles were almost exclusively domestic. One woman stated, "Women always work: cooking, washing clothes, and other things like that." These duties were viewed as requiring less formal education.

Cultural tradition may also be apparent in the observation that more males initiated interaction with the teacher. Such a male-oriented society would naturally favor a male taking on an assertive role. In contrast, a girl might expect that her subordinate position in the community would require that she be less dominant in the classroom. Her hesitancy to participate may also increase as she is ridiculed in front of the class. In one case, a teacher made several jokes to the class when a girl was unable to recite a poem correctly. It was also common to see students laughing at girls who would rather hide their heads under their pañuelos than answer a teacher's question. It would seem logical that such negative reinforcement would amplify women's shy behavior in the future. Moreover, the practice of avoiding discussion and evading response seemed common among adult women with whom we attempted to speak on the streets.

As indicated, male students seemed to cause a majority of the disruptions, although the nature of the problems differed according to gender. Males demonstrated more physical or outspoken distractions such as fighting, yelling, or teasing. Disciplinary problems involving females were, for the most part, less physical, but in many respects no less disruptive. Females generally seemed to be either inattentive or overly social. Girls often congregated in small bunches in the classroom to socialize with friends. Such patterns were also common throughout the town because of the nature of the activities in which women typically participate. These ranged from weaving with family members to conversing with other women while washing clothing at one of the various public *pilas* (sinks).

We questioned the teachers to determine whether they perceived differences in behavioral problems according to gender. Of those teachers who perceived marked differences in behavior between males and females, some commented that boys tended to fight and bully more, to be *más inquietos* (more restless), generally causing more disruptive behavior. One female teacher also felt that males are more difficult to discipline. Some problems noted with girls: they chewed gum in class, returned late from recess because they played basketball, and were sometimes bossy with younger students.

In one second grade class, the teacher spoke with a mother, her son, and another boy because the students had been fighting. The instructor later explained that one of the two boys was particularly violent because his father was an alcoholic and had no interest in his son or in controling his son's behavior. The boy was allowed to view karate videos which were shown at a home-based video parlor. The teacher blamed the boy's hostile behavior and lack of self-control on violent examples in the movies. Because many males were not curbed in their aggressive behavior in the home or at school, this teacher feared that boys might tend to exhibit such actions more frequently as they grew older and eventually manifest aggressiveness in their own marriage and family relationships. He also believed that such videos go against traditional Maya cultural teachings, such as *paciencia y disciplina* (patience and discipline) and focus instead on modern attitudes of *violencia y egoísmo* (violence and self-centeredness). Many people, including the justice of the peace, mentioned such videos as the cause of violence and lack of discipline among the youth of Nahualá.

Some teaching practices also seemed to perpetuate the overt gender differences. Several classes physically segregated students according to gender by placing them in different rows or groups. One male fifth grade teacher with such an arrangement consistently stood on the boys' side of the room and interacted with the male students for nearly an entire one-hour period.

Some other instructors also reinforced female non-participation by making comments in front of the class such as "*las niñas no hablan*" (girls don't talk) and "*sus bocas no mueven*" (their mouths don't move). Such generalizations could inhibit future participation by girls, who may feel they have already been assigned a label by their teacher. It would seem difficult to oppose such predisposed expectations and easier to fulfill them instead. At the same time, some teachers used such labels as "*molestón*" (disruptive) and "inquieto" (restless) in reference to male students. This could also initiate a self-fulfilling prophecy, where boys felt they had already been categorized and could act out the traits of such labels by being rowdy and disruptive.

Differences in gender roles could also become more defined by the division of responsibilities in the classroom. Female students were typically assigned to wash the cups for refacciones, mix the powdered milk, and mop the floors. Such duties were perhaps viewed as more domestic and therefore more appropriate for girls, but they also gave the connotation of subservience and allowed these feelings to manifest themselves in other areas of life.

On the other hand, several teachers utilized methods that would seem to ameliorate gender difference barriers. Some classes had students randomly and somewhat evenly dispersed according to gender, making it more difficult for a teacher to favor a certain area of the classroom. Some teachers encouraged students, rather then demeaning or embarrassing them, creating a more inviting environment for participation by the frequently more timid female students. One teacher explained that *"mujeres y hombres son uno, tenemos los mismos derechos"* (women and men are alike, we have the same rights). Here a sense of comraderie could have helped combat feelings of greater or lesser worth according to one's gender. Frustration undoubtedly arose in teachers who received no feedback or participation from extremely shy girl students. The reaction of some teachers was to vent these frustrations by reprimanding or excluding these students. Other teachers had learned to work in a way that overcame cultural norms and expectations to some extent, through patience and by not allowing females to hide behind their gender stereotypes. It seemed that although many women had accepted and grown accustomed to their position in society, not all were happy about or supportive of such situations. One young girl revealed her dream of continuing her education, but said that family responsibilities were more important.

CONCLUSION

Our research has shown pervasive, but not universal, gender bias in the school classroom. Both male and female teachers were oriented toward male students more than toward female students. Male students disproportionately disrupted the operation of the classroom, compared with female students. Male students also initiated more non-disruptive interactions with teachers than did female students. We interpret these observations to be consistent with and understandable within the widespread cultural assumptions and behavioral practices that accorded priority and status to males and granted them the public, dominant roles.

We empathized with women's dissatisfaction in occupying a less prominent societal status. We also often identified with a teacher's frustration at the lack of participation on the part of many of the girls in class. One female teacher showed this frustration when talking about how young girls *tienen vergüenza* (feel ashamed) and do not like to talk in class. While female students were subjected to much unfair treatment, their reactions to this treatment seemed to hinder rather than improve their situation. It is unlikely that change will be initiated by a male population accustomed to holding a dominant position. If change is to take place for the women and girls in this male-dominant society, much of that change will need to begin within women themselves.

NOTES

1. $X^2=59.319$, with one degree of freedom. Probability this distribution is due to chance is ≤ 0.001.

2. $X^2=33.9$, with one degree of freedom. Probability this distribution is due to chance is ≤ 0.001.

3. $X^2=26.513$, with one degree of freedom. Probability this distribution is due to chance is ≤ 0.001.

4. Female teachers delivered 20 positive interactions to 102 female students and 42 positive interactions to 110 male students. $X^2=6.23$, df=1, p=0.013. Boys had significantly more positive interactions from female teachers than the girls did.

5. Male teachers delivered 41 positive interactions to 167 female students and 97 positive interactions to 197 male students. $X^2=14.531$, df=1, p <0.00. Boys had significantly more positive interactions from male teachers than the girls did.

6. Female teachers delivered 8 negative interactions to 102 female students and 14 negative interactions to 110 male students. $X^2=1.221$, df=1, p=0.269. There was no statistically significant difference between female teachers' negative interactions with boys compared with girls.

7. Male teachers delivered 32 negative interactions to 167 female students and 29 negative interactions to 197 male students. $X^2=1.056$, df=1, p=0.304. There was no statistically significant difference between male teachers' negative interactions with boys compared with girls. Given that boys caused a disproportionate share of disruptions, the failure to find a statistical difference in teachers' negative interactions with them demonstrates a bias in favor of boys.

About the author: *In October 2002, I came to work for the State of Utah in the Governor's Office of Planning and Budget. As the health analyst, I help develop the state's budget for Medicaid and other health programs. Previously I conducted performance audits for the California State Auditor's Office on various programs including information technology and domestic violence. In 1998 I received my Master's of Public Administration from Brigham Young University. As part of a research assistantship during that program, I co-authored a study on the use of program evaluation in not-for-profit organizations that lent small amounts of money to individuals through a "micro-credit" model. In 1996, I completed my undergraduate studies in International Relations at Brigham Young University.*

Reflections on the 1995 field experience: *One lesson I drew from my fieldwork was the relative nature of poverty. I had previously lived in Argentina for two years and had seen extreme poverty existing next to relative wealth. People in those circumstances could easily define their poverty by looking down the street to see how their neighbor lived. Before arriving in Santa Catarina Ixtahuacán, I wondered if the seclusion of the town would stifle the impulse of its residents to compare their status with that of bustling Guatemala City. However, I found that the residents' trips outside the town, along with their exposure to mass culture through television and radio, had left them with concrete aspirations for increasing their earnings and changing their lifestyle. Now, as my wife and I raise our three children in the suburbs of the United States, we, too, face the challenge of defining our status and sense of well-being while we are bombarded with images of wealth from television and we see the lifestyles of our neighbors. As with the residents of Santa Catarina Ixtahuacán, I have found these perceptions of wealth can cause me to feel "left behind."*

CHAPTER 8

"BY THE SWEAT OF THY BROW"
Development, Religion, and Culture
in Santa Catarina Ixtahuacán

Nathan Checketts

The people of Santa Catarina Ixtahuacán expressed a definite awareness of their poverty and relative deprivation. The recent arrival of televisions and the longtime presence of radios underscored the idea, already felt from Ladino influence, that the Mayas were not getting their full share of what was available. This sense of being *atrasado* (behind or underdeveloped) had spawned a great desire for "advancement." Progress was seen as necessary and desirable by everyone in the town. There was little questioning of whether this progress might be detrimental to the social structure and cultural existence of the town. Quite the contrary: there was a universal push to get ahead economically and leave poverty behind at both community and family levels.

A municipal report (Proyecto Salquil 1992:35–37) states that the average family income in Ixtahuacán was less than two thousand quetzales each year (with a ratio of approximately Q5 to US $1). To acquire this meager income, farmers worked small plots using hoes and machetes. Many did not use fertilizers, pesticides, or improved seeds. The report claims the municipality had an infant mortality rate of 70.46 per 1,000 live births, with most of the deaths occurring in the first twenty days of life. According to the report, as of the last census 54 percent of the population was illiterate. As seen from these numbers, the community's perception of their socioeconomic deprivation was well founded.

The people not only recognized their general level of poverty, but they had specific needs that they hoped to fill. One of the most commonly mentioned needs of the community was for a paved road from their town to the international highway. From the highway, a rocky, narrow road snaked ten kilometers down a steep grade to Santa Catarina Ixtahuacán. The people believed that a paved road would allow more buses and trucks to enter Ixtahuacán, enabling them to buy goods at lower prices and sell goods to outside markets at higher profits. Townspeople cited the example of Nahualá, claiming that the main difference between Nahualá and Ixtahuacán was the highway. "It has brought modernization and advancement to Nahualá." In contrast, Ixtahuacán was said to be isolated, backward, and lawless because it lacked easy access to the highway.

Another major problem of the community involved its forests. Much talk and many educational programs focused on the importance of the forests in Guatemala. One man said, "It is bad to cut down the trees because there will not be any trees for our children. People say that if there are not any trees there will not be any water." The community's sensitivity to the need to maintain the forests was demonstrated by the two major disturbances of village tranquility during our fieldwork, both of which involved wood-cutting disputes. The community was especially aggressive against the use of chainsaws to cut down trees for sale outside the community. The hillsides around Ixtahuacán showed major deforestation caused by the pressure for wood and farmland. For example, a group of young brothers had recently inherited their father's land. It was undeveloped, heavily forested land at a considerable distance from the town center. A North American had come and offered to buy the land so that he could set up a hydroelectric system there. The brothers refused because they felt it was more important to preserve the forests.

Community members also complained about the inadequate school buildings. The elementary school opened a second wing in June 1994, doubling the number of classrooms. Nevertheless, the school director predicted that the expected increase in the number of students next year would force them to hold classes in a dilapidated old school building. The high school was currently holding classes in a borrowed building.

Other needs included skilled laborers and shops for carpentry, weaving, and sewing. The absence of these industries was attributed to the lack of a paved road. Informants also mentioned the desire for a more frequent meat market. Meat was only brought into town once a week on Saturday. People stored the meat in their houses without refrigeration until it was used. More frequent meat delivery, it was felt, could alleviate the problem of possible food spoilage from prolonged storage in homes without refrigeration.

On the family level, the most pressing necessity that people mentioned was that of better housing. Many lived with dirt floors, leaky roofs, and open-fire cooking facilities. There was also a sense of overcrowding because grandparents, children, and grandchildren often slept together in one or two rooms. Many homes in rural hamlets lacked latrines, sewer systems, wash-basins, running water, or electricity. In the urban center, most of the homes had these amenities, but the residents perceived a need for improvement.

Although many saw housing as their most pressing concern, others felt that food and clothing were needed most. Many families reported not having enough corn to make tortillas or tamales, the staples that accompanied every meal. One man explained that, "Just like gasoline makes a car go, tortillas make people go."

Community officials shared the views of ordinary citizens because most of the officials were from the community and maintained daily contact with the people. The officials mentioned the same needs as the others: schools, health clinics, running water, the highway, prevention of deforestation, sources of income, and housing.

Outsiders, such as Ladino representatives of government agencies, often saw different problems not shared by the community residents. For example, a truck driver from Panajachel told me that Ixtahuacán needed active policemen and more law and order because they did not respect the federal authorities that came to town. A secretary from Quezaltenango said that the town needed schoolteachers who would be willing to teach in the outlying villages. She also mentioned the necessity for adult literacy programs in those areas. The official secretary of a neighboring town felt that the people needed more education to take advantage of the democratic powers that they had acquired in recent years. One woman from Nahualá simply classified those from Ixtahuacán as "lazy, just waiting to be helped by the [aid] projects." These and other outsiders' views missed the mark of Ixtahuaquense needs. Indeed, they simply expressed their own needs as outsiders.

THE AID PROJECTS

The first thing that caught my attention about aid and development was the sheer number of development projects in Ixtahuacán. I identified ten groups working in Ixtahuacán, each with its own history, goals, and activities. In general, these projects seemed to be a reflection of the town's self-image of poverty and the people's desire to move ahead.

Origins

Aid projects came to Ixtahuacán in two ways. Usually, individuals in the community came together with a desire either to improve their family's living standard or to improve the community in general. Seven of Ixtahuacán's ten projects had such grassroots starts. Few of these groups had any source of consistent funding, yet they maintained their group in the hope that some advancement would take place. The *Salquil* project provides the most successful example of the genesis of self-help projects. The founder of Salquil had lived on the coastal plain in a caserío of Ixtahuacán, where he was an elementary school teacher. Through his dealings with the children, he realized they had many health and sanitation problems that impeded learning. He started classes to educate the parents and began organizing youth and adult groups. He also worked to build a school, but there was no funding for his efforts. In 1970, he came in contact with the U.S.-sponsored Christian Children's Fund and obtained sponsors for the children. He wanted the municipal town center of Ixtahuacán also to benefit from the project. He moved to Ixtahuacán and opened a branch of the project in 1972.

The other genesis for projects came when an outside funding source perceived a certain need and created a project to address it. Three projects in Ixtahuacán started that way. Part of the reason that some of these projects were started in Ixtahuacán is that the town's Catholic priest is from the United States. The three projects are partly the result of his efforts to bring in aid from his home diocese in the United States to his parish in Ixtahuacán. The Familia a Familia (Adopt-a-Family) project was created when a couple from the diocese visited Ixtahuacán. Since then, a second family-to-family sponsor program has been developed. The program was directed by an American nun for the first five years and then by a woman from Ixtahuacán.

The third outside aid project was the town's agricultural extension agency, DIGESA, which was funded by the Guatemalan government. DIGESA was the only government agency that was generally classified by the people as an aid project. Although the project was meant to serve the agricultural needs of the town, contact with the community was limited because the director came only once every two weeks to train participants.

Goals

Each project had its own set of goals, which could be categorized in three groups: community improvement, training, and subsistence. Many projects included plans to improve the community. Familia a Familia, in addition to its family aid, had a tree nursery and a reforestation program. The Salquil project had been working for a long time to develop transportation that would allow goods and people to move more quickly in and out of

Ixtahuacán. They purchased a bus and van line to serve the community. Generación de Maíz sought to put health clinics in all villages in the municipality. These projects, aimed at community improvement, shared several characteristics. First, they benefited the entire community and not just a few people. They also required the active participation of the community to plan and build. Those who participated were not paid but received both prestige and the benefits of the communal project. These programs were paid for mostly out of village donations or what they could obtain from private sponsors. They did not expect to receive much government help because it was rarely forthcoming.

Another goal involved the training of community members in life and job skills. Familia a Familia and Pan de Vida were two of the most active training programs. Some courses focused on marketable skills such as carpentry, shoe repair, poncho making, sewing, embroidering, and sandal making. Other courses taught things that were useful in the home, such as health classes, bread making, and women's civic education. Scholarships were offered to youths so that through their academic skills they could become self-sufficient. One senses the range of *Familia a Familia*'s mission in its motto: "To sponsor families for a time so they can have a more human way of life, break the vicious cycle of poverty, and become more self-sufficient."

The third goal involved subsistence. These programs sought to keep the individual fed and clothed but offered no plan for development other than to "reduce poverty," with the hope that the individual would continue to improve independently. Groups tried to provide a better physical situation for participants, such as roofing, bedding, latrines, and sewers. Nutrition programs fell into this category. Some examples include Salquil's food basket, Hermano Pedro's lunch snacks and meals, and DIGESA's distribution of foodstuffs. Much of the food that was given out by the projects came from USAID or the European Community. They experienced mixed success with the food that was sent. Staples such as corn and beans were very well received. However, some foods, such as canned Danish pork, were rarely eaten by the families, and stacks of the cans could be seen for sale at markets. The goal of such programs, while not always successful, was to fight malnutrition and hunger.

Funding and Distribution of Funds

One of the biggest problems that impeded the advancement of these projects was funding. Almost all grassroots projects suffered at one point or another from a lack of funding. Most had gone to the government and been rejected. Project Santa Cruz, however, obtained Q30,000 from FONAPAZ (Fondo Nacional para la Paz) to build a chicken coop, and another group obtained Q90,000 to create new classrooms for the elementary school. However, such funding was rare. Many projects had no way to finance their activities. Indeed, they hoped that when this research study was published, groups in the United States would sponsor them.

Two projects, Hermano Pedro and Salquil, were funded by programs in the United States. Children sponsored by these projects were listed on an information sheet that provided their date of birth, height, weight, and year in school. It also included information about a family's size, income, housing, presence of bathroom and washing facilities, and the like. This information, along with a photo of the child, was sent to the main center of the program in the United States. When the connection was made, the center sent a letter back to Ixtahuacán saying that the child had been accepted by a sponsor in the United States. Sponsors agreed to send a monthly payment to the center for the child, of whom they were often considered godparents. The international group connected to Hermano Pedro, the Christian Fund for Children and the Aging, sent eight to nine dollars (Q40–Q45) each month for each child. Salquil received Q100 (about US$18) each month per sponsored child from the Christian Children's Fund.

Some money sent by sponsors went directly to the children in Ixtahuacán. If the sponsor chose to send more than the agreed-upon monthly payment, it was considered a gift to the child or the family. Often these were birthday, Christmas, or Easter gifts. Most of the money contributed was used to fund the different programs that benefited the child. At Hermano Pedro, the workers informed the child's family that their child had received an amount of quetzales. The workers determined the needs of the child, bought whatever was needed, and gave it to the child. A photo would be sent back to the sponsor showing that the gift was received and delivered. The program used to give the money straight to the family, but often it was not spent on the child's needs. These gifts provide no income to the project's staff, but composed an important part of the services provided.

Familia a Familia sponsored entire families in a program like that of Hermano Pedro and Salquil. Familia a Familia was unique in the way it distributed its funds. When a new family was accepted, they planned with the director what to do with the money they would receive each month. For example, the family might decide to participate in a sewing class and buy a sewing machine. The sponsorship money in the United States was collected monthly, but it was only sent to Ixtahuacán when a specific need had been identified and communicated to the U.S. headquarters. This system of financing insured that the family was involved in planning and that it was correcly spending the funds. It also made the office in Ixtahuacán responsible for the money it distributed.

Staffing

All staff members for the projects were Guatemalans. Two were from neighboring communities, but the rest lived in, and were natives of, Ixtahuacán. Projects with a fixed source of external funding paid their staff, generally including a director, at least one fieldworker, and a secretary. They also had a full-time accountant to balance the books and document expenses. The two largest projects (Hermano Pedro and Salquil) had additional paid positions including social worker, librarian, photocopier, and correspondence coordinator. They worked forty hours a week and received a monthly salary. Most had a high school education, and many had just recently graduated. Those over twenty seemed to have made this their career, and they planned to continue working at the project for a long time. The younger workers talked about going to a university in a couple of years.

For those projects that lacked funding, there was usually a volunteer staff who worked irregular hours. Often, these offices were located in someone's house and were open just once a week. The volunteers viewed their participation as community service rather than a job. They were often part of the original parent group that had founded the project. Most worked as volunteers, ten to twenty hours a week, on the projects. In Pan de Vida, the workers received a small reimbursement for their time, but it hardly constituted a salary. However, most groups said that if they were to receive full-time funding, they would need full-time, salaried workers to handle all the different activities of the project.

AID PROJECT SUCCESSES

Several projects excelled in education. Many of the youth at the junior high and high school were on scholarships provided by aid programs. All participants in the programs reported having received school supplies. Yet, even in this area, teachers still reported that there was a serious lack of supplies. The Paraíso Maya high school, founded in 1993 without government support, was a great achievement, but in 1996, the program was hampered by lack of funds and there was uncertainty regarding how the teachers would be paid. A Danish aid program, however, agreed to finance the construction of a school building and pay the teachers' salaries for three years.

Another area of success was that of training workshops. Many people supplemented their milpa farming by working part-time in trades learned through involvement with training projects. The additional income helped keep a family fed without the father having to leave the highlands to work in the plantations on the coast. One old man remarked that people always used to go down to the coffee and sugarcane *fincas* to work, but now people have more work to do in Ixtahuacán. For example, one man learned carpentry and spent his spare time making furniture, working out of his home. Another man sat in the plaza doing shoe repair. Many women spent several hours a week making clothes to sell to American tourists—all skills learned through the projects. Although the demand was not enough to create full-time jobs, the projects provided training in trades that helped many obtain a greater degree of self-sufficiency. Familia a Familia helped several families achieve self-sufficiency through trout farms. The fish farm became a self-sufficient cooperative in three years. This reflects Familia a Familia's commitment to help families eventually become capable of sustaining themselves without outside aid.

Some of the projects benefited the community as a whole. Salquil had great success with its truck and bus line. Salquil bought two busses and ran a daily early-morning departure from the town center to the international highway.[1] Funds from the Christian Children's Fund sponsors have also been channeled into the transport program and thereby provided an invaluable service to the whole community. Salquil has now formed a separate company that operates the buses and a heavy-freight truck.

AID PROJECT IMPEDIMENTS

The big successes described above are not the rule however. Although many improvements have been made, the projects' goals were many times not achieved. What are the reasons for their inability to achieve what they set out to do?

Many people did not participate in development projects despite the apparent advantages of doing so. Some declined for reasons related to religion and doctrinal beliefs. Others were deterred from active participation by rumors about the project and its effect on the people. There also seemed to be a cultural resistance to the basic philosophy behind the project system. Though well respected by some, the projects did not have the complete support of the community.

Religious Affiliation and Doctrinal Resistance

Although the sponsors of a particular project might be decidedly Catholic or Protestant, all projects provided their services to people of any faith. Moreover, none of the projects recorded the religious affiliation of the participants. The director of the program usually knew the religion of those in the program, but only because he or she knew the families intimately. Despite this open acceptance regardless of faith, religion played an important role in the founding of projects and continued to play a role in people's participation in them.

One of the most obvious problems came when a Protestant-funded program attempted to enter the community. Despite the inroads made by various Protestant religions, the majority in Ixtahuacán were Catholic. Protestant-supported Visión Mundial was asked to fund a group in Ixtahuacán in 1990. The group consisted of heads of households who were hoping to find additional aid for the children in the community; Visión Mundial accepted the proposal and agreed to sponsor the local group. However, the Catholic Church reacted negatively. One person reported that the priest came to the home and said, "Why don't you look for help in the parish? Visión Mundial will change the people. If you cancel [their sponsorship], I will help you find another program." The Catholic heads of families held a meeting and decided to cancel their affiliation with Visión Mundial. The priest fulfilled his promise and the local group is now associated with a group from Kansas City that is not as overtly Protestant as was Visión Mundial. Although this type of religious furor has not stopped all projects from entering Ixtahuacán, it influences which types of projects will be allowed to work here.

Catholics were not the only ones who opposed projects based on the project's religious orientation. Protestants showed a similar hesitancy to participate with any project that was Catholic in origin. When I asked one Protestant pastor why he did not participate in any of the projects, he said, "They don't share my religion." Although only a few projects were funded from solely Catholic sources, all project leaders and most workers were Catholic. This gave rise to the perception by some Protestants that the projects were in the hands of the Catholics, and, therefore, only Catholics should participate in them.

Yet, there was more to the nature of religious impact than a simple Catholic/Protestant division. I found that all the Protestant pastors and one Charismatic catechist opposed participation in *any* project. Catholic control of projects, however, was not their concern. The most common reason they gave for not participating in the projects was "We don't know the origin of the money." The fear of not knowing the source appears to come from a sense of being compromised by the process of receiving monthly or weekly aid. One pastor went so far as to characterize occasional aid as being "from the heart" but recurrent aid as being "potentially soul-threatening" because one did not know where the aid was coming from. Pastors and members alike feared that one possible source of this unknown aid was the "anti-Christ."[2] One evangelical preacher warned,

> The devil will come offering things and performing healings. If you want anything, the anti-Christ will give it to you. Thessalonians says that the devil, the anti-Christ, will come offering things. The Bible says this person is false, and if anyone believes in him, he will lose his spiritual life.

Another pastor said, "He [the devil] traps people through the aid. In the epistle of St. John it says that in the last days, he will be offering aid. It is better not to get involved to avoid problems." Perhaps there could have been no stronger deterrent to devout Christians than to tell them that they would lose their souls for participating in the projects. From this point of view, it was rational to go without the few extra dollars from the aid projects to avoid being trapped by the anti-Christ.

Several pastors had chosen to preach this position out of their interpretation of the Bible. At least one reported that a general directive to that effect was sent to all pastors in his church, issued by the church's council of experienced pastors in Guatemala City.

Another reason for Protestant resistance to the projects and other forms of aid was based on a scripture from the Old Testament. Many informants cited Genesis 3:19: "By the sweat of thy brow shalt thou eat bread." They used this to imply that people must expect to work for themselves. Conversely, anything that came without work was not of God. One Protestant man, after quoting this verse, said that he would work and fulfill the needs of his own family and not look for anyone to do it for him. He took pride that he had paid his son's schooling costs without receiving any outside aid. This work ethic,

along with other factors previously mentioned, gave Protestants good reason
to avoid participating in the projects.

Generalized Cultural Resistance

The entire community understood and lived by the "sweat of thy brow"
ethos because the Mayas have always valued work generated by sweat. While
Catholics did not interpret this logic as a mandate to avoid aid projects, they
also applied the principle by valuing work over laziness. Non-workers in a
Maya community were likely to be stereotyped as Ladinos. A person thus
labeled could possibly lose his or her integral place in the community.
Watanabe (1992:56) says that "to Maya, Ladinos are by nature arrogant, lazy,
and untrustworthy." He also describes a *cholil*, or highway robber, who
usually got his reputation from his lack of work in the community. Therefore,
by association, being labeled as a non-worker was one step toward being
pushed out of the Maya community and being labeled Ladino or cholil.

The work ethic, characterized by the "sweat of thy brow" also included
a strong distrust of non-Maya outsiders. Because self-reliance within the
community was the goal, any connection that created dependence on outsiders
came under high suspicion. This helps us understand the hesitation that Maya
Protestants had regarding outside aid. Both Catholics and Protestants said
that the anti-Christ would come in human form, but that the person's physical
characteristics would not be known. Thus, any outsider coming in offering money
immediately came under suspicion that he or she might be the anti-Christ.

While the idea of an anti-Christ is post-Columbian, it has many of the
same characteristics ascribed to the Maya "earth lords." Watanabe (1992:74–76)
describes these *witz* (earth lords) as beings with Ladino-like features and
clothing who "intercede in human affairs only when it suits them, usually to
enslave souls or to make Mephistophelian pacts with greedy or ambitious
souls." Compare this description to those listed earlier regarding the anti-
Christ, who is also predisposed toward giving away material wealth to trap
the souls of those who are foolish enough to involve themselves. Whether
it is the traditionalist witz or the Evangelical anti-Christ, the message is the
same: do not get involved with outside, unknown sources of wealth because
unearned wealth corrupts a person.

Part of this fear of outsiders has been linked to past periods of military
violence in the country. One public official told of rumors that people were
killed for receiving aid from development projects during the 1980s.[3] The

people considered those rumors as a lesson: do not accept aid or the military
may kill you. Others openly speculated that these projects were connected
with the U.S. military and government and with their plans for Guatemala.
Some of the project workers themselves feared the aid might have hidden
ties to U.S. policy. One worker asked if the U.S. sponsor program was really
private or if it represented some agreement between the president of the
United States and the president of Guatemala.

Another core part of the "sweat of thy brow" concept was the personal
work ethic. Although it was important to help each other out in farming the
milpa, the basic belief was that each man must sustain himself and his family
in his own agricultural plot by his own work. One older man, referring to
anyone who was without enough corn to feed his family, said, "It's his own
fault if he does not have corn, because he does not work." Anyone who
received aid was open to criticism because great importance was placed on
work and independence. One pastor said, "Some participate because they are
needy, but others because they are greedy." Most people considered themselves just as needy as the next family. Given the pervasive sense of *"envidia"*
(envy), they accused those who participated of being greedy.

Other Obstacles

One of the biggest obstacles to the success of aid projects was a general
lack of funds. The goals of a project may have matched the needs of the community, but many projects lacked money. Examples included the construction
of a road linking the southern hamlets to Santa Catarina Ixtahuacán, and the
construction of health clinics in rural hamlets. Unfortunately, government
funding was limited and often directed to activities other than what the community viewed as necessary. The only other option for the projects was to
obtain private sponsors with the funds and vision to complete large projects.
In most cases this meant that an international non-governmental source had
to be found.

Sometimes projects failed because their goals did not match the community's needs. For example, Salquil built two large, modern silos west of
town to create a communal grain storage warehouse that would buy and sell
maize at a stable price throughout the year. However, the people decided to
sell their grain outside of the community, and consequently the grain silos
remained empty. Not only were the silos not being used, but the town was
still forced to rely on outside sources of corn during the periods of scarcity
that land-short milpa farming entailed.

Part of the disjunction between goal and need arose because many of the projects were now being run by career workers who had lost contact with their original parent groups. This disconnection between project goals and people's needs will only get worse if the projects require more administration and fail to take active measures to discern the wants and needs of those they serve.

Finally, people distrusted those who worked for the projects, and thus undermined the accomplishment of their goals. The most commonly held belief was that the workers were getting rich from their involvement in the projects. One pastor said, "We have seen the money get to Salquil. The workers do not do what is right. They use the money for themselves. Many have built two-story houses. They steal the money that should go to the children." Another man suggested that the projects manipulated people and that they even threatened to discontinue sponsorship if the family did not participate in the correct political group. Regardless of the validity of these accusations, they reflect the community's distrust of those who staffed the projects. This lack of confidence was reflected in the little time and effort many people gave to the projects.

CONCLUSION

Santa Catarina's isolation contributed to its underdeveloped status. Yet many development projects were working there. New groups were forming because of the apparent inability of the previous projects to meet communal and family needs. The result was an unorganized attempt to meet almost limitless needs with limited resources. The projects kept some families at a moderate standard of living. However, they had yet to make anything more than small inroads in the overall needy situation of the community. The projects were more like an aspirin to lower a fever than a penicillin shot to cure the infection.

The people felt a pervasive sense of their impoverishment and responded by creating self-aid associations and by connecting with outside aid sources. Several projects have been highly successful and helpful. Because many of the projects were locally organized, project goals tended to match community members' interests. The receipt of outside funding had debilitating implications because local culture strongly encouraged independence. Its self-help work ethic, supported by Catholic and Protestant interpretations of the Bible and by Maya mythology, and further supported by many centuries of Ladino exploitation, justified a wariness of outside money and connection.

However, these villagers had insufficient funds to self-finance their own projects. Thus, the funds came either from the government, which was inaccessible and culturally prejudiced, or from private sources—which meant, for the most part, religious groups. Although the religiously funded projects accepted all participants regardless of their religion, community residents, encouraged by their clergy, held back to avoid feeling entrapped or obligated by another religion. In addition, limited funds, occasions when projects did not match community goals, and distrust and envy of local aid project employees undermined aid efforts.

NOTES

1. The bus route continued to Quezaltenango and Mazatenango on the coastal plain and turned around upon reaching the most remote coastal hamlet of Ixtahuacán, returning to Ixtahuacán center in the afternoon.

2. Andrew Sherman (n.d.) found this concept hindered development efforts in Nahualá, too.

3. In fact, during the eighties, the Guatemalan government extensively targeted Catholic leadership and its organization and development project leadership.

About the author: *My father's job in the U.S. Air Force provided opportunities to see many parts of the world. These experiences sparked my interest in different cultures and languages. I attended Brigham Young University, majoring in sociocultural anthropology and minoring in Spanish. While at BYU, I went with the 1996 field-study group to the highlands of Guatemala. I later spent a year-and-a-half in Paraguay as a missionary for the Church of Jesus Christ of Latter-day Saints. I returned to Guatemala in 1999 and 2000 as the student facilitator of the field school. Upon graduating, I attended Central Michigan University, completing a master's degree in TESOL (Teaching English to Speakers of Other Languages). My husband, James Nuttall, and I now live in San Diego, California, with our son Isaac.*

Reflections on the 1996 field experience: *A significant landmark in my life was the spring of 1996 when I had the opportunity to go with the international field study program of Dr. Hawkins and Dr. Adams to Santa Catarina Ixtahuacán. Conducting anthropological research in Guatemala was an incredible hands-on learning experience. While immersed in the everyday life of the village, I focused my efforts on an ethnography of women and development in the community. By synthesizing the concepts of international development and applied anthropology, I came to see how these Maya women are changing along with the world around them. While working with them, I was personally enriched by their insights, their examples, their plans, and their dreams. They are not women who will sit and watch the world go by; they are caretakers of their homes and catalysts for action within their community. They inspired me to commence a graduate program that I could relate in a significant way to international development. I wanted to be equipped with a skill I could apply cross-culturally. I decided that within the discipline of education I could make a practical and positive impact. My first experience in Guatemala and my subsequent returns to the country as the facilitator of the program have provided me with amazing opportunities for learning and growth. I applied my cross-cultural research knowledge as a graduate student, and I plan to continue to build upon it in my future endeavors.*

CHAPTER 9

"WE ARE VERY CAPABLE"
Women and Development
in Santa Catarina Ixtahuacán

Kristyn Roser Nuttall

"I wake up early, start my fire, wash corn, go to the mill, and return to prepare food for my sons and husband." So begins a typical day for a woman in Santa Catarina Ixtahuacán. It is a day focused on caring for family and preparation of food—tasks that renew themselves each time the sun rises. A woman's hands slap tortillas, wrap tamales in corn leaves, scrub clothes over rocks, lift children into rainbow-colored blankets, weave symbols into textiles, and light fires—a woman's hands work to develop the community. This study focuses on women's roles in Santa Catarina Ixtahuacán and their participation in community development. What do women do? Who is involved? What factors influence women's participation in development?

I became familiar with development organizations in the town, attended meetings and activities, and interviewed Protestant and Catholic women to discover their worldviews and why they participated in community development organizations. Most of the interviews were conducted with the aid of a translator because many of the women spoke only K'iche'. In this paper, I blend my understanding of development and anthropology to explore how Maya women are helping to change their world and how they are, in turn, changed by the world around them. I will demonstrate women's potential in development by discussing the varied roles they play in the home and community. I also highlight some of the many factors—religion, group leadership, *machismo*, and economics—that influence women's participation in community development organizations.

DAILY LIFE AS INFORMAL DEVELOPMENT

The vital roles women played in the community affected their participation in development. Women were the binding threads in the multicolored
fabric of the Maya family. First and foremost, they stood as mothers. They
knew they should educate their children both formally and informally. The
children first spoke the language of their Indian identity in the home; the
sounds of K'iche' surrounded them from birth. Thus the mother's role as an
informal educator in the home was invaluable. The acquisition of Spanish
came later, in public schooling. Many mothers encouraged their children to
receive formal schooling. According to Cristina, "One of the most important
responsibilities of a woman is to tell her children to go to school and study."
Mothers were the first to set the example of what it meant to be a good member
of the community—to show respect for the community elders and maintain
values of honesty, generosity, integrity, and, especially, hard work. Moreover,
a woman's influence continued and expanded as she aged and had grandchildren. The grown children took care of both the grandmother and grandfather,
showed them respect, and continued to seek their guidance.

Women commonly had seven to eleven children and sometimes more.
Birth control was not an option for many because of religious prohibitions;
as a result, most women had children throughout the span of their child-
bearing years. However, due to lack of access to adequate health care facilities
and other problems, including malnutrition, women often lost one or more
children. Such experiences were harsh; but, if they were to survive, the
mothers had to be strong in the face of such hardships.

Notwithstanding the loss of children, families were comparatively large,
and the influence of a woman was great as she raised her own surviving
children and watched over those of her friends and relatives. The demands
of motherhood created a great strain on the mother both mentally and physically. Mothers strove to meet the nutritional and emotional needs of each
child, and child care became almost a lifetime career. Yet the mothers were
not with their children every hour of the day. Older siblings and cousins light-
ened the load by watching over the littlest ones. Mothers took turns looking
after each other's children in a type of neighborhood daycare network in
which children roamed in groups from household to household. Women thus
created a significant support system with other women.

Preparing meals and doing general housework consumed much of their
time. Women arose early every morning and took the corn to the mill to be
ground so there would be enough dough to make sufficient tortillas and

tamales for the family. After bringing the dough back from the mill, the women ground it again with their *piedra de moler*[1] to ensure that the dough was not grainy and coarse. They gathered with their daughters around the stove (which usually consisted of a wood-fueled fire on a raised brick hearth, covered by a sheet of metal) to perform the daily ritual of making tortillas. The little girls learned by watching their mother and sisters, beginning as soon as their hands were coordinated enough to shape the dough.

In addition to being homemakers, some women also served as teachers, others as *comadronas* (midwives), and still others as *curanderas* (healers)—all highly respected roles in the community. Most midwives and healers received a spiritual call to these duties and subsequently underwent special training, both as apprentices to practicing midwives and as trainees in nationally sponsored public health courses. Midwives not only aided in the birthing of children, but also gave constant care to women throughout their pregnancies. They visited the women, advised them, cleansed them in the *temascal*,[2] and massaged the woman's stomach if the fetus needed to be rotated into the proper birthing position. As healers and midwives, they performed various curing rituals, drawing upon their medical, religious, and herbal knowledge, passing their knowledge on through the generations as the midwives and healers continually trained other women.[3]

Women also raised the livestock, such as cattle, chicken, and pigs, feeding the animals every day and watching over them. The men helped care for the animals, but the women usually did this because they considered themselves best qualified. Many women commented that they thought the men would probably forget to feed the livestock. Men spent most of their time working in the cornfields; the women cared for the entire household—including the animals.

Weaving was another important role of K'iche' women. They engaged in backstrap weaving, an art form that was a legacy of their ancestors. Hours evaporated as they counted out threads in the traditional vigesimal system and shuttled different colors through their looms to create designs of eagles, flowers, serpents, monkeys, chickens, squirrels, and various geometric designs. Most often, they created huipiles (the traditional blouse), fajas (belts), and pañuelos (multipurpose woven squares used for head-coverings, baby wraps, shawls, and cargo carriers). Women wove to clothe the female members of their families.[4] Some women sold their weavings at the market to help the financial situation of their families.

They often marketed produce and other commodities. Ixtahuacán celebrated market day on Thursdays and Sundays; people from the town and from surrounding hamlets descended into the town center. However, the market was comparatively small in relation to those of neighboring towns, such as Nahualá's Sunday market, and women often traveled to other markets if they wished to sell their goods.

In addition to serving as vendors at markets, women did most of the buying of necessities for their families. The male was considered head of the household, and his income was generally spent on corn and firewood. Although female earnings were usually a secondary or tertiary source of household income, many rural families depended on the female-generated income to buy food, a pattern also documented by Ehlers (1990:43).

Women seemed to be more aware of the family needs than their husbands. According to one woman, "When it is time to clean out the cornfields, I myself have to tell my husband it is time to clean them. I must also remind him when we run out of food." To prepare the meals and clothe the family, the woman must have some control of the family finances and must carefully budget the household expenses. Thus, the wife's role overlapped with that of her husband in making sure her family's temporal needs were satisfied.

Women's Formal Organizations and Efforts

Because women were the examples, the teachers, and the binding threads of the family, they played an important part as catalysts for change. Women seemed to be more active than men in development projects because, as care-takers of the home, they were more aware of the family's needs. Increasing numbers of women were becoming involved with development groups for the benefit of their families.

Women worldwide stand as the major providers of food for millions of families, contributing more than 50 percent of the total food production and about 25 percent of the total industrial work force in the developing world (Roy et al. 1996:vii). Many analysts recognize that women are significant agents of change. Recent projects show that sustainable economic development of the world community requires significant improvement in the socioeconomic status of women. Women throughout Latin America participate in neighborhood associations, mothers' clubs, and communal kitchens. Such activities involve women simultaneously in community and family development (Jelin 1990:95).

In Ixtahuacán, formally organized women's development groups offered cooking classes, nutritional lectures, literacy classes, and workshops in such skills as gardening, sewing, and child care. In addition, they provided economic aid and contributed foodstuffs to the most needy families. Josefina, the coordinator of Familia a Familia,[5] commented that female participation far outnumbered males:

> In the short time I have worked with the women, I have seen that they are very capable. The woman is very qualified to take part in development. Her first priority is the role she plays in the development of the family, and her second priority is the development of the community as a whole, because the indigenous communities are very community oriented. As women, *somos muy capaces*—we are very capable. The focus of a woman is more broad and all-encompassing. She thinks more about her family and has greater responsibility. We have 95 percent participation by the women, but only 40 percent participation by the men. The woman has more participation, but perhaps this is because the women are more able to. The men can not afford to lose time working because their salary is very minimal as it is, only about twelve quetzales a day [two American dollars].

As Josefina explained, Maya women had an important function in development activities because of their diverse capacities. Nevertheless, men could not be faulted for their lack of involvement because of their responsibility to work and provide for their family. Their wages were meager and no income could be sacrificed.

Women often had more time and incentive to become involved in development groups. Moreover, they could channel what they learned and the benefits they received to the direct aid of their families. Manuela commented, "I am learning many new things: for example, how to make baskets. I plan to teach these skills to my children. I am also learning about nutrition and new foods that I can cook for my family." Pascuala continued this sentiment: "I decided to attend a group because I wanted to learn new things to improve the situation of my family." In addition to workshops on marketable skills such as sewing and embroidering, women also attended literacy classes. In the last official census report, 54 percent of the people were illiterate. Most of these were women because they had not had the same opportunities to study as men. However, that was beginning to change. Twice a week, about thirty women crowded into a small schoolroom near the central plaza to attend literacy classes. By educating themselves, they knew they could better educate their children.

However, their time was limited. These were very busy women. As Rosa said:

> The woman is always caring for the household, weaving, washing, and cooking. She must always carefully plan her day. For example, if she wants to participate in a development group, she must think, well, "Tomorrow I'm going to get my washing done in the morning so that I'll have time to go to the meeting." Such is the life of a woman, very busy. Only at night do we have time to relax. But even in the nighttime there are visits to be made and visitors who come.

Many elements influenced whether or not these women participated in various development organizations. The available time and desire to learn were factors, but a more profound influence was religion.

RELIGIOUS INFLUENCE

Santa Catarina has undergone a great religious upheaval in recent years. Although it was once completely Catholic, many people—a third or more—in the town center now participated in various Protestant or Evangelical religions. The arrival of these religions required different ways of thinking, acting, and working and different ways of relating to the community. According to Annis (1987:84), "There is a Protestant ethic, and the draw of the new creed at the village level is closely related to the fact that it encourages personal rather than collective uses of wealth." Thus, the Protestant religions might be expected to move their congregations away from community integration, resulting in decreased involvement in development organizations within the community.

Protestant women did indeed participate in development organizations less frequently than Catholic women. One Protestant woman commented, "The majority of women involved in development groups are Catholic because they like to participate, and they have more liberty because the majority of the groups and institutions are Catholic based." Most of the development groups in the town had a Catholic origin. Familia a Familia, for example, was a privately funded development organization, but it originated with the help of the town's Catholic priest. Several groups, such as DIGESA,[6] had no religious affiliation, yet, this group still was overwhelmingly Catholic in membership. Most projects were not funded solely from Catholic sources, but the project leaders and workers were Catholic. Thus, many Protestants perceived development projects as having an inherent Catholic religious affiliation, even though most projects remained open to people of any faith.

In addition, many Protestant pastors claimed that it was a sin to participate in such groups. I found among women the same belief in "sweat of the brow" logic and distrust of outside money as Checketts (ch 8., this volume) found for men. Protestant women, more than Catholic women, repeatedly emphasized that they were forbidden to receive *cosas regaladas* (handouts). Thus, Catholics had more liberty to participate.

Not only did the institutions and groups tend to have a Catholic identity, but project participation correlated with the Catholic emphasis on seeking to improve the present world. In contrast, the Protestants seemed to be going to the opposing extreme by focusing on the spiritual world to come. Many Protestants felt that the second coming of Christ was near and therefore, there was no point in focusing on the temporal needs met by development. Julia suggested, "We, as Protestants, have to nurture carefully our spiritual life because we don't know what is going to happen in these last days, and the second coming of Christ is approaching." As an alternative to participating in women's development groups within the community, Evangelical women involved themselves in prayer groups. While many Catholics found sisterhood, support, and companionship in the development organizations, Protestants satisfied this need by attending their church's prayer groups.

Yet the equation was not so simple. It would be easy to say that the Protestant women did not attend development groups because their religion forbade it or they just did not care to; but there was more behind their hesitation. One Evangelical convert told me her daughters had been attending a Catholic development program through the parish clinic. However, one morning a Catholic catechist reproved her daughters for coming to receive medicine and vitamins, saying, "You no longer have the right to come here because you have your own separate religion." The woman then went to the clinic and told the man in charge to remove the names of her daughters and grandchildren from the receiving list. Other Protestant women admitted that they would like to participate in development organizations but did not want to be the subject of Catholic women's criticism or gossip. Juana stated,

"Now we do not go to receive aid because we do not want the other women to criticize us. The Catholics are the ones who participate in the groups. There are still a few Protestants but not more."

Religious affiliation thus significantly influenced a woman's decision to participate. Although exceptions existed among both groups, the Catholic acceptance and promotion of development projects contrasted with the general hesitation of Protestants to participate.

Group Leadership

Group leadership also influenced whether women participated in development programs. The more a woman culturally identified with the leader of the group, the more likely she was to participate. The social dynamics of leadership are visible in the two *Amas de Casa* (homemakers) groups sponsored by DIGESA. The women in one group called themselves Las Flores. This group was organized in October 1994 by an Indian woman, Silvia, who worked as a paid DIGESA representative. The other group, Las Catalinas, was organized in November 1994 by Mónica, a Ladina educator from Quezaltenango, also employed by DIGESA.

According to Silvia, founder of the first group, Las Amas de Casa was for the "woman who works in the home, caring for her children." This organization provided cooking lessons, craft demonstrations, educational discussions, and various vocational skills. Silvia saw nutrition as the main focus of Las Amas de Casa because, she said, most of the women lacked knowledge of food preparation and cooking. In contrast, Mónica said that the central objective of this organization was for women to "come to learn how to create their own micro-enterprises." None of the women in Mónica's group, however, emphasized micro-enterprise as a central objective of the group. On the contrary, most of these women said that they planned to focus on incorporating their new skills into their homes and families and saw marketing as secondary. Thus, Monica's objectives did not seem to mirror those of the Indian women with whom she worked.

Moreover, the meetings of these two groups were conducted very differently. I give an account of each from my field notes:

> I glance around the room looking for Silvia and notice her sitting on the floor talking with two other women. Her position as leader is not obvious. Silvia steps forward quietly and gives a nutrition talk while

making *mox*.[7] She clearly announces what she is doing in K'iche' as the women attentively look on. She adds twelve spoonfuls of milk powder to the boiling water. Silvia makes a joke about how she was weaving the other afternoon. She explains that she told her son to get some firewood, and he said he did not want to, so she told him that in that case he could do the weaving and she would get the firewood. He quickly changed his mind. The women all laugh, sharing the humor of underlying cultural roles that everyone understands. Silvia acts like one of them. She is their leader, but she performs her role in such a way that there is no uncomfortable distance between her and the group. In fact, everyone stands huddled together.

The meetings held by Mónica had a different atmosphere:

Everyone assembles in the DIGESA office across from the central plaza next to the schoolrooms. Mónica comes in and commands attention with her penetrating presence. Her white sweater and blue jeans create a distinct contrast with the colorful traditional huipiles and long skirts of the other women. She walks to the front of the room, and the first thing she says (all in Spanish) is, "Have you figured out what your project is yet?" Mónica does not speak K'iche', and I immediately perceive that this is a barrier between her and the other women. Although a good number of the women can understand and speak Spanish, many of them do not. As a result, everything that Mónica says must be translated into K'iche'. The women murmur among each other in K'iche'. Finally, Timotea speaks up and says, "communal bank." Mónica asks if everyone is sure this is what they want to do. More murmuring—the women discuss the project. Mónica becomes frustrated with the murmuring in K'iche' and launches into a description of what the communal bank will entail.

The cultural differences and the manner in which these women conducted their meetings was undoubtedly an influential factor in the overall participation of the women of Ixtahuacán in development. In the second year that the groups were in existence, the organization cut the local representatives—people like Silvia—from the payroll. Mónica offered to take over Silvia's group, but the women refused her. According to Silvia,

Well, it is true that when she arrives at her meetings, the first thing
she does is chastise the women. Because the women were aware of
her impatient nature, they would not receive her. So they asked me
to do them the favor of continuing to lead and support the group
even without a salary. In the first place, I thought, "I am going to
continue because this is my community, my people, and I cannot
desert them." In the second place, many of my relatives are in the
group, and if I stop working with the group, then who knows what
will happen to the money we are saving in the bank? It is for these
reasons that I continued working with the women's group.

When I asked Mónica why she was involved with these women's development groups, she answered simply, "because it is my job." Undoubtedly,
these women differed in their motives to serve as leaders. Silvia felt a loyalty
to her community and people, while Mónica felt more of a commitment to
a line of work. The participating women were very aware of this difference.

Trust was another area where the two leaders differed greatly. Silvia
expressed trust and dependency on the other women in the group to help
her accomplish her goals. Because of her experience and leadership skills,
the other women also trusted her, and she had a deep dedication and respect
for them. When asked why the two groups did not work together more,
Tomasa replied, "Perhaps it is because of envy (envidia)."

In fact, women from both groups commented on how jealousy existed
between the groups because the women in Mónica's group could see how
well organized and cohesive Silvia's group was in comparison to their own.
Mónica did not nurture the ideal of trusting the group. Rather, she seemed
to have a condescending attitude. When questioned on what she thought
would be some of the difficulties of starting a communal bank with the
group, she replied, "The women will probably steal the money or take it and
give it away to their friends and relatives."

The two leadership styles had obvious differences, and their effective-
ness was both a reflection of the leader's personality and of the ethnic group
to which she belonged. Silvia was affable; she radiated a charisma that drew
the other women to seek her guidance. More importantly, Silvia was a K'iche'
woman of Ixtahuacán, making her a cultural insider, one who understood the
needs of the women. She spoke their language and could communicate in a
means far beyond grammar and vocabulary. She expressed an accepted
sense of humor and a familiar way of doing things with which all the
participants could identify. This was manifest in the joke she told about her

son, in the way she sat among the women, and the way they gave her their undivided attention.

On the other hand, Mónica was a Ladina, making her a cultural outsider not only in the way she dressed, but also in how she carried herself as a leader. She was direct, knowledgeable, and capable—but also irritable, intolerant, and always in a hurry. I was told that Mónica had been refused as a leader by women in surrounding hamlets and by the other women's DIGESA group in the town. Was this because she was a Ladina or because her personality was so difficult? Several women replied, "It is because of her angry nature and because she is a Ladina, both." Apparently her sour demeanor and her ethnic standing as a Ladina combined to make her leadership unwelcome, and most of the women were unwilling to tolerate it. Because she was Ladina, many of the women felt that she could not truly relate to their situation.

Problems always surfaced because of Mónica's condescension and her inability to directly communicate with the women. When I discussed the groups with the DIGESA regional representative, he explained that miscommunication was the major problem with Mónica's groups. Thus, the leadership of the development groups had a significant impact on women's participation. I observed that for development groups to achieve success, a key factor was incorporating local leadership in order to provide a clear line of communication and participation.

MACHISMO

Machismo was another factor that could influence women's participation. In the Latin American tradition, the patriarchal family constitutes the basic unit around which daily life revolves. The relationships between genders and generations are measured on a hierarchical scale, which involves a definite division of labor (Jelin 1990:7). Women assume the domestic tasks of the home related to the maintenance of the family. Men are supposed to be the breadwinners and are responsible for the areas relating to the public sphere of social and political life.

As one Ixtahuaquense put it, a common definition of machismo was "when the man believes that he is superior to the woman, and he has control over everything in his family—the children and everything else. The wife is then under his command." Women had to seek permission from their husbands before becoming involved in any sort of group. According to the coordinator of Familia a Familia, "The women always say, 'I have to go talk with my husband to see if he will give me permission.' In this respect, the woman is very dependent on the man." Pascuala elaborated on this point:

> Before deciding to become involved in Familia a Familia, I spoke with my husband so that we could both try to find the money they were asking. Between the two of us we made the decision. I had to go to my husband because I alone could not give the necessary money—only with the help of my husband and with his permission. However, many women do not have the support from their spouse that I have, and this is why they do not participate in development groups.

A member of Las Amas de Casa agreed: "The majority of the men dominate over their wives and often refuse them permission to participate in community groups." Some men did not want the women to go and gossip. According to Catarina, "Because of this, husbands admonish their wives to be careful and refrain from speaking badly of other persons because if one day the husband happens to hear something dishonorable that the wife has done or talked about, he will hit her." Women also mentioned that, though married, many men had lovers, and they feared that if they gave their wives too much freedom, the women would do the same. Thus, Rosa noted that for women to be involved as group leaders, they could not have jealous husbands.

Along those same lines, one woman gave an example of a more rigid machismo in years past: "My grandfather, when he was living, was the focus of respect in our home. He said that all of his clothing had a special place and that it was a bad thing to mix the clothing of a man and a woman together." Furthermore, in 1996, it was still customary for many women to kneel on mats on the floor in the kitchen, while the men sat at a table. At celebrations, only men sat at the tables, and they were served first.

When asked if the women had a voice in their community, Sebastiana replied,

> Almost none, because the husbands don't allow their wives to participate. In spite of this, though, there are women who do have a space in the city government. In whatever place, in whatever activity in the community, women will at times participate; but, in these cases, others will criticize them. Either they do not like the women or think ill of them because they receive a salary. There is a lot of

jealousy driving these feelings. But there are women who do not care, and thus they participate even though there are those who will criticize them. Yet, the majority of the women are in the home. Yes, it's true that machismo is something that exists, and it violates the rights of women. But now the situation is not as serious as it was before.

Thus, the community activities of women have traditionally been significantly impeded by encultured gender constraints and by a cultural disposition toward male control and distrust of women.

Where does this idea of machismo come from? One Protestant woman explained:

That is how it is written in the Bible. Because of this, the man feels superior to the woman. And they also say that the woman should not be permitted to go out anywhere. Yes, machismo exists here because men do not give permission for the woman to participate in [development] groups. The men are afraid that the women are going to go out and do bad things, and the women are likewise afraid that the men will do bad things when they go out.

While some gave biblical reasons, others commented that machismo was the result of misunderstandings between the couple. Machismo, of course, long predates Protestant influence and biblical justification in these communities. All things considered, many women were limited in their participation by husbands who felt threatened, were jealous, or felt the need to exercise overt domination in the home. However, this trend of domination was undergoing dramatic change as women increasingly completed more education. As one woman stated, "The man did not put value on the rights of a woman because neither of them had the opportunity to study."

In the past, when teachers came to the houses to enroll the children, parents hid their little girls and did not give them permission to go to school. This rarely happens now. Now that more women are able to attend school, they are also able to learn Spanish. Most women over thirty struggled with Spanish because they never really had the opportunity to learn it. They became even more dependent on their husbands for travel, doctor visits, and communicating with anyone who did not speak K'iche'. Dominga remarked, "It is necessary in a woman's life to learn Spanish to communicate with other people that don't speak her language. For example, I can't speak Spanish, only K'iche'; even though I want to speak it, I can't. Because of this, I tell my children to make sure their daughters have the opportunity to go to school." Such statements indicate that the situation was changing. Josefina elaborated,

> At least now there are groups that are making the men aware that women have the same rights and privileges as men and should be able to participate in whatever type of meeting. So, admittedly, the men are now more than ever permitting their wives to participate in community groups. They realize that the women are not wasting time when they take time to participate in development groups because they are learning valuable ways to help their families. However, as far as allowing them to speak in public and declare their thoughts, men are still not willing to permit women to do this. I don't know why.

It must be noted that even though machismo is the prevailing concept, there were many exceptions indicating the trend was beginning to reverse. For example, at a birthday party for one of the children in the neighborhood, the father worked in partnership with his wife and daughters. The women cooked the food; the father served everyone, cleared the dishes, and helped clean up afterwards. Moreover, another woman emphasized that her husband did not fit the machismo stereotype because he helped her prepare meals and gave their children religious training.

Other women mentioned that the situation seemed to be improving for their daughters' generation. Dominga remarked that she was setting a good example for her daughter so that her daughter would not suffer as she suffered. "My daughter is blessed with an understanding husband who helps her take care of the children and do the domestic chores." Rosa proudly reported her husband's support, saying, "My husband has always given me permission to participate for the fifteen years that I have been seeking opportunities to learn [from] whatever course or group is available." Thus, the attitude of husbands was a significant factor in women's ability to participate in community development. However, in the day-to-day game of survival, poverty motivated several women to reap the benefits of development groups. In the face of economic despair, even the most dominating husbands relented and allowed their wives to participate.

Economics

The average household income in Santa Catarina Ixtahuacán was about two thousand quetzales per year. As noted, infant mortality remained high. Many resided in conditions that were considered impoverished even by Guatemalan standards, with dirt or cement floors, tin roofs, cardboard ceilings, and cramped facilities. Moreover, a few in town and many in the hamlets lacked sewage systems, running water, and electricity. The most pressing concern, though, seemed to be having enough food to feed one's family and enough money to clothe them. Such needs made religion, machismo, and group leadership secondary concerns.

Some Protestant women, who were admonished not to receive "handouts," found themselves unable to turn down the relief that some development organizations offered. According to a Protestant who was one of the few of her faith participating in a development organization, "It is necessary for [development] groups to be here because there are very needy people— people in extreme poverty, without economic means." A Catholic woman also illustrated the need for these groups: "[Development] projects are very important because it is through these that many people are improving the lives of their families. For example, the projects that give food to the children, such as Pan de Vida, help the families whose children do not have food to eat in the morning to be able to have healthy lunches during the week."

Groups such as Familia a Familia offered needy families the opportunity to exchange participation and service for the benefits they received. After a new family was accepted, they talked with the director of the program to plan how they could best use the twenty to thirty dollars a month they would receive. The family could decide to build a house or participate in a sewing class, according to their needs. Instead of being given the money directly, they were given the materials or had their classes paid for them. Moreover, because the necessary materials in Familia a Familia were paid for, participation at group meetings was high. The program director pointed out that all the women attended the funded classes and projects and came at the designated hour. No one was missing unless they were sick. A member of this organization commented, "It is good that the program provides the necessary materials to the family because it is very difficult for the family to buy their own materials." By providing funding for classes and project materials, Familia a Familia met basic needs and facilitated active participation by women.

Women were also motivated to participate in other groups because of available aid. Pascuala explained the economic incentives behind her participation in Pan de Vida and DIGESA:

> I saw the need of my family before I participated in the project Pan de Vida. I had young children at the time, and because my baby needed food, I joined and participated in the project because they gave food to those with young children. However, when my children got older, Pan de Vida would no longer accept us. I knew I had to find help, though, because we did not have sufficient money to buy essential things like oil. Because of this I joined the Las Amas de Casa through DIGESA.

The women in the DIGESA groups were enrolled in a two-year program. Foodstuffs were distributed to them monthly. They received forty-four pounds of corn, seven pounds of fish, six pounds of beans, twenty-two pounds of flour, and two bottles of cooking oil. A participant explained the importance of this food distribution to her family.

> We participate because of our needs, the needs that we have in the family. For example, we lack resources—economic resources—and in DIGESA they give us corn. And of course you know that we eat corn all day long. If we want to be able to sufficiently feed our families, we turn to these groups.

The women were required to contribute twenty quetzales every month to remain in good standing. Five quetzales were allocated to DIGESA to pay for the food. Fifteen quetzales were deposited in the local women's group bank account, to be used by the group in a future project. The basic theory behind this was *capacitación a través de los alimentos* (empowerment through food). The money that the women would otherwise have spent on food they now invested.

The women of Ixtahuacán recognized the economic needs of their families and sought to attain important resources through various development groups such as Familia a Familia, Pan de Vida, and DIGESA. Their poverty motivated them to participate and gain access to the proffered aid.

Conclusion

The women of Ixtahuacán provided a variety of answers in response to the question of what development meant to them:

> For me, development means the betterment of the town. And it is good, but something that needs much strength on the part of the people if the town is going to improve.—Dominga

> Development only happens by sharing knowledge; one does not know everything and must begin by learning from others.—Cristina

> Through our organizations, we as women learn new things and create development in the community. I plan to teach others what I have learned.—Pascuala

> The most important thing to know before starting a development group is the needs of the people.—Tomasa

> In order to have good development in the community, we should communicate and participate.—Silvia

As indicated by their responses, the women of Santa Catarina Ixtahuacán had a penetrating vision of what communal development entailed. They emphasized that to begin a project one must understand the needs of the people and their cultural boundaries. They recognized key elements such as communication, participation, learning, cooperation, and sharing. Moreover, they highlighted a prime determinant of sustainable development: the desire to teach what they learned to others.

The significant roles of women in the families and community of Ixtahuacán qualified them to be effective initiators in the field of development. Among other activities, they served as mothers, teachers, healers, midwives, and merchants. They were in influential positions and had the potential to affect the lives of many. While the men were often bound to their daily occupations, primarily working in the fields, the women had more opportunity to become involved with various development organizations in the community. Furthermore, women's participation was more beneficial to the family because whatever they learned or received was almost always immediately invested into the home.

However, women's participation in development was affected by many factors such as religion, group leadership, machismo, and economics. Religious affiliation influenced and sometimes dictated whether a person felt comfortable being involved in one of the town's development groups. Catholics had more liberty to participate, while many Protestants felt inhibited or were opposed outright to the ideas associated with development organizations. Group leadership stood as another significant issue. The women were far less likely to be involved in a development organization led by someone who did not speak their language or understand their way of life. It seemed that those best qualified to develop a community were the people themselves—local leaders who were aware of the needs, cultural background, and capabilities of their peers. Machismo was another reality that could not be ignored. In Ixtahuacán's patriarchal society, some men saw women's participation in groups as a threat to their power. However, due to increasing levels of education, more husbands were supporting their wives in development activities. Nevertheless, economic need was all-pervading. Many merely survived day-to-day within the poverty cycle and could not afford to reject the financial benefits offered by development organizations. Any hesitation that might be caused by religion, group leadership, or machismo melted in the face of dire financial need.

At first glance, the women of Santa Catarina Ixtahuacán appeared to live a simple life in seclusion from the outside world. They still engaged in traditional activities such as weaving and washing their clothes on rocks. However, the local reality of huge Orange Crush advertisements painted on house walls, little boys wearing Power Rangers T-shirts, and television programs portraying *Dallas* in Spanish illustrated another side to the story. These women did not live in a bubble.

Though isolated, they lived as a part of the modern world; they were not immune to the influences of the global market, technological advancement, and social change. All of the issues discussed here formed an extremely complex equation, resulting in the decision of women to participate or not in community development groups. The women had forces pulling them in multiple ways as they stood at these transitional crossroads. Whatever decisions they made would have an undeniable impact on their children and on the future of the town itself. These were not women who would stand back and let the world go by. They were active catalysts for change, especially in the area of development. They strove to do all in their power to improve their home situation through what they learned and their earning potential, because they were, indeed, *"muy capaces"*—very capable.

NOTES

1. *Piedra de moler*: a large, flat stone (metate) where corn and corn dough are ground with a hand-held stone (mano).

2. *Temascal*: a small sweat hut used by Maya for bathing, personal cleansing, and curing, known locally as a tuuj.

3. For additional material on midwives and birthing, see K. Wilson (n.d.).

4. See Semus, ch. 5, this volume.

5. Familia a Familia: literally, Family to Family, or Adopt-a-Family. See Checketts, ch. 8, this volume.

6. DIGESA: Dirección General de Servicios Agrícolas.

7. *mox*: a hot oatmeal gruel.

REFLECTIONS ON THE ETHNOGRAPHY OF NAHUALÁ AND SANTA CATARINA IXTAHUACÁN

Walter Randolph Adams and John P. Hawkins

An important focus of this volume has been the professionalization of undergraduate students through their participation in a field school and the resultant publication of their research. This being the case, we believe it incumbent to keep the focus of this chapter on two themes: how the field school affected their research and how their research presents a corpus of ethnographic information consistent with the findings of their peers and those of other, more senior investigators.

IMPACT OF THE FIELD SCHOOL

The students who contributed papers to this volume were undergraduate participants in a field school. The brief student autobiographies at the beginning of each chapter and an occasional reference in a few of the papers reveal the profound effect this experience had on their lives. The three-month duration of the field school provided them the opportunity to become at least temporary members of the community, demonstrated by their inclusion in several intimate aspects of family life such as participating in marriage rituals (Araneda), learning how to weave (Semus)—an activity which caused her to be "missed" when she left—assisting school officials in helping a victim of rape (Thompson and Hanamaikai), and engaging sensitively with the practitioners of the disparaged traditional Maya religion (Morgan). The insights these students received, and reported, in these pages would not have been possible had they not been accepted by the communities and their inhabitants.

These and other activities were made possible by the standard anthropological field method known as participant observation. While none of the chapters specifically documents that the students had learned this or other field methods in our field school classroom setting, the Morgan chapter and the Hanamaikai and Thompson chapter refer to other methods described in one of the books (Bernard 1995) they were required to use in the methods course. The use of these additional methods either helped clarify phenomena observed or provided the students with insights that would not have been possible otherwise. In short, a methods course should be an integral component of a field school even if students have had such a course before. Moreover, faculty need to require that students use diverse field methods. We observed that, of the students who had not taken a pre-field methods course, only one used any field method other than participant observation and interviewing.

Another observation that we should offer pertains to field notes. While all students were informed about the importance of field notes—both in class lectures and in their reading of Bernard (1995)—the quality ranged from very detailed and rich ethnographic information to cursory notes with little detail. The papers in this volume were written by students who produced among the richest notes. Those students whose field notes were weaker in quality also produced papers that were weaker in quality and scope and not suitable for publication. It is extremely important to encourage students to write detailed notes as they conduct their research.

We also can report that the length of the field school was sufficient to make the students aware of their ethnocentrism. While all of the students to date have undergone this transformation (even those who had done missionary work in Guatemala previously), many of the students are aware that the transformation occurred in themselves and refer to this in their prefatory autobiographical statements. In some cases, students' concerns that their views might be construed as ethnocentric appear in the papers themselves (Thompson and Hanamaikai, Hatch). As field directors, we find this transformation one of the most satisfying and exhilarating rewards of directing a field school, and it continues to elate us even ten years later.

The field school has also had an impact on the communities. Perhaps the most obvious is that the presence of the students has been an additional source of wealth—not only due to the purchase of textiles (Semus), but also because the students pay families for their room and board. As a result, many of the families have been able to add rooms, buy better food, or acquire appliances. The increased wealth of these host families, unfortunately, has been a factor contributing to feelings of envy on the part of other families. As a result, community leaders have suggested that we should be more democratic and distribute the students among more families, which we have done.[1]

The communities have benefited by our presence in other ways. During the first year of our project and some subsequent years, our students offered an evening course, teaching English to those who attended. Other students have taught English to their host family members. In addition, an Eagle Scout looking for a culminating project contacted one of the directors, got connected with us, and collected and delivered thirteen large boxes of medical supplies to Nahualá's health center. More recently, we have begun to assist the community to develop a treatment and prevention program for alcohol abuse among its adolescents and young adults. This program also strives to keep these young people from getting involved with youth gangs.

INTEGRATING THEMES

As might be expected when studying a people for whom maize is critical, milpa agriculture is a predominant theme. Morgan writes that milpa is important in order for the K'iche' in Nahualá and Santa Catarina to remain self-sufficient. Self-sufficiency is essential to the survival of a rural group of people who, for the most part, have been ignored by the state. R. N. Adams and Bastos (2003:100) remark that "No Guatemalan government since Arbenz (1951–1954) has seriously confronted the difficult problem of developing the rural sector nor has any government resolved how to deal with the needs and necessary forms of adaptation of a population that remains predominantly rural."

Yet, for the past 125 years, Indians in Guatemala have had to contend with forced labor, usurpation of lands due to an expansion of the Ladino population, and persistent indigenous population pressures and resultant land shortage (R. N. Adams and Bastos 2003:81). These forces have made it necessary for the Mayas to shift from a self-sufficient milpa economy to a market economy. In keeping with observations reported by other scholars, as the milpa becomes insufficient to meet a family's needs (Araneda), they sometimes supplement their farming by working part-time in trades learned through craft training programs provided by religious groups (Checketts) or by becoming paid personnel in these programs (Nuttall).

Recent contact with world churches other than Catholicism constitutes another important change, yet one, except for Morgan, that is under-represented in our collection.[2] Catholicism successfully created a hierarchy that mirrored and operated within community and national government. The new religions, however, broke Catholicism's religious hegemony and provided alternate routes of social contact (Garrard-Burnett 1998) that further undermined the formerly useful fiction of an (albeit relatively) "closed corporate community" (Aguirre Beltrán 1979; Wolf 1957).[3]

While no Guatemalan Indian community was ever fully isolated, Nahualá and Santa Catarina Ixtahuacán have gone through a sea change of increased access to the outside world and consequent diminution of the relative strength and practical application of community orientation (see Morgan). This change is demonstrated by a decline in interest on the part of the youth to participate in traditional positions of authority, such as the cofradía system (Morgan) and the k'amal b'e (Araneda). Conversely, they now manifest interest in becoming involved in the non-governmental organizations proliferating in the communities (Morgan, Checketts), interacting more fully with tourists (Semus), and receiving a better education (Hanamaikai and Thompson).

The students also observed that the rivalry between the Protestant churches and the Roman Catholics have engendered conflict in these communities (Morgan, Checketts, Nuttall). They also report that Protestants are either openly pushed away from using services offered by Catholic organizations (Nuttall) or feel that they might be if they were to participate in these organizations (Checketts). In either case, the result is that people tend to look for services provided by their own church, and the rivalry between the Protestants and Catholics continues to simmer.

These transformations result from forces that also drive the integration of the Mayas into larger political-economic systems. We witness this emerging Mayanness in Nahualá and Santa Catarina. Morgan, Araneda, Nuttall, and Checketts imply this is occurring when they remark that Ixtahuaquenses are increasingly becoming leaders in non-governmental organizations that provide assistance of various sorts, including trying to find resolution to the serious problem of malnutrition in these communities (Morgan, Checketts, Nuttall).

Globalization is inherently implicated in these endeavors, as indicated by Checketts's observation that one of the food programs sent tins of imported Danish meat to the residents. In Nahualá and Santa Catarina, we have seen increasing interest in and participation in NGOs; access to new media including television, Internet, and e-mail; and internal recognition and communication between Nahualenses or Ixtahuaquenses and other indigenous peoples as Mayas rather than as persons of a particular village or town. These mirror the processes reported by Nash (2001) in Chiapas, Mexico, and by Fischer (2001) in Tecpan and Patzicia, Guatemala. In a word, "community" is still a mobilizing ideal in Santa Catarina and Nahualá, but community cohesion has been greatly modified and continues to be eroded by external contact and the rising respect for youth-based external knowledge and power rather than seniority-based and locally focused knowledge and respect. Moreover, new forms of communications abound. Video parlors, televisions, telephones and cell phones; access to movies, newspapers, and radio; as well as the expansion of bus traffic and road access to Quezaltenango, Guatemala City, and points beyond, all have contributed to a proliferation of contacts beyond the community, as exemplified in the chapters by Morgan and Checketts.

Finally, as a result of the economic conditions in Guatemala and processes of increasing access to the world, many families in Nahualá now count heavily on remittances from (mostly male) family members who have successfully journeyed to the United States in search of jobs. Here, Santa Catarina follows more slowly; its first immigrants traveled to the United States as of the year 2000 (to be discussed in a forthcoming volume). The proliferation of two- and three-story structures and pickup trucks, many of the latter sporting glittering letters across the windshield or back window proclaiming the vehicle was a "*regalo de Dios*," provide silent testimony to the importance remittances have had in the communities. All of these processes contribute to the erosion of the community as their focal point of reference.

Concurrently, we witness processes consistent with the "imagined community" (R. N. Adams and Bastos 2003:42–45), linking individuals from these two communities to a much larger group. Women wearing huipiles from other communities and interest in Cosmovisión Maya (Lima Soto 1995) and Mayan resurgence (R. Wilson 1995) provide testimony.

The importance of women in Maya culture—at least in these two communities—emerges in several papers in this volume. The papers present two contrasting pictures. One shows that Indian women are integral to the maintenance of traditional Maya cultural values and depicts forces at work that keep them in positions of subjugation viz-à-viz the men. For example, Thompson and Hanamaikai—as well as Semus—show that women are only thought to be important to serve the needs of men. Several chapters refer to the custom of women sitting on the floor while men and boys sit in chairs, and men and boys eating the better foods. The subordination of women is also observed in schools by Hatch and in the gender bias that puts greater attention on the boys, reported by Hanamaikai and Thompson.

These observations point to the interpretation that formal education may not be important for women, but weaving and performing other domestic functions are critical to family economics (see also Nuttall), especially given the level of poverty found in Nahualá and Santa Catarina. As a result, there is a conflict between whether girls should go to school to receive a formal education or stay at home to help meet the family's needs.[4]

On the other hand, Morgan, Araneda, and Thompson and Hanamaikai note that women expect to be abandoned by their husbands or common-law partners, so parents now want daughters to complete school. Hanamaikai and Thompson's study lends further support to this trend by their finding that 79 percent of girls (as opposed to 83 percent of boys) graduated to the next grade in 1994. This statistic would have been incomprehensible even a decade before. Araneda also remarks that men are becoming increasingly aware that they may not be able to support their families adequately.[5] As a result, they either leave the community in search of work elsewhere (thereby essentially, if not in fact, abandoning the women) or have to accept that their wives become actively involved in the labor market. It is no wonder, then, that women jockey for positions of authority within the textile industry, as Semus reports, or that they seek increasing involvement in non-governmental organizations, as Nuttall discusses. Given these conditions, we clearly appreciate why Nuttall comments that women "were active catalysts for change."

Given the ethic of community, conflict ought not exist, but it does—intensely, in the community and even within a single family (Semus). Indeed, conflict is fostered by the contradictions between an ethic of egalitarian Indian poverty and the reality of a range of new opportunities that differentially brings wealth, contact, power, or respect to various members of the community. Being Indian, conceptually, means being rooted in communities that were set up to facilitate colonial control and extraction of wealth. For all but the *cacique* power brokers, that meant being relatively equal, poor, and powerless vis-à-vis the Spanish system.

The papers at hand, however, show a variety of ways in which individuals distinguish themselves in relative access to wealth or power. Some are resident in the community center and have more access than those from the outlying hamlets (see chapters by Morgan and Semus). Some have better access to roads or markets, either as individuals (Morgan) or as whole communities relative to each other, as is so clearly the case between Nahualá and Santa Catarina (Checketts). Some individuals have better contacts than others through development projects, religious groups, wealthy patrons, or government jobs (Checketts, Nuttall). Some may have succeeded in getting an education—even from institutions of higher education in the United States or elsewhere. In all these ways, individuals have improved differentially their ability to compete for the limited available resources both inside and outside the municipio.

The culturally accepted and repeatedly experienced response to the disjunction between culturally expected equality and actually experienced inequality is envy (envidia) (Checketts, Nuttall, Semus). Envy ought to be manageable by individuals using trustworthy institutions of mediation. Unfortunately, distrust, rather than trust, is the underlying premise within the community, apparently inculcated, at least since the colonial conquest, by the Spanish practice of forcing village caciques to extract the required and relatively fixed taxes of both products and labor from a population in decline (MacLeod 1973). More recently, distrust among villagers was inculcated by the Guatemalan army and its use of the Civil Patrols (Montejo 1999:78). Morgan, Thompson and Hanamaikai, Checketts, Nuttall, and Semus have all remarked on the extent to which distrust is present in these two communities.

While there may have been a time when leaders in the two communities were able to administer decisions with relatively little personal interest, today that is rendered difficult. Council members inevitably are suspected of having "interests," given the emergence of highly differentiated opportunities for connection. The ethic of envy and distrust seems likely to make the indigenous municipio increasingly unmanageable and incoherent even while it promotes a community's linkage with the state.

EXTERNAL CONSISTENCIES

Although many of the papers do not place their fieldwork in the context of phenomena occurring in the larger Guatemalan context, they present information consistent with the descriptions and views of other, more senior, scholars.

Six of these papers derive from the field school conducted the year prior to the signing of the Guatemalan Peace Accords. Two were based on 1996 fieldwork, the year the accords were signed. Because this was a delicate period politically, we instructed the students to refrain from delving deeply into political issues. In the main, the students did as they were told; only two of the papers in this volume make any reference to Guatemala's civil war (Morgan, Nuttall). It is possible that even if students wanted to learn about that bloody period in Guatemala's history, they would have been frustrated in their attempts because, as Morgan states, people did not want to talk openly about the war. This is not just a K'iche' Maya phenomenon, nor does it necessarily reflect an inherent inability of undergraduates to elicit this sort of information. Wilkinson (2002) found it difficult to discuss this topic in the Ladino community of La Reforma, San Marcos, too, and was only able to do so after several years of visiting that community. Our students, by contrast, were limited to a single field season.

The theme of community, long a focus of anthropological research in Guatemala, as demonstrated by the multiple ethnographies written between the 1940s and the 1990s (Annis 1987; LaFarge 1947; Oakes 1951; Reina 1966; Wagley 1941, 1949; Warren 1978; Watanabe 1992; R. Wilson 1995—the list can be much extended), continues to be a vigorous concept among the inhabitants of Nahualá and Santa Catarina Ixtahuacán. Community provides a primary source of identity—epitomized by the distinctiveness of village traje—and this orientation to identity shows up repeatedly in these essays and in the collective experiences of many authors whose works have focused on weaving (Otzoy 1996).

The phrase "community of identity" represents the close articulation of the two concepts. Indeed, in Santa Catarina Ixtahuacán center, community identity may still exceed ethnic identity in emotive power, as was so clearly the case throughout Guatemala in the 1930s (Tax 1937). During the ten years we have been in Santa Catarina Ixtahuacán, the community has mobilized several times: to confront an external lumber company over communal forest thefts (see Checketts), to assemble for a school cleanup (see Hatch), and to deal with the aftermath of a hurricane. Likewise, community seemed to remain the focus of marital selection, for none of the informants of any age questioned by Araneda explicitly mentioned the conscious awareness of movement toward more frequent out-of-community marriages, though we are aware of a few in Santa Catarina and several in Nahualá.

For Nahualá center, by contrast, commercial connection seems to have diminished the ability to mobilize the sense of community that is still there. In Nahualá, individual identity remains tied to the community, but group action on the basis of that identity is difficult to mobilize. The only issue of sufficient importance to mobilize Nahualá, in our experience, has been land and boundaries. Nahualenses have assembled several times against Santa

Catarina Ixtahuacán (Nuttall n.d.) and against Argueta, a community to the east, the episodes resulting in violent conflict. However, we have not seen the entire center of Nahualá mobilize, as Santa Catarina Ixtahuacán has, perhaps because the diversity of individual enterprises and demands overwhelms the residents' ability to focus on community-centered issues.[6]

In Santa Catarina Ixtahuacán and even in Nahualá, adhesion to community remains a profound source of indigenous power. From the colonial era to the present, the potential of an idigenous community to mobilize has constituted a threat that could elicit a favorable response from the external government. Morgan, for example, saw the government back down in the face of a Nahualá hamlet's collective mobilization, though space does not permit our including the episode in this volume. The capacity to mobilize still has power, though it seems that Santa Catarina Ixtahuacán center (prior to 2000), and the Nahualá hamlets exercise this sense of self more than present-day Nahualá center.

Nevertheless, the remaining sense of community and the power it confers are threatened by the dendritic connections that arise from entrance into the world market. The process seems to be today's version of economic modernization. While we are well aware that world markets have been penetrating the Guatemalan highland since before the arrival of the Toltecs, the inhabitants of Nahualá in the last three decades and the inhabitants of Santa Catarina in the last decade have experienced a qualitative change and temporal speed-up in the quantity and process of their world economic access, matters exemplified in Morgan's chapter.

The papers in this collection make clear that Nahualá and Santa Catarina do not exist in a vacuum. They interact with national and international systems. The inhabitants of these communities, like other people throughout Guatemala, are becoming more actively involved and concerned with the social, political, and economic situation of the republic. The papers also make it clear that while structural impediments remain, the Nahualenses and Ixtahuaquenses are tired of being second-class citizens and are actively trying to improve their situation and rectify errors of the past.

One of the ways this is manifested is by an intensified and expanded connection beyond the municipios to national politics (Portillo 1998; Tuyuc 1998). Indeed, the political election of 1999, which put Portillo in office as president and Tuyuc as *diputada*, was the first in which the indigenous population turned out en masse. Our papers do not touch on this significantly, but both Santa Catarina and Nahualá have, à la Brintnall (1979) and Watanabe (1992), arrived at post-gerontological and post-municipal politics, having had municipal activities incorporated into national politics and parties, and having supplanted the collective group of the respected community elders with a variety of options to connect through the politically motivated youth, the young evangélicos, and the young development project technicians. Part of Javier Tzoc's pathos, as expressed in Morgan's paper, derives from this country-wide displacement of the formerly respected and well-positioned community elders.

The two communities under study here show close parallels to other Maya Indian communities with respect to deforestation. Morgan states that Nahualá had virtually deforested the area around that community, while Checketts shows that the Ixtahuaquenses were taking care not to do the same. Severe deforestation has occurred in Guatemala; R. N. Adams and Bastos (2003:111–18) state that the amount of land covered by forests declined by 40.33 percent between 1977 and 1992. They also report that, with the exception of Alta Verapaz, there is a strong positive correlation (0.651) between departments with a high Indian population and the area covered by forest in 1992 (R. N. Adams and Bastos 2003:112, 113).

Similarly, tired of the "siege on Indianness," as Morgan refers to the phenomena, characterized by the forced changes in how Indians are to dress, speak, and believe, the K'iche' in Santa Catarina are clearly fighting back and demonstrating pride in being Indian, while at least some of the older individuals in Nahualá are wondering what happened and if the change is for the good. It is still not too late for Nahualá, though; because, as Morgan says, the Mayas are not interested in assimilating. To their benefit, the Guatemalan Peace Accords recognize that Guatemala is culturally pluralistic and that Ladino and Indian manifestations must be allowed to coexist. This, at least theoretically, puts an end to the assimilation policies of the Republican and Liberal periods (R. N. Adams and Bastos 2003). While compliance with the principles inherent in the peace accords may not have been all that apparent during the Portillo administration, the Berger administration, which came into being in January 2004, has made it clear that it intends to abide by those accords and has named Rigoberta Menchú as ambassador of the peace accords. It is possible, then, that cultural pluralism will finally become the actual policy, and not one that merely exists on paper, as it has in the past. To be sure, cultural erosion has occurred in both communities. However, as Morgan notes, resurgent Maya pride movements, such as Cosmovisión Maya (Lima Soto 1995), seek to limit further cultural erosion and help to redefine the Mayas so they are no longer simply milperos (Valladares 1957, 1993).

NOTES

1. Initially, we were limited to housing students with a small number of families because we had to ensure that the students would be kept healthy. As remittances came into the communities, more families were able to improve their housing to the level suitable for the students. This facilitated our ability to house students with more families.

2. The central focus of the 2003 field season was religion. In addition to a discussion of the rapid demise of traditional cofradía organizations, we examined evangélicos, carismáticos, and traditional variants of the region's major faiths. The results of that field season will be provided in a forthcoming volume.

3. Other writers referring to such phenomena have considered this "self-segregation" to be a defensive strategy (Aguirre Beltrán 1979) or, more recently, "a positive desire to be with one's own people who share the same mode of thought" (R. N. Adams and Bastos 2003:358).

4. Hatch notes that this is also a problem for boys, who are regularly absent from class so they can help the family find firewood or help in the weaving process, but it seems that girls are more likely than boys to be kept from school.

5. This alteration in the expectations of gender roles may contribute to violence against women because men confront increasingly limited economic options in the community. Thus, while Thompson and Hanamaikai report that community members said that rape was not a frequent event in Nahualá, the frequency with which this crime may be committed in the future may increase.

6. We will lay out the events and evidence of this matter in a future volume, which focuses on the fission of Santa Catarina Ixtahuacán between the fall of 1999 and January 2000. The schismatic group set up its community on land purportedly controlled by Nahualá. On the decline of community mobilization, see Cancian's (1992) discussion of a somewhat parallel case in Zinacantán, Chiapas, Mexico.

GLOSSARY

KEY

K'i.:   A term in K'iche'
Lit.:   "Literally"
Sp.:   A term in Spanish
Mam: A term in Mam (of the Maya language family)

Agricultor: (Sp.) Farmer.

Ajiitz: (K'i.) Shaman-priest devoted to or accused of imposing evil in the way of others. Lit. "worker/master" of (*aj*) "misfortune/evil" (*iitz*).

Ajq'iij: (K'i.) Shaman-priest devoted to or thought of as beneficial to others and the community; Sp. *zajorín*.

Alcalde: (Sp.) Mayor of a *municipio* (Sp.).

Aldea: (Sp.) Large hamlet.

Ama de casa: (Sp.) Homemaker.

Antepasados: (Sp.) Ancestors; those who have passed on.

Atiteco(s): (Sp.) A person from Santiago Atitlán.

Atrasado: (Sp.) Behind; underdeveloped.

Azadón: (Sp.) A hoe with a blade generally of 20 cm width by 15 cm height (or larger), used for plowing, planting, weeding, and shoveling.

B'inb'al: (K'i.) Cash gift to bride's parents. Lit. "the go-instrument."

Barranco: (Sp.) Ravine.

Básico: (Sp.) Junior high school.

Brujo: (Sp.) Witch, *zajorín* (Sp.).

Caballería: (Sp.) Unit of land measure equal to 1,000 *cuerdas* (Sp.).

Cabecera municipal: (Sp.) Administrative town-center of a *municipio*.

Cacique: (Sp.) Leader of a group, a central power broker, a chief.

Caldo de res: (Sp.) Beef stew.

Camino Real: (Sp.) In the colonial period, a principal highway, and literally the principal road that connects a king's realm.

Cantón: (Sp.) Neighborhood, a quarter of a town, and now, a populated subdivision of a *municipio*.

Cargo: (Sp.) Civil-religious responsibility.

Carismático: (Sp.) A charismatic Catholic (noun). One who participates in the Catholic Renovación, the renovation movement, wherein Catholics seek Pentecostal gifts of the spirit and manifest Evangelical styles of worship and preach abstinence from alcohol, dance, and fiesta excess (adj.).

Caserío: (Sp.) Small hamlet, a rural subdivision of a *municipio*.

Catarineco: (Sp.) A person from Santa Catarina.

Catequista: (Sp.) Religious educator.

Centro de salúd: (Sp.) Health center. The apex of the national public health care service system found in rural areas. It has a permanent public health physician, nurses, health care technicians and other personnel. Found in most municipal centers (Santa Catarina Ixtahuacán is an exception. Because the Centro de Salúd in Nahualá is located close by, and because Santa Catarina does not have as large a population as Nahualá, there is no Centro de Salúd in Santa Catarina Ixtahuacán.)

Chiapaneco: (Sp.) A person from Chiapas, Mexico.

Cholil: (Mam) Highway robber, possibly from the Sp. *cholero*, "cowboy."

Chuchqajaw: (K'i.) Respected senior shaman. Lit. "(our) mother-our-lord-father."

Chupb'al q'aaq': (K'i.) Marriage ritual. Lit., "instrument to extinguish fire."

Cinta: (Sp.) Belt-like headpiece, K'i. *xaq'ab*.

Código civil: (Sp.) Civil code; the tort and contract law of the country.

Código penal: (Sp.) Penal code; the criminal law of the country.

Cofradía: (Sp.) Custodial caretakers (men and assisting women) for a saint and its associated ritual celebrations.

Comadrona: (Sp.) Midwife.

Compradrazgo: (Sp.) Ritual kinship, interlacing godparental ties.

Compromiso: (Sp.) Commitment.

Copal: (from Nahuatl) Resin from the *copal* tree that is burned in traditional ceremonies as a kind of incense.

Corte: (Sp.) Indigenous ankle-length skirt of hand woven or foot-loomed cotton.

Cosas regaladas: (Sp.) Gifts, things unearned.

Cosas típicas: (Sp.) Indigenous crafts.

Cosmovisión Maya: (Sp.) Maya worldview. The set of precepts associated with Maya revitalization and its political manifestation in such groups as the Movimiento Maya.

Costumbre: (Sp.) Traditional Maya religion.

Costumbrismo: (Sp.) The panopoly of practices entailed in traditional religion, as practiced alone or managed under the guidance of the shaman-priests.

Costumbrista: (Sp.) One who practices costumbre.

Coyote: (Sp.) Illegal guide for transit to the United States.

Cuaderno(s): (Sp.) School notebook(s), copybook(s).

Cuerda: (Sp.) The basic unit of land measure, generally a piece of land 25 *varas* by 25 *varas* (or the equivalent), a *vara* ("rod") being 32 inches in length. In practice, a unit of land whose agricultural task (planting, weeding, plowing) constitutes roughly a day's labor.

Culto: (Sp.) Religious church services. Specifically used with respect to Evangelical Protestant church services. Catholics use the Sp. terms *celebración* or *servicio* to refer to analogous religious services, and *misa* to refer to Mass.

Cumbre, el: (Sp.) The highest point of a mountain or trail.

Curandera: (Sp.) A female healer who uses herbal remedies, ritual, and body manipulation to effect cures.

Cuxa: (K'i.) An illegally produced, home-brewed alcohol beverage; moonshine.

Cuxero: (Sp. adaptation of *cuxa*) One who produces *cuxa*.

Despedida: (Sp.) A sending-off, especially of a bride; a good-bye.

Día del campo: (Sp.) A field day.

Diputada: (Sp.) Congresswoman; a designated representative.

Dueño: (Sp.) Owner.

Dueño del mundo: (Sp.) Owner of the world; mountain spirit or divinity.

Egoismo: (Sp.) Egoism; self-centeredness.

Encomienda: (Sp.) A requirement that Indians pay taxes in the form of products and services delivered to overlords.

Envidia: (Sp.) Envy.

Faja: (Sp.) Belt, sash.

Finca: (Sp.) A plantation, usually for export crops such as coffee or sugar cane.

Guardia de hacienda: (Sp.) Tax and fiscal duty police.

Guaro: (Sp.) Liquor, possibly from the Sp. *agua ardiente*, lit. "water that burns."

Guerrilla(s): (Sp.) Insurgent(s).

Hacer hilo: (Sp.) To prepare thread.

Hierba: (Sp.) Greens; a dish made of the boiled leaves of any edible plants other than corn. The term is also used to refer to herbal remedies.

Huipil: (Sp.) Indigenous blouse, generally hand loomed and brocaded. Traditionally the term referred to shirts worn by males and females, but today it refers only to those worn by women.

Indígena: (Sp.) An Indian (noun); indigenous (adj.).

Inquieto: (Sp.) Restless; not quiet or subdued.

Ixim: (K'i.) Corn grain.

Ixtahuaquense: (Sp.) A person from the municipio of Santa Catarina Ixtahuacán.

Juramentaciones: (Sp.) Oaths, sworn statements.

Juyub: (K'i.) Mountain or hill. In context, may refer to spirits or divinities inhabiting a mountain.

K'amal b'e: (K'i.) Marriage go-between.

K'iche': (K'i.) One of several languages in the Maya language family; one who speaks that language.

Karelaq'aaj: (K'i.) Elopement; a traditional capture-like phase of marriage; Sp. *robo*. From *kä* (incompletive), *r* (third person singular), *elaq'a* ("to steal"), *j* (transitive marker).

Koxtaar: (K'i.) Men's skirt; probably a K'iche' modification of the Sp. *costal*, "burlap bag."

La: (K'i.) Respectful second person singular. *La* following a verb denotes respect for the second-person singular, and operates like *Usted* in the *Usted/tú* distinction in Spanish.

Ladino: (Sp.) In western Guatemala, a non-Indian, Spanish-speaking person oriented toward national interests and international consumer symbols.

Leña: (Sp.) Firewood.

Limpieza: (Sp.) Cleaning, cleanliness.

Lo que llega: (Sp.) That which arrives.

Machismo: (Sp.) An orientation toward male priority and dominance, manifest especially in the physical control, spatial restriction, and behavior monitoring of women in general and wives or daughters in particular.

Madrina: (Sp.) Godmother.

Magisterio: (Sp.) Normal school; a high school curriculum track for those preparing to be primary or secondary teachers.

Mala gente: (Sp.) A bad person or people.

Malcriado: (Sp.) A brat; bratty; misbehaved person.

Mano: (Sp.) The hand-held stone of a non-motorized corn grinder. Used with a *metate* (Sp.).

Marimba: (Sp.) A native xylophone.

Mayordomo: (Sp.) Custodian of the saints; wedding assistant.

Metate: (Sp.) The base block stone of a non-motorized corn grinder. Used with a *mano* (Sp.).

Milpa: (Sp.) Corn plot cultivated by hoe; by extension, any small hand-worked field, corn in the field, or, occasionally, corn for consumption.

Milpero: (Sp.) One who practices subsistence cultivation of corn.

Ministerio: (Sp.) A major department of national government.

Molino: (Sp.) Mill.

Mox: (Sp.) Oatmeal gruel.

Multa: (Sp.) Fine; penalty.

Mundo: (Sp.) Local mountain spirit or diety, generally conceived of as Ladino.

Municipio: (Sp.) Municipality; a township-like political subdivision in Guatemala.

Nahualense: (Sp.) A person from the *municipio* of Nahualá.

Natural: (Sp.) Native.

Negociante: (Sp.) A businesswoman or -man. Specifically referring to someone who sells agricultural or craft products in a local market for cash.

Norteamericano: (Sp.) A North American.

Novia: (Sp.) Girlfriend. Connotes commitment.

Novio: (Sp.) Boyfriend. Connotes commitment.

Paciencia y disciplina: (Sp.) Patience and discipline.

Padrino: (Sp.) Godfather.

Palabras antiguas: (Sp.) Old words, referring to ceremonial speech; K'i. *tz'onob'al tz'iij.*

Pañuelo: (Sp.) A multi-purpose cloth one meter square or larger for carrying bundles or babies, generally backstrap woven.

Paraje: (Sp.) Place; area.

Pasado: (Sp.) An elder indigenous male who has passed through the stages of the civil-religious hierarchy. Today, an elder male who has served the community much.

Pedir disculpas: (Sp.) To ask forgiveness.

Peña: (Sp.) A cliff; a large boulder that threatens from above.

Peraje: (Sp.) Shawl.

Petate: (Sp.) A woven mat made with tule reeds.

Piedra de moler: (Sp.) Grindstone; *metate* (Sp.).

Pila: (Sp.) A household wash tank; a multi-stall public wash tank.

Pinos: (Sp.) Pine trees.

Plantillo: (Sp.) Vegetation.

Político: (Sp.) A politically involved or powerful person.

Poom: (K'i.) *Copal*

Pre-primaria: (Sp.) Preschool; kindergarten.

Popol Vuj (or Popol Wuj): A colonial transcription of a prehispanic K'iche' religious and historical text.

Primaria: (Sp.) Primary school; elementary school.

Primer consejal: (Sp.) Lit. "first counselor," the second to top person in the cargo system.

Principal: (Sp.) A respected male elder.

Probacíon: (Sp.) Test.

Puesto de salúd: (Sp.) Health outpost, subordinate to a *centro de salúd*. Generally found in larger non-municipal settlements. Its highest level functionary is a nurse practitioner or rural health promoter. It is also the highest level health care provision center in Santa Catarina Ixtahuacán, owing both to the proximity and larger population of Nahualá.

Quetzal: (Sp.) The Guatemalan unit of money.

Reducción: (Sp.) The process of resettling indigenous rural residents in town centers under Spanish governmental and ecclesiastical control. A town center of those so reduced.

Refacción(es): (Sp.) Snack(s).

Regalo: (Sp.) Gift.

Regalo de Dios: (Sp.) Gift of God.

Regidor: (Sp.) A municipal mayor's respected top advisor, who is acting mayor in the mayor's absence.

Reglamento de la escuela: (Sp.) School regulations.

Robo: (Sp.) Elopement. *See Karelaq'aaj.*

Sexto grado: (Sp.) Sixth grade.

Siéntense bien: (Sp.) Sit properly (a command).

Solicitud de matrimonio: (Sp.) Marriage licence.

Sombrero: (Sp.) Three-hundred-sixty-degree brimmed hat.

Suyacal: Rain protection.

Tamalitos: (Sp.) Little tamales.

Tarjeta de calificación: (Sp.) Report card.

Temascal: (from Nahuatl, incorporated in Sp.) Sweat hut used for bathing and for many curing rituals; K'i. *tuuj*.

Tienen vergüenza: (Sp.) Lit. "They are ashamed."

Tierra fría: (Sp.) Cold country; highland mountainous areas.

Traje: (Sp.) Handmade costume, often woven, that usually indicates the wearer is indigenous.

Tuuj: (K'i.) Sweat house. *See Temascal.*

Tziite': (K'i.) Seeds used in divination.

Tzut(e): (K'i.) A modification of K'i. *su't*. Head wrap; cloth.

Tzuultaq'a: (Q'eqchi') Mountain god; earth lord.

Tz'onob'al Tz'iij: (K'i.) Ceremonial speech of betrothment. Also known as *palabras antiguas* (Sp.), "ancient words."

Videos de karate, los: (Sp.) Karate videos; videos and cinematic violence.

Violencia, La: (Sp.) Lit. "The Violence." The undeclared war. Scholars generally agree that it began in 1979 or 1980 and gradually tapered to an end by 1985. The Peace Accords, however, were not signed until 1996.

Wa: (K'i.) Corn foods; food in general.

Witz: (Mam) Earth lord.

Xaq'ap: (K'i.) Belt-like headpiece; *cinta* (Sp.).

Xela: A shortened form of *Xelaju*, the K'iche' name for Quezaltenango, Guatemala's second largest city, located an hour's bus ride from the project area.

Xokte'b'al: (K'i.) The son's entering of a mother's house.

Zajorín: (Sp.) To Ladinos, any shaman-priest, usually thought of negatively as a *brujo*, or "witch." To Indians, the term may be applied to the shaman-priests of the highest level, who bless the communities and are thought of as doing good and teaching lower-level shamans.

WORKS CITED

Adams, Betty H. 1994. "The Cost of Producing Coffee." *World Coffee and Tea* 35:39–42.

Adams, Richard N. 1970. *Crucifixion by Power: Essays on Guatemalan National Social Structure, 1944–1966.* Austin: University of Texas Press.

———. 1988. *The Eighth Day: Social Evolution as the Self-Organization of Energy.* Austin: University of Texas Press.

———. 1994. "Guatemalan Ladinization and History." *The Americas* 50, No. 4: 527–43.

———. 1995. "Ethnic Conflict, Governance and Globalization in Latin America, with Special Attention to Guatemala." In *Ethnic Conflict and Governance in Comparative Perspective*, edited by Ralph Espach. Washington, D.C.: Woodrow Wilson Center.

———. 1997. "Surgimiento de la identidad Maya." In *Historia general de Guatemala*, edited by Jorge Luján Muñoz. Vol. 6, *Época contemporánea: De 1945 a la actualidad*, edited by J. Daniel Contreras R. 317–46. Guatemala: Asociación de Amigos del País, Fundación para la Cultura y el Desarrollo.

Adams, Richard N., and Santiago Bastos. 2003. *Las relaciones étnicas en Guatemala, 1944–2000.* Antigua, Guatemala: Centro de Investigaciones Regionales de Mesoamérica.

Adams, Walter Randolph. 1988a. "Fission, Maintenance, and Interaction in an Anishinabe Community on Keweenaw Bay, Michigan, 1832–1881." PhD diss., Michigan State University.

———. 1988b. "Tzeltal-Tojolabal Religious Interaction: The Pilgrimages." In *The Linguistics of Southeastern Chiapas, Mexico*, edited by Lyle Campbell, 183–98. Papers of the New World Archeological Foundation, No. 50. Provo: Brigham Young University.

————. 1993a. *Exploraciones en la factibilidad de realizar proyectos al nivel local.* Report prepared for DELTA PLAN/SEGEPLAN/BCIE project, "Desarrollo Integral a Nivel Local en el Departamento de Jalapa."

———— 1993b. "On the Origins of Ethnic Groups: The r-K Selection Theory in Relation to Indians and Ladinos in Guatemala." Paper presented at the 13th International Congress of Anthropological and Ethnological Sciences, Mexico City.

————. 1997. "Processes and Dynamics of Community Fission and Maintenance: An Ojibway Case." In *Explorations in Anthropology and Theology*, edited by Frank A. Salamone and Walter Randolph Adams, 209–31. Lanham, Md.: University Press of America. Reprinted in Walter Randolph Adams and Frank A. Salamone, eds. 2000. *Anthropology and Theology: Gods, Icons, and God-talk.* Lanham, Md.: University Press of America, 363–90.

————. 1999. "Alcohol Production and Consumption in a Highland Guatemalan Maya Community." *Bulletin of the Alcohol and Drug Study Group* 34 (2): 1–9.

Adams, Walter Randolph, Hugo Ramos, and Cornelius Hugo. 1993. *Effects of the Structural Adjustment Program on the Demand and Consumption of Basic Grains in El Salvador.* Manhattan, Kans.: Kansas State University, Food and Feed Grain Institute, Technical Report 134.

Aguirre Beltrán, Gonzalo. 1979. *Regions of Refuge.* Edited by Deward E. Walker. Washington, D.C.: Society for Applied Anthropology.

Ajpacajá Tum, Florentino Pedro. 2001. *Tz'onob'al tziij: Discurso ceremonial k'ichee'.* Guatemala City: Cholsamaj.

Annis, Sheldon. 1987. *God and Production in a Guatemalan Town.* Austin: University of Texas Press.

Beals, Alan R. 1970. "Fieldwork in Gopalpur." In *Being an Anthropologist: Fieldwork in Eleven Cultures*, edited by George D. Spindler. New York: Holt, Rinehart and Winston.

————. 1980. *Gopalpur: A South Indian Village, Fieldwork Edition.* New York: Holt, Rinehart and Winston.

Bernard, H. Russell. 1988. *Research Methods in Cultural Anthropology.* Newbury Park, Calif.: Sage Publications.

————. 1995. *Research Methods in Anthropology: Qualitative and Quantitative Approaches*, 2nd ed. Walnut Creek, Calif.: Altamira Press.

————. 2002. *Research Methods in Anthropology: Qualitative and Quantitative Approaches.* 3rd ed. Walnut Creek, Calif.: Altamira Press.

Bertrand, Lauri Ellen. 1999. "Nutritional Assessment of a Maya Village." Undergraduate Honors Thesis, Brigham Young University.

Boas, Franz. 1974. "The Jesup North Pacific Expedition [1898]." In *The Shaping of American Anthropology, 1883–1911: A Franz Boas Reader*, edited by George W. Stocking, Jr. 107–16. New York: Basic Books.

Brintnall, Douglas E. 1979. *Revolt Against the Dead: The Modernization of a Mayan Community in the Highlands of Guatemala*. New York: Gordon and Breach.

Cancian, Frank. 1992. *The Decline of Community in Zinacantán: Economy, Public Life, and Social Stratification, 1960–1987*. Stanford: Stanford University Press.

Carlsen, Robert S. 1997. *The War for the Heart and Soul of a Highland Maya Town*. Austin: University of Texas Press.

Carrithers, Michael. 1992. *Why Humans Have Cultures: Explaining Anthropology and Social Diversity*. New York: Oxford University Press.

Cassell, Philip. 1993. *The Giddens Reader*. Stanford, Calif.: Stanford University Press.

Cojtí Cuxil, Demetrio. 1997. *Ri maya' moloj pa iximulew: El movimiento maya (en Guatemala)*. Guatemala City: Centro Educativo y Cultural Maya.

Coombs, Gary, Jean I. Hess, and Kathleen Killorin. 1977. "The Urban Anthropology Field School: Design, Implementation, and Retrospective," *Urban Anthropology* 6 (2): 155–64.

Dirección General de Cartografía. 1961. *Diccionario geográfico de Guatemala*. Vol. 1. Guatemala: Tipografía Nacional de Guatemala.

———. 1962. *Diccionario geográfico de Guatemala*. Vol. 2. Guatemala: Tipografía Nacional de Guatemala.

Dirección General de Estadística. 1994. *X Censo Nacional de Población y V de Habitación Guatemala*. Guatemala: Tipografía Nacional.

Durkheim, Emile. 1951. *Suicide: A Study in Sociology*. Translated by John A. Spaulding and George Simpson. New York: Free Press.

Ebers, Christine. 1995. *Women and Alcohol in a Highland Maya Town: Water of Hope, Water of Sorrow*. Austin: University of Texas Press.

Ehlers, Tracy Bachrach. 1990. *Silent Looms: Women and Production in a Guatemalan Town*. Boulder: Westview Press.

Epstein, A. L., ed. 1967. *The Craft of Social Anthropology*. London: Tavistock Publications.

Fischer, Edward F. 2001. *Cultural Logics and Global Economies: Maya Identity in Thought and Practice*. Austin: University of Texas Press.

Fluehr-Lobban, Carolyn. 2003. "Darkness in El Dorado: Research Ethics, Then and Now." In *Ethics and the Profession of Anthropology: Dialogue for Ethically Conscious Practice*, 2nd ed. Edited by Carolyn Fluehr-Lobban, 85–106. Walnut Creek: Altamira Press.

Foley, Douglas E. 1999. "The Fox Project: A Reappraisal." *Current Anthropology* 40(2): 171–91.

Gall, Francis. 1981. *Diccionario geográfico de Guatemala.* Vol. 2. Guatemala: Instituto Geográfico Nacional.

García Kihn, J. 1995. "La ruta de la pobreza." *Crónica Semanal* (June 16–22): 39–40.

Garrard-Burnett, Virginia. 1998. *Protestantism in Guatemala: Living in the New Jerusalem.* Austin: University of Texas Press.

Gluckman, Max. 1945. "The Seven-Year Research Plan of the Rhodes-Livingstone Institute of Social Studies in British Central Africa." *Rhodes-Livingstone Institute Journal* (1945): 1–32.

Gmelch, George, and Sharon Bohn Gmelch. 1999. "An Ethnographic Field School: What Students Do and Learn." *Anthropology and Education Quarterly* 30 (2): 220–27.

Grant, Linda, Josephine Beoku–Betts, William Finlay, and Gary Alan Fine. 1999. "Fieldwork in Familiar Places: The UGA Workshop in Fieldwork Methods." *Anthropology and Education Quarterly* 30 (2): 238–48.

Hawkins, John P. 1984. *Inverse Images: The Meaning of Culture, Ethnicity and Family in Postcolonial Guatemala.* Albuquerque: University of New Mexico Press.

Inter-American Development Bank. 2002. *Managing the Competitive Transition of the Coffee Sector in Central America.* Discussion Document Prepared for the Regional Workshop: The Coffee Crisis and its Impact in Central America: Situation and Lines of Action. Antigua, Guatemala.

Jelin, Elizabeth, ed. 1990. *Women and Social Change in Latin America.* London: Zed Books.

Kottak, Conrad Phillip. 1982. *Researching American Culture: A Guide for Student Anthropologists.* Ann Arbor: University of Michigan Press.

Kulbeth, Jared. n.d. "'I'll Sell until I Die': The Nahualá Market and Its Vendors." Unpublished manuscript. Brigham Young University, Anthropology Department.

La Farge, Oliver. 1947. *Santa Eulalia: The Religion of a Cuchumatán Indian Town.* Chicago: University of Chicago Press.

Lee, Brandon. n.d. "Living Off the Sacred Earth: Conceptions of Land, Tenure, and Community in Santa Catarina Ixtahuacán." Unpublished manuscript. Brigham Young University, Anthropology Department.

Leonard, H. Jeffrey. 1987. *Natural Resources and Economic Development in Central America: A Regional Environmental Profile.* New Brunswick, N.J.: Transaction Books.

Levine, Linda. 1999. "Comment on 'Special Reflections from the Field: Mentoring Apprentice Ethnographers through Field Schools.'" *Anthropology and Education Quarterly* 30 (2): 249–50.

Lima Soto, Ricardo E. 1995. *Aproximación a la cosmovisión maya*. Guatemala City: Universidad Rafael Landívar, Instituto de Investigaciones Económicas y Sociales.

Lovell, W. George. 2000. *A Beauty That Hurts: Life and Death in Guatemala*. Austin: University of Texas Press.

McCreery, David. 1994. *Rural Guatemala: 1760–1940*. Stanford: Stanford University Press.

McGoodwin, James R. 1978. "Directing an Ethnographic Field School: Notes and Advice." *Anthropological Quarterly* 51 (3): 175–83.

MacLeod, Murdo J. 1973. *Spanish Central America: A Socioeconomic History, 1520–1720*. Berkeley: University of California Press.

Mair, Lucy. 1971. *Marriage*. Baltimore, Md.: Penguin Books.

Marcus, George E., and Michael M. J. Fischer. 1986. *Anthropology As Cultural Critique: An Experimental Moment in the Human Sciences*. Chicago: University of Chicago Press, 1999.

Mendelson, E. Michael. 1965. *Escándalos de Maximón: Un estudio sobre la religión y la visión del mundo de Santiago Atitlán*. Translated by Julio Vielman. Seminario de Integración Social Guatemalteco 19. Guatemala: Tipografía Nacional.

Montejo, Victor. 1999. *Voices from Exile: Violence and Survival in Modern Maya History*. Norman: University of Oklahoma Press.

Morales Urrutia, Mateo. 1961. *La división política y administrativa de la República de Guatemala*. 2 vols. Guatemala: Editorial Iberia Gutenberg.

Nash, June C. 2001. *Mayan Visions: The Quest for Autonomy in an Age of Globalization*. New York: Routledge.

Nuttall, Kristyn Roser. n.d. "The Genesis of Exodus: The Relocation of Santa Catarina Ixtahuacán." Unpublished manuscript, Brigham Young University, Anthropology Department.

Oakes, Maud. 1951. *The Two Crosses of Todos Santos*. New York: Pantheon Books.

Otzoy, Irma. 1996. "Maya Clothing and Identity." In *Mayan Cultural Activism*, edited by Edward F. Fischer and R. McKenna Brown, 141–55. Austin: University of Texas Press.

Oxfam International. 2002. *Mugged: Poverty in Your Coffee Cup*. Oxford: Oxfam International.

Portillo, Alfonso. 1998. "Una reforma política para la paz." In *Guatemala after the Peace Accords*, edited by Rachel Sieder, 228–37. London: University of London, Institute of Latin American Studies.

Proyecto Salquil. 1992. Diagnóstico socioeconómico de Santa Catarina Ixtahuacán, Sololá. Limited distribution technical report. Santa Catarina Ixtahuacán.

Rabe, Jeremy. n.d. "The Public Market in Santa Catarina Ixtahuacán." Unpublished manuscript. Brigham Young University, Anthropology Department.

Reina, Rubén E. 1966. *The Law of the Saints: a Pokomam Pueblo and Its Community Culture*. Indianapolis: Bobbs-Merrill.

Rivers, W. H. R. 1901. *Reports of the Cambridge Anthropological Expedition to Torres Straits*. Vol. 1. Cambridge, England: University Press.

Rodríguez Guaján, Demetrio. 1992. "Maya Culture and the Politics of Development." In *Maya Cultural Activism in Guatemala*, edited by Edward F. Fischer and McKenna Brown, 74–88. Austin: University of Texas Press.

Rojas Lima, Flavio. 1988. *La cultura del maíz en Guatemala*. Guatemala: Ministerio de Cultura y Deportes.

Roy, Kartick C., Hans C. Bomquist, and A. T. Clement, eds. 1996. *Economic Development and Women in the World Community*. London: Praeger.

Saravia, Albertina E. 1983. *El ladino me jodió: Vida de un indígena*. Guatemala: Editorial José de Pineda Ibarra.

Schensul, Jean J., and Margaret D. LeCompte, eds. 1999. *The Ethnographer's Toolkit*. 7 vols. Walnut Creek, Calif.: Altamira Press.

Sekaquaptewa, Emory. 1972. "Preserving the Good Things of Hopi Life." In *Plural Society in the Southwest*, edited by Edward H. Spicer and R. H. Thompson, 239–60. New York: Interbrook.

Sexton, James D., ed. and trans. 2001. *Joseño: Another Mayan Voice Speaks from Guatemala*. Narrated by Ignacio Bizarro Ujpán. Albuquerque: University of New Mexico Press.

Sherman, Andrew. n.d. "'That's How Life Is': Grassroots Development in Nahualá." Unpublished manuscript. Brigham Young University, Anthropology Department.

Spradley, James P. 1979. *The Ethnographic Interview*. New York: Holt, Rinehart, and Winston.

Spradley, James P., and David W. McCurdy. 1988. *The Cultural Experience: Ethnography in Complex Society*. Prospect Heights, Ill.: Waveland Press.

Stocking, George W., Jr., ed. 1974. *The Shaping of American Anthropology: 1883–1911, a Franz Boas Reader*. New York: Basic Books.

Stoll, David. 1993. *Between Two Armies in the Ixil Highlands of Guatemala*. New York: Columbia University Press.

Tarn, Nathaniel. 1997. *Scandals in the House of Birds: Shamans and Priests on Lake Atitlán*. New York: Marsilio.

Tax, Sol. 1937. "The Municipios of the Midwestern Highlands of Guatemala." *American Anthropologist* 39 (3): 423–44.

———. 1988. "Pride and Puzzlement: A Retro-Introspective Record of 60 Years of Anthropology." *Annual Review of Anthropology* 17:1–22.

Tedlock, Dennis, trans. 1985. *Popol Vuh: The Definitive Edition of the Mayan Book of the Dawn of Life and the Glories of Gods and Kings*. New York: Simon and Schuster.

Tierney, Patrick. 2000. *Darkness in El Dorado: How Scientists and Journalists Devastated the Amazon*. New York: W. W. Norton.

Tuyuc, Rosalina. 1998. "Los acuerdos de paz, los pueblos indígenas y la reforma política." In *Guatemala after the Peace Accords*, edited by Rachel Sieder, 238–42. London: University of London, Institute of Latin American Studies.

Valladares, León A. 1957. *El hombre y el maíz: etnografía y etnopsicología de Colotenango*. 2nd ed. Mexico City: B. Costa-Amic.

———. 1993. *Culto al maíz en Guatemala*. 2nd ed. Guatemala City: Oscar de León Palacios.

Villa Cases, María, ed. 1999. *Café amargo: por un comercio norte-sur justo*. Barcelona: Setem.

Vogt, Evon Z. 1994. *Fieldwork among the Maya: Reflections on the Harvard Chiapas Project*. Albuquerque: University of New Mexico Press.

Wagley, Charles. 1941. *Economics of a Guatemalan Village*. Memoirs of the American Anthropological Association 58. Menasha, Wis.: American Anthropological Association.

———. 1949. *The Social and Religious Life of a Guatemalan Village*. Memoirs of the American Anthropological Association 71. Menasha, Wis.: American Anthropological Association.

Wallace, James M. T. 1999. "Mentoring Apprentice Ethnographers Through Field Schools: Introduction." *Anthropology and Education Quarterly* 30 (2): 210–19.

Ward, Martha C. 1999. "Managing Student Culture and Culture Shock: A Case from European Tyrol," *Anthropology and Education Quarterly* 30 (2): 228–37.

Warren, Kay B. 1978. *The Symbolism of Subordination: Indian Identity in a Guatemalan Town*. Austin: University of Texas Press.

———. 1998. *Indigenous Movements and Their Critics: Pan-Maya Activism in Guatemala*. Princeton: Princeton University Press.

Watanabe, John. 1992. *Maya Saints and Souls in a Changing World*. Austin: University of Texas Press.

Weber, Max. 1996. *Protestant Ethic and the Spirit of Capitalism*. Translated by Alcott Parsons. Los Angeles: Roxbury.

Werner, Oswald, and G. Mark Schoepfle. 1987. *Systematic Fieldwork: Foundations of Ethnography and Interviewing*. Vol. 1. Newbury Park, Calif: Sage Publications.

Wilkinson, Daniel. 2002. *Silence on the Mountain: Stories of Terror, Betrayal, and Forgetting in Guatemala*. New York: Houghton Mifflin Co.

Wilson, Kevara Ellsworth. n.d. "'Your Destiny is to Care for Pregnant Women':
    Midwives and Childbirth in Nahualá." Unpublished manuscript. Brigham
    Young University, Anthropology Department.
Wilson, Richard. 1995. *Maya Resurgence in Guatemala: Q'eqchi' Experiences*.
    Norman: University of Oklahoma Press.
Wolf, Eric. 1957. "Closed Corporate Peasant Communities in Mesoamerica and
    Central Java." *Southwestern Journal of Anthropology* 13 (1): 1–18.

INDEX

expectations read, 110; commitment
concept, 110; community orientation, 110; divorce versus separation
after, 109; marriage license 109–10;
mayor as officiator, 109–10; penal
sanctions recited, 110; vows recited,
110
Civil-religious hierarchy. *See* Cofradía
Civil war, 66, 91–93, 95n21, 188n3;
limited discussion of, 217; religion
and, 92–93
Closed corporate community, 48, 51,
54, 57, 71, 135, 213
Clothing, indigenous, 69–71; child
care and, 139; clothing and ethnic
identity, 80; community identity
and, 141–42; description of, 62,
69–71; economic value of women's,
147; ladino ridicule of, 70–71;
Pan–American Highway and change
of, 69–71; women and production
of, 141–42; xaq'ap (head band) in
wedding, 111
Coffee industry crisis, 46, 59n7
Cofradía, 63–64, 66; collapse of,
82–83, 122n4; mayordomos in,
75–76; organization and activities
of, 63–64; rituals of, 82
Community: anomie in, 55–57; closed
community, 135–36, 220n3; collective action in, 49–50; community of
identity, 217–18; economic change
and waning of, 90–91; endogamy
waning, 217; envy and unmanage-
ability of, 216; erosion of sense of,
214; fiction of closed corporate community, 213; fiction of isolation, 8;
fission of Santa Catarina Ixtahuacán,
8; "imagined community," 214;

impact of field school on, 211–12;
indigenous power and, 218;
mobilization of, 217–18; religious
change and waning of, 90–91; town
meetings, 49–50
Community fission, 8, 220n6
Corn, 39, 43, 54, 177, 192–93
Corte. *See* Clothing, indigenous
Cosmovisión Maya, 55, 74–75, 214;
appeal to elites, 83
Costumbre. *See* Religions, Maya
Courtship, 57, 99–104; cultural change
impact on, 101–102; economic
change impact on, 102, 115–16;
economic uncertainty and change of,
117–18; education impact on, 102;
influence of ladino patterns on, 117;
media impacts on, 116–17; parental
anger during, 118–20; recent period,
101–102; San Simón and, 102;
traditional (pre-1945), 100–101;
transitional period (circa
1955–1965), 101
Courtship and marriage case studies,
112–15; patrilocal residence, 116;
recent period, 114–15; traditional
period, 112–13; transitional period,
113–14
Craft industries, local, 39–40, 45; lack
of, in Santa Catarina Ixtahuacán,
47–48, 176
Crops of region, 39–40, 45
Cultural accommodation. *See*
Synthesis, cultural
Cultural synthesis. *See* Synthesis,
cultural
Culture change, 57, 61–62, 64–91,
215; attitudes toward marriage
undergoing, 120–22; evangelical